This book is to be returned on or before
st

# ENVIRONMENTAL ISSUES IN EDUCATION

This is the second volume of a series entitled

**Monitoring Change in Education**

# Environmental Issues in Education

edited by

*Gill Harris*

*and*

*Cynthia Blackwell*

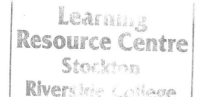
© The contributors 1996

Published by
Arena
Ashgate Publishing Limited
Gower House
Croft Road
Aldershot
Hants GU11 3HR
England

Ashgate Publishing Company
Old Post Road
Brookfield
Vermont 05036
USA


**British Library Cataloguing in Publication Data**

Environmental issues in education – (Monitoring change in education)
    1. Environmental education
    I. Harris, Gill  II. Blackwell, Cynthia
    333.7'07
ISBN 1 85742 331 3

**Library of Congress Catalog Card Number:** 96-83262

Printed in Great Britain at the University Press, Cambridge

# Contents

# Notes on contributors

**Dr Chris Gayford** is head of the Department of Science and Technology Education at the University of Reading. His research interests include the nature and purpose of environmental education, support systems at local, national and international levels and methodologies for the evaluation of the affective aspect of environmental education.

**Professor Cedric Cullingford** is head of the Post-Graduate Sector in the School of Education at the University of Huddersfield. His recent books include 'Children and Society', 'The Inner World of the School' and 'The Effective Teacher'.

**Dr Martin Stanisstreet** of the Department of Environment and Evolutionary Biology, and **Dr Edward Boyes** of the Department of Education are members of the Environmental Education Research Unit at the University of Liverpool. The aims of the unit are to research children's thinking about, and attitudes to environmental issues, to enable the effective targeting of educational strategies and resources.

**Liz Lakin** is a lecturer at the Cheltenham and Gloucester College of Higher Education, where she is involved in both teacher education and the delivery of environmental modules within the Science Faculty. She is chair of the Association for Science Education Environmental Education Task Group.

**Dr Paul Oliver** is a principal lecturer in the School of Education at the University of Huddersfield. He has published articles on comparative religion and multicultural education, and is interested in the ethical dimensions of environmental education.

**Dr Walter Leal Filho** is director of the European Research and Training Centre on Environmental Education (ERTCEE) at the University of Bradford. The centre is involved in environmental education research across the European Union.

**Pam Green** and **Linda Platten** are respectively lecturers in biology and geography with particular interest in environmental education; **Dr George Raper** is director of the Post-Graduate Certificate in Education and co-ordinator of secondary science studies. All are members of the Institute of Education at the University of Warwick.

**Dr Hayley Randle** is a lecturer in quantitative methods, with research interests in cattle behaviour and welfare. **Ian Kemp** spent a number of years working in conservation and countryside management, both as manager of the Plymouth Urban Fringe Project and as Heritage Coast Officer for South Devon. He is now senior lecturer in countryside management. Both are members of the Seale-Hayne Faculty of Agriculture, Food Studies and Land Use at the University of Plymouth.

**Dr Jonathan Horner** is a senior lecturer in environmental studies in the Department of Environmental and Geographical Studies at Roehampton Institute London. His teaching and research interests encompass aspects of environmental monitoring and management. He is especially concerned with pollution monitoring and environmental policy.

**Robert Stephenson** is a research fellow in the Faculty of Education, Sport and Leisure at the University of Brighton. He is a member of the Tidy Britain Group Schools Research Project, developing an environmental management system for schools entitled 'Eco-schools: towards a sustainable lifestyle'. His involvement in environmental campaigns has included the establishment of a community recycling scheme, co-founding a cycling campaign and working for Brighton's Local Agenda 21 mechanism, the Brighton Community Environmental Partnership.

**Dr Roger Firth** and **Dr Malcolm Plant** of the Faculty of Education, Nottingham Trent University, run a MA in Environmental Education by distance learning, which has attracted students from the UK and overseas. Their current research interests include the transformation of the teaching culture in a primary school through action research and the development and testing of a socially critical approach to environmental education within higher education respectively.

# Foreword

Environmental education has long been a Huddersfield speciality; the teaching of Geography dates back to the 1850s, when it was offered by the Huddersfield Mechanic's Institute, one of the institutions that eventually became the University of Huddersfield. Geography became a BSc honours degree in 1976 and has always had an applied and problem solving emphasis which has increasingly focused on the contribution that geographers can make to the solution of environmental problems and to resource management.

Geography is of course, a widely taught subject, but Huddersfield has a unique claim as the home of the first British degree in Human Ecology. This four-year BSc honours degree, with a full year spent in supervised work experience, was introduced in 1975 in response to the growth of the environmental movement of the 1960s. Its central aim was 'an integrated approach to human society and associated problems and the development of an awareness of the complex interrelationships existing between man and his environment'. This course has continued to thrive and now has formal collaborative links with similar courses across Europe. A growing number of graduates are involved in environmental education in the classroom, in non-governmental organisations and in policy-making positions.

The continuing need to provide a greater environmental input into the training of scientists led, in 1992, to the development of a BSc in Environmental Analysis. This joint venture between Chemists, Geographers and Human Ecologists will produce its first graduates in 1996. In addition, the University has three specialist centres linked to the department of Geographical and Environmental Sciences: the Centre for Water and Environmental Management, the Limestone Research Group and the Institute for Environmental and Policy Analysis are actively engaged in environmental research projects with both industry and the public sector.

The University continues to have a major role in environmental education at the Higher Education level. This book, the result of collaboration between the Department of Geographical and Environmental Sciences and the School of Education, explores the wider aspects of environmental education and will be of interest to those involved in this important area of work at any level.

Professor John Gunn
Head of the Department of Geographical and Environmental Sciences
University of Huddersfield

# Preface

The changes that have taken place in our understanding of environmental *Blueprint for Survival* and *Stockholm Conference*, both in the early 1970s, led to a transformation in environmental awareness particularly at government level. From this has stemmed the need for a greatly enhanced sense of environmental responsibility in every citizen, young and old, yet this cannot be achieved without a comprehensive programme of education, particularly within the school context.

For today's school children, the environmental concerns of the 1970s have little significance, but the ripples created by these events are rapidly becoming the tidal wave that is sweeping environmental education into the 21st century. An analogy of this kind seems appropriate: the slow, but steady increase in environmentally oriented courses at university level during the 1970s, coupled with the gradual integration of an environmental perspective into field work and the launch of Environmental Studies as an examination subject within the school curriculum, all served to foster concern for the environment amongst the younger generation. The launch of the *World Conservation Strategy* in 1980 provided further impetus and a framework for thinking about the environment on a world wide basis. However, concern has not been restricted to the formal classroom setting or just to the young. Increasing media coverage of important issues has done much to stimulate interest and concern for the environment among the general public as the steady rise in membership of groups such as the National Trust, the royal Society for the Protection of Birds, Friends of the Earth and the Greenpeace indicates.

But what of the current decade? The launch of the Agenda 21 initiative at the 1992 UN conference in Rio de Janeiro has done much to ensure that the environment remains at the forefront of our thinking. However, some would argue that the constraints of the National Curriculum have checked the tide of environmental education in schools. Others see cause for much optimism in the Education and Environment conference organised jointly by DOE and DFE in February 1995 which concluded that priority must be given to practical help for teachers in delivering environmental education throughout the National Curriculum.

In Further and Higher Education the Toyne Report of 1992 has focused attention sharply on the need to develop increasing levels of environmental knowledge, skills and understanding across the campus and has done much to reinforce the aims of the Greening of Higher Education Council established in 1991.

Whatever our level of involvement, education is clearly the key to the development of environmental responsibility in both current and future generations. The papers in this book explore issues related to the delivery of environmental education from the primary school to the higher education sector. CHRIS GAYFORD begins by considering the changing nature of environmental education from its origins in ecology and fieldwork, and goes on to look at recent influences on its development. It is now generally agreed that environmental education should include the development of values and attitudes as well as skills and understanding: the tripartite model of education *about*, *in* and *for* the environmental. However many differing attitudes to the environment still exist, even among environmentalists and those involved in environmental education.

CEDRIC CULLINGFORD's work with young children provides a fascinating insight into their emerging attitudes to their local environment, while MARTIN STANISSTREET and EDWARD BOYES demonstrate that children's understanding of global environment issues remains overgeneralised, in thinking for example, that all pollutants contribute to all environmental problems. In a second study, even primary school teachers were shown to be unclear about certain aspects. This suggests that instead of young children's ideas and misconceptions being challenged by teachers, mistakes and misunderstandings could well be perpetuated or reinforced. Ways in which children might be helped to develop their thinking about global environmental issues are then discussed.

LIZ LAKIN considers the progressive marginalisation of environmental education during the evolution of the National Curriculum and discusses the need to promote environmental education as a cross-curricula theme. She describes the role of the Environmental Education Task Group, set up by the Association for Science Education, to identify and promote good practice in schools and to address the provision of environmental education within initial teacher training. PAUL OLIVER looks at environmental education within a multicultural setting and points out that sensitivity to the environment and the importance of living in equilibrium with it has been an intrinsic part of the culture and religion of a number of other societies. Teachers should therefore be aware of the contribution that pupils from various ethnic groups can make and in so doing will make a positive statement of respect for other cultures.

To provide a European perspective, WALTER LEAL FILHO describes a survey involving over 20,000 school children in sixteen member countries of the Council of Europe, regarding their knowledge of, and attitudes to the environment. His paper gives an insight into the methodology used in such a large scale survey, as well as the difficulties encountered and how these were overcome. Initial findings are presented, with a view to the identification of areas for further research.

What support is available to those involved in environmental education? CHRIS GAYFORD looks at the role of various central and local government as well as non-governmental organisations in the provision of support networks and materials. He also reports the results of a study of the type of support required by teachers, which demonstrates that a pre-evaluation of the great variety of resources already available would be the most helpful factor. The next paper describes the development of a wetlands site, the result of a partnerhsip between the University of Warwick and the National Rivers Authority. PAM GREEN, LINDA PLATTEN and GEORGE RAPER show how this has provided an exciting teaching and learning resource which is used by school pupils and students of all ages, including trainee teachers.

Many changes have also taken place within the post-compulsory sector, HAYLEY RANDLE and IAN KEMP trace the development of Seale-Hayne from its origins as an agricultural college, training farm workers to maximise food production during the first part of this century, to its incorporation into the Faculty of Agriculture, Food Studies and Land Use at the University of Plymouth, offering courses on rural resources management, countryside management and tourism. JONATHAN HORNER looks at the 'greening' of further and higher education, examining the extent to which institutions have developed environmental policies in response to the Toyne Report. He concludes that the response so far is patchy and lacking in co-ordination. However, case studies of successful collaborative projects between students on degree programmes and local business, industry and educational establishments are presented to show what can be done.

Much 'environmental education' takes place in an informal way, and ROBERT STEPHENSON gives an overview of the range of environmental education experiences available to people in the normal course of work and leisure activities. He provides a critical review of various environmental initiatives and looks at how the type of publicity they are given can increase environmental awareness. The importance of tailor projects, materials and information to identifiable target groups is emphasised, together with the need to involve people through their own concerns at the local level.

Finally, how does the environmental educator know when environmental education is working? Many of the papers presented in this volume suggest that there is much scope for improvement, both within and outside the formal education setting. ROGER FIRTH and MALCOLM PLANT question the assumption on which much of the environmental education is based and seek to establish indicators that will enable the effectiveness of environmental education programmes to be evaluated. The transformation of the rhetoric of environmental education into practical action for the environment at individual and community level is the next major challenge to be faced. Only through a full understanding of the complex issues involved at this level can the young people of today take full responsibility for the global environment in the future.

# Acknowledgements

We wish to thank members of the 'Monitoring Change in Education' Editorial Board in the School of Education at the University of Huddersfield, particularly Cedric Cullingford, Philip Mitchell and Paul Oliver, for their support and guidance. We would also like to thank Louie Carr, Librarian and Dionne Glennon, Administrative Assistant for their help, and Jackie Hepworth for her painstaking preparation of the camera-ready copy.

Gill Harris and Cynthia Blackwell

October 1995

# 1 The nature and purposes of environmental education

*Chris Gayford*

## Abstract

This paper outlines some of the thinking behind the purposes of environmental education, with emphasis on changes in ideas over the last few years. The need for a more holistic view, which is in contrast to the reductionist approaches of traditional education, is considered, as well as links with development education, the concepts of *sustainability*, 'green consumerism' and *life cycle analysis* of goods and services. The unavoidably political implications of environmental education are also considered.

The discussion is mainly focused on schools, but not exclusively so. The constraints felt by teachers are discussed, together with the results of a brief study of motivated primary and secondary teachers involved with environmental education. The study was an enquiry into the teachers' attitudes and practice in relation to some of the new thinking in environmental education. The findings indicate that while teachers are aware of the changes in emphasis that occurred, and many included important elements in their teaching, very few were willing to address the implicit political dimensions.

## Introduction

The objective of environmental education is to increase awareness to the problems in this field, as well as possible solutions, and to lay the foundations to a fully informed and active participation of the individual in the protection of the environment and the prudent use of natural resources.

(Council of Ministers of the European Community, 1988)

Those who have observed the progress of environmental education over the last two decades or more may be excused for being rather puzzled over why it has not had a more profound impact on all aspects and all levels of education, both formal and non-formal. It has been widely argued (Her Majesty's Government, 1991; Smyth, 1995), and now it is generally accepted throughout society and by governments, that environmental education is an essential requirement for the future survival of humanity, and therefore should be treated as a central concern for all areas of education. The call has been for both a more environmentally literate workforce and a more environmentally aware public. In a whole succession of major international reports on the environment (see for example the *Bruntland Report*: World Commission on the Environment and Development, 1987; or the United Nations Conference on the Environment and Development (UNCED), 1992) the case has also been made again and again for the importance of environmental education. In addition these ideas have been reflected by regional or national bodies, for example The Council of Ministers of the European Community (1988), and the Department for the Environment in the UK (1994). An important question must be that, with all of this support, why is environmental education not being followed through energetically in schools, colleges and in non-formal contexts all over the world? On the other hand the underlying fact that essential aspects of environmental education are unavoidably political (Orr, 1992) must always be taken into account as a contributory factor to this overall reluctance.

Many of the problems faced by environmental educators, particularly in relation to aspects of formal education, revolve around its nature and purpose (Fien, 1993; Smyth, 1995). This is a matter over which there is a continuing debate and the particular outcome at the time determines the direction in which environmental education goes in the future. The fact that there is no real consensus of views has been seen as problematic in establishing environmental education within the formal curriculum and elsewhere. Some practitioners wish to clearly define environmental education in the belief that in doing so their energies can then be turned to implementation and practice. Others feel that the debate should continue and be renewed, thus ensuring a healthy growth of ideas to inform environmental education. Another difficulty has been that environmental education has grown organically, particularly in recent years, so that perspectives and priorities have changed even among long-standing, experienced practitioners.

During the relatively short time that environmental education has been recognised it has had a chequered history, and it may be helpful to identify some of the most influential strands in its development, concentrating on some of the most recent aspects of the process of change. The history of environmental education has been well documented (see for example Sterling, 1992; Goodson, 1993 and Gayford and Dorion, 1993) and therefore it is not intended to pursue this much further here. However, it should be appreciated that the term environmental education was coined only recently. Some consider that it was in the early 1970s when it was first used, conjunction with The Countryside in the 70s Conference (Royal Society of Arts, 1970). Here the concept was still closely associated with ideas related to the natural environment and its care and conservation. This followed a tradition of ecology and fieldwork which was clearly recognisable to the educators of the day. This emphasis is still firmly embedded in the minds of many practitioners world-wide. It was not until a few years later that a more holistic notion of the environment and environmental education was appreciated with the *Belgrade Charter* (UNESCO-UNEP, 1976) where the emphasis in environmental education was focused on values and attitudes as well as skills and understanding. In 1977, the UNESCO-UNEP Conference on Environmental Education in Tbilisi (USSR) saw the establishment of an overall philosophy with a degree of international acceptance, even if it was accompanied by fragmentation in practice (UNESCO-UNEP, 1978). As recently as 1992, Sterling writes that despite consensus on the principles of environmental education, in practice a number of approaches or emphases have evolved. These reflect the different importance given to aspects of the environment, such as the natural environment, the built environment and the social and cultural environment.

Environmental education as an explicit activity has had its roots in the school curriculum in subjects such as biology and geography, with particular emphasis on the elements of field studies (Goodson, 1993). The links between the knowledge and understanding of the underlying principles and concepts of the natural environment and environmental education have remained in the minds of many people. However, some of the more recent statements about the purpose of environmental education have extended this perception and placed emphasis on methodology to include problem solving and decision making (UNESCO-UNEP, 1978), also skills and attitude development (National Curriculum Council, 1990), as well as moral and ethical dimensions (Caduto, 1985). The theoretical base of environmental education is in both the environment, or environmentalism, and in education. An understanding of this is essential when considering its purposes and directions (Greig *et al*, 1989). Recent developments have broadened the purposes of environmental education even further in the minds of many environmentalists and some of these influential ideas will be explored in this chapter.

## Some recent major influences on environmental education

In recent years there have been a number of significant changes in thinking about the environment and the impact of human activity on the environment. These have had a profound effect on the way that environmental education is currently perceived. There is now a realisation of the extent and scope of the interconnectedness of the whole field, where issues concerned with the environment are all related to each other (Smyth, 1995). By considering one issue, elements of others are seen to be involved, thereby creating a complex web of interrelated ideas. In addition to this, each issue has many dimensions which include scientific, technological, economic, aesthetic, political, ethical, cultural and spiritual. Balanced views require contributions from specialists working in all of these spheres, making collaboration essential. Those involved in environmental education now need to be able to work holistically, rather than in a fragmented and specialised way (Sterling, 1992; Fien, 1995).

The major issues now tend to be considered on a global scale with nations no longer being able to operate separately or unilaterally. There is an understanding of shared responsibility for environmental problems, whereby the actions of one community impact themselves on others in different, often remote, parts of the world. The notion of global commons, such as the atmosphere and oceans, together with our individual and corporate responsibilities, are an important part of this discussion. However, for the majority of people, personal and local contexts are more likely to have the most direct impact on their thinking and subsequent behaviour. From recognition of this situation the idea of *thinking globally and acting locally* has emerged as an influential slogan (United Nations, 1992) with the development of *Local Agenda 21* initiatives (Local Government Management Board, 1993) in many parts of the UK and elsewhere. The emphasis here is upon ways in which the behaviour of individuals or communities can be seen to impact on wider, more remote or global issues. From this has emerged two important dimensions to environmental education. One is the significances of personal participation in active environmental improvement programmes. The *World Conservation Strategy* (IUCN *et al*, 1980) strongly advocated environmental action by participation as a strategy for achieving the purposes of environmental education. This notion has been further extended to include community education as a vehicle for environmental education (Smyth, 1995). The other aspect is raising the awareness of consumer behaviour and how this relates to environmental issues. Green consumerism is now well established in the consciousness of many people (Mori, 1987 and Mintel, 1994); it is claimed that more than 60% of the UK population make purchasing decisions partly based on their knowledge of the environmental consequences of the production, use and disposal of a wide range of common goods and services. The concept of *Life Cycle Analysis*, whereby individuals study the impact on the environment of methods of production, regular use and disposal of waste, related to the goods and services they use, is an important step forward in measuring the environmental costs of production and consumption (Redclift, 1993). This type of approach can provide a valuable link between local action and impact and global effect.

It is now widely recognised by many involved in environmental education that the relationship between knowledge and understanding of the underlying principles relating to environmental issues and the behaviours that educators state that they wish to foster in the public are not simple (Costanzo *et al*, 1986). In the past there has been a general assumption that there is a clear link between knowledge and understanding of an issue and the related attitudes and behaviours of individuals. It has been assumed that by acquiring deeper, more detailed, or a wider grasp of the 'facts', the appropriate course of action in terms of personal behaviour becomes obvious and will be followed. Consequently, emphasis has been placed on the development of knowledge about the environment and the outcomes of behaviour (see, for example, Department for the Environment, 1994). Studies of a broad range of examples of human behaviour have shown that the relationship between changes in knowledge and understanding and behavioural change is complex and that knowledge is only one component in the decision-making process and the reasons behind actions (Fishbein and Ajzen, 1975; Ajzen, 1988). Elaborate models have been developed which take into account the influences of social norms, peer groups, and the degree of control that people perceive that they have over situations, as well as the understanding that people have of the outcomes of their own behaviour. If behavioural modification is an important outcome, then these factors which are thought to affect behaviour all need to be considered when developing new approaches to environmental education.

There has, however, been a significant reaction in recent years (Robottom and Hart, 1993; Fien, 1993) against the notion that environmental education is mainly about the development of responsible environmental behaviour as advocated, for example by Hines *et al* (1986) or the National Curriculum Council (1990a). The arguments are that such education is too individualistic and relates to 'green consumers' as the beneficiaries of economic development and that the teaching methods used are too behaviouristic. There is a call from these critics of the behavioural modification philosophy for an approach to environmental education which strives for greater political literacy with active as well as informed citizenship.

The views of environmentalists about the most important areas of emphases for environmental education have changed considerably over the last two decades or so. In the 1970s when environmental education began to be recognised, there was a major debate which focused on the *Limits to Growth* (Meadows *et al*, 1972). Here concern was particularly about the human impact on the environment through the exploitation of non-renewable resources, especially fossil fuels and other minerals. There was at the same time an optimistic attitude that technological innovation would solve these problems (Redclift, 1994). More recently attention has shifted towards the long term damaging side-effects of unrestrained commercial exploitation of the environment, such as climate change through the build up of greenhouse gases, ozone depletion and the reduction of biodiversity, mainly through habitat destruction (United Nations, 1992; Department of the Environment, 1994).

## The sustainability debate and green awareness

One of the most important changes in thinking in relation to environmental education has been the association between environmental concerns and development issues. From here the notion of *sustainability* has emerged as a central concept (WCED, 1987; UNCED, 1992). While, as yet there is no commonly agreed definition of sustainability there are many aspects where there is a measure of agreement; this includes linking the ability to provide for present needs with an ability to provide for the needs of the future. However, there is considerable controversy about some of the underlying assumptions, for instance, that the term *sustainability* is often transformed to *sustainable development*. In the minds of most people the notion of development means growth and the various interpretations of this idea (Orr, 1992). Schleicher (1989) argues for a paradigm shift in human attitudes and actions towards the environment which does not require a growth of the kind usually envisaged. This thinking is further developed in *Caring for the Earth: a strategy for sustainable living* (IUCN, UNEP and WWF, 1991) which argues for an essential role for education, to ensure that people accept the principle that living 'sustainably' depends on acceptance of the need to seek harmony with other people and with nature.

The linking of environmental education with development education is of fundamental importance since it acknowledges the idea that a good deal of environmental degradation is the direct result of poverty. In the richer, often called 'developed' countries, environmental concerns have frequently emphasised the amenity value of the environment (Redclift, 1994) with a consequent urge for conservation based on the requirement for areas that can be used for leisure and relaxation. In poor countries the need to use environmental resources on a short-term basis in order to survive predominates. In these two different contexts the notion of conservation has different implications. The fact that development is frequently the result of economic associations between rich and poor countries has even further implications and these are being explored in the context of environmental education (see for example *Reaching Out*, World Wide Fund for Nature, 1993).

Studies of so called, 'green awareness' (O'Riordan, 1981; Cotgrove, 1982; Witherspoon and Martin, 1993) have shown that environmental attitudes, far from being consistent across interested groups, are heterogeneous. Studies have shown that those who profess environmental concern fall into several groups. For example there are those with a particular interest in the protection of wildlife and their habitats. There are others who are especially concerned about matters of pollution such as vehicle emissions, nuclear waste or greenhouse gases. Their interest often focuses on the effects on human health. Others have been variously described, and O'Riordan (1981) calls them 'deep ecologists' or 'dark green'. This group concentrates on the inter-relatedness of much of human behaviour and the impact that this has on the environment. This wide range of attitudes to the environment is reflected in the variety of people involved in environmental education. Their motivations for involvement often differ and they have different views of the purposes that they pursue. This is another factor contributing to the complexity of the change process in environmental education.

## Environmental education in schools

The development of environmental education in schools in England, Wales and Northern Ireland in recent years has occurred at a time of profound change in the whole education system. Bowe *et al* (1992) list the introduction of local management of schools, the establishment of the National Curriculum, records of achievement and Standard Assessment Tasks (SATs) as being the most significant. The demise of the Local Education Authorities, with their provision of central services, as well as changes in the arrangements for in-service training (DFE, 1992) and the new inspection regulations (OFSTED, 1993) are also significant. Each of these would require a chapter to themselves to explore their implications for education and how these have impacted on environmental education, but for the purposes of the present discussion it should be understood that this larger educational backdrop needs to be appreciated in order to follow the changes in attitude to environmental education in schools.

The heritage of environmental education largely came from the tradition of fieldwork in the secondary schools and topic work in primary schools. For many years in the secondary curriculum there has been a continuing debate about the place of environmental education in the curriculum (see Gayford, 1986 and 1992; Ebutt, 1992; Goodson, 1993). This is not simply an academic argument with little practical significance, it has serious implications for how environmental education is treated in teaching programmes. Part of the basis of the discussion is whether environmental education should be treated as a separate subject in the curriculum, with its own timetabled space and examinations, or integrated across the curriculum. The former stance presupposes a body of knowledge which can be taught separately from other subjects and which can be assessed through formal examinations. This thinking emphasises the importance of the subject material, and there is an expectation that this helps to raise the status of environmental education in the curriculum. The alternative view is that environmental education should be integrated into the whole curriculum where, it is argued, it enables the subject matter to be taught in the context of traditional established subjects, and it can also become more easily suffused into the whole ethos of the school. Primary schools have fewer difficulties with the concept of environmental education as part of a whole school curriculum since this idea conforms more closely with their traditional methodologies, often involving topic work (Dorion, 1993; Neal and Palmer, 1994).

For a time, the place of formal environmental education in the curriculum in England, Wales and Northern Ireland appeared to be settled following the Education Reform Act in 1988, with the introduction of the National Curriculum. At that time a number of cross-curricular dimensions, skills and themes were identified (National Curriculum Council, 1990b). These were expected to permeate the school curriculum; among them was environmental education. Guidance of a non-statutory kind was provided in the form of *Curriculum Guidance No. 7: Environmental Education* (National Curriculum Council, 1990a). The isolation of the so called, 'adjectival' education forms, (Sterling, 1990) of which environmental education is one along with health, economic and industrial understanding, careers education and citizenship, which resulted from this approach to the whole curriculum, has meant that there is frequently competition for space in curriculum time rather than a determined attempt to integrate. This situation has now been further changed following the *Dearing Review* of the Curriculum (Schools Curriculum and Assessment Authority, 1994), which was set up to simplify what was admitted to be an over-prescriptive, over-complex and over-assessed curriculum. The resulting inclusion of elements relating to the environment was perhaps more encouraging than had been anticipated (Gayford, 1995). However, the introduction of the discretionary 20% of time for schools to use has raised serious questions about the position of environmental education and the other 'adjectival' forms of education within the curriculum. A significant problem for environmental education in most of the UK and elsewhere in the world is that there is a preoccupation with the statutory curriculum and the assessed elements of learning which makes it difficult to move the thinking of senior managers and planners away from some of the simpler and somewhat outmoded ideas of the nature and purpose of environmental education.

One of the predominant models of environmental education in current literature presents it as consisting of three interlinked forms of education (Schools Council, 1974 and the National Curriculum Council, 1990a). These are described as education *about* the environment, which is concerned with developing knowledge of environmental principles and processes and education which involves learning *in* the environment, where the environment is used as a resource which may be likened to an extended classroom and the emphasis is on developing skills and awareness. The third strand is education *for* the environment which is aimed at addressing values. This tripartite model of environmental education is probably the most influential in the UK and in many other countries.

There have been criticisms of the model (Ebbutt, 1992) from the viewpoint that the term *about* the environment implies that the understanding of the ecological principles upon which environments are based is sufficient without deeper understanding of the ways in which human populations impact on the environment through the processes of production and consumption. Education *in* the environment seems to emphasise the place where learning should take place rather than how it should be done. Finally education *for* the environment suggests that environmental education should result in a particular viewpoint and fails to take account of different possible value systems; consequently, however well intentioned it may be, the result may be more akin to indoctrination rather than education. Fien (1993) feels that education *about* and *in* the environment are of value only in so far as they develop the knowledge and skills which support the transforming purposes of education *for* the environment. Fien goes on to argue for what he describes as a 'critical approach' within environmental education and which Sterling (1992) describes as 'socially critical'. They take the *Tbilisi Declaration* (UNESCO-UNEP, 1978) as a starting point, and develop five overarching features for this type of education:

1   Critical environment education which emphasises the development of an environmental consciousness based upon holistic views, which consider the interdependence of natural and social systems, historical perspectives of environmental issues, the study of causes and effects of problems with alternative solutions and the examination of ideology, economy and technology and links between local, regional, national and global governments and economies.

2   Critical environmental education which emphasises critical thinking and problem-solving skills through a range of practical and interdisciplinary learning experiences, focusing on real problems and involving the study of a wide range of sources and types of information.

3   Emphasis on the development of an environmental ethic based on sensitivity and concern for the quality of the environment.

4   Emphasis on the development of attitudes, understanding and skills which relate to political literacy which promotes participation in different forms of social action to help maintain and improve the environment.

5   Teaching methodologies which are consistent with these aims.

(Based on Fien, 1993)

Huckle (1993), building on the tripartite model of environmental education, suggests a correspondence between this and three ideological positions. One is education for management and control of the environment, with emphasis on the technological aspects of human interests, which he relates mainly to education *about* the environment. Another is education for environmental awareness which is concerned mainly with interpretation and corresponds most closely to education *in* the environment. The last is education for sustainability which focuses on aspects of critical human interest, relating most to education *for* the environment. While different combinations of these can be seen in practice in different teaching situations there is significantly much more emphasis on education for management and control. Also it is perhaps significant that the language of business management has become pervasive within formal education. This type of language reflects assumptions about the way that education should be managed and often this is in contrast to the consensus forms of curriculum management advocated by environmental educators.

Recent surveys of the teaching profession have shown that while many teachers approve of the inclusion of environmental education in the school curriculum and feel that it is something in which all schools should be involved, there remain a number of important concerns which affect their overall enthusiasm. It may be helpful at this stage to consider what these are and to reflect on their consequences if further development of environmental education is to occur in our schools. These are considered in no particular order of importance but give an idea of the range and nature of the reservations expressed. They are based mainly on evidence gathered by Gayford (1991) which has recently been up-dated. By taking account of and then addressing these concerns, it is hoped that future progress in environmental education in the formal sector can be assisted.

## Reservations about environmental education expressed by teachers

Firstly, the concepts of the environment and environmental education that has been promoted by many of the international agencies and conferences is so wide that it easily subsumes the whole of education. Consequently teachers of environmental education find it difficult to identify their main aims and to communicate these to others, be they teachers, pupils, parents or governors, who may not share their enthusiasm (Gayford, 1991).

Also environmental educators often appear to be particularly concerned with the major issues related to the environment. This may include tropical rain-forest destruction, nuclear power, pollution and many others. The effect of this can be that environmental education becomes 'issue based', thus lacking the coherence and rigour expected by those planning and organising the educational experiences of pupils (Goodson, 1993). Many of the issues raised in the context of environmental education are broad and complex and there are no straightforward answers. Frequently, rational people may hold opposing views. Teachers and pupils often find this situation confusing, frustrating and unsatisfactory in comparison with other curriculum areas. The holistic nature of environmental education can be a problem for teachers who, having been educated themselves in a reductionist and fragmented tradition of education, feel unable to cope with the multiplicity of concepts and differing ideas that need to be brought to bear on individual issues (Smyth, 1995).

Subject chauvinism is well established, particularly in the secondary school curriculum and there is considerable unwillingness for teachers to engage in integrated or inter-disciplinary areas (see Layton, 1972; Gayford, 1986). In addition, there is less support from the professional subject associations which are more clearly oriented to the needs of subject specialist teachers. Cross-curricular areas often experience difficulties since no particular subject specialist teacher is willing to take responsibility for these aspects of the curriculum or if they do so, specialists in other areas are inclined to leave it to those in the area where some responsibility has been acknowledged. This phenomenon has a profound effect on the processes of planning and co-ordination across the curriculum (Gayford and Dorion, 1993).

There is a genuine concern amongst educators that environmental education may be treated as a form of indoctrination; this relates to the fact that a good deal of environmental education deals with values, attitudes and behaviour. It is also seen as problematic that it is frequently taught by teachers with enthusiasm for this part of the curriculum who may have what are considered to be extreme views, and who may take the opportunity to promote their particular ideology. The concerns have an even more obvious basis when it is appreciated that a good deal of discussion related to environmental issues has explicit political implications (Orr, 1992).

There are particular problems over the assessment and evaluation of environmental education in its broadest sense, whereby traditional methods have been shown to be inappropriate. In most countries there is a preoccupation with educational measurement of performance, often to the extent that there is a danger of assuming that if the qualities to be developed cannot be measured, then they cannot be suitable priorities of education. This creates an important conflict over the fundamental purposes for education. Environmental education is concerned with either higher order learning objectives, such as problem solving or decision making (UNESCO-UNEP, 1978) or else it relates to affective aspects of pupils' development; both require innovative methods to effectively cover their assessment or evaluation. Few would be surprised at these reservations but there are powerful counterbalancing arguments to be taken into account, which have been set out in this article.

# A recent study of attitudes of teachers to environmental education

This is a brief account of an enquiry carried out by the author into the attitudes of 87 secondary teachers and 95 primary teachers involved in environmental education in state maintained schools in urban and rural areas across much of England and Wales, which took place in early 1995. Rather than ask about all aspects of the environmental education with which they were currently involved, it was decided to focus particularly on a range of questions related to sustainability and 'green attitudes' which reflect issues of the broad debate on environmental education. The questions related to the following:

1   The use and application of the concept of *sustainability* to their teaching and what this might mean for personal behaviour and lifestyles. Each teacher was asked to write a paragraph stating what they understood by the term and what they thought were the most important factors from a teaching perspective.

2   The extent to which they considered the most important purpose of environmental education to be the development of environmentally responsible behaviour among their students. Teachers were asked what qualifying statement they would wish to add.

3   The inclusion of elements of *life cycle analysis* in their teaching to enable students to understand the impact on the environment of goods and services that they use. Teachers were asked whether they included this in any of their teaching and if so, what importance they gave to it. To answer this part of the question teachers were given three options which were: very important, fairly important and not important.

4   The encouragement of student participation in environmental maintenance and improvement initiatives around the school or in the locality. Teachers were asked whether: (a) they undertook any of this type of activity or (b) they thought it important as part of environmental education. Again they were given three options, as in 3 above.

5   The extent to which they felt that the environmental education that they carried out in their schools is concerned with raising political awareness and understanding of appropriate ways of participating in the democratic process.

13

6   Whether the teachers felt that the main emphasis of their own motivation for involvement in environmental education lay in: (a) the care of wildlife and wildlife habitats, (b) the reduction of the impact of lifestyles on the environment, e.g. resource depletion or pollution or (c) a holistic approach where a multidimensional understanding is required with the possibility of a paradigm shift in outlook.

The results are summarised in Table 1.1. From this it can be seen that the teachers were aware of the concept of *sustainability* and many used it in their teaching. Within their answers to this question, the impact of poverty (69% primary and 83% secondary), the current economic strategies, particularly those of the 'developed countries' (62% primary and 75% secondary) and the increasing expectations of most consumers (58% primary and 72% secondary) were cited as the most important factors affecting progress towards sustainability.

All teachers stated that the most important purpose of environmental education was the development of environmentally responsible behaviour, but this was qualified in two main ways: (a) that this should be through a deep concern and respect for the environment (88% primary and 82% secondary) or (b) to understand the issues involved and to make their own judgements (65% primary and 78% secondary). Many felt that it was important that students were not taught to have particular attitudes, but that an open-minded approach should be part of the educational process.

Most teachers (65% primary and 56% secondary) included elements of *life cycle analysis* in their environmental education and a majority felt that this was an important part of their work (81% primary and 70% secondary). The additional statements made by teachers from both phases were that it helped to give relevance to their teaching and that it clearly demonstrated links between local actions and global impacts.

Participation in the maintenance or improvement of the environment showed that while a large proportion of the sample of teachers considered that it is an important part of environmental education (85% primary and 69% secondary), fewer actually became involved (47% primary and 53% secondary).

The answers to the next question (Question 5) showed that very few teachers felt that explicitly addressing the political dimension of environmental issues was part of their concern (4% primary and 18% secondary). Their main motivations for being involved in environmental education showed a fairly even distribution between: (a) care of wildlife and their habitats (41% primary and 34% secondary) and (b) the reduction of the impact of lifestyles in the environment (42% primary and 30% secondary). Fewer felt that the holistic approach with a possible paradigm shift was their priority (15% primary and 23% secondary).

**Table 1.1   Responses of teachers to questions on sustainability and 'green attitudes'**

|  |  | Primary % | Secondary % |
|---|---|---|---|
| 1 | (a) Teacher awareness of the concept of *sustainability* | 100 | 100 |
|  | (b) Use of the term *sustainability* in teaching | 41 | 89 |
| 2 | The main purpose of environmental education is to develop environmentally responsible behaviour | 100 | 100 |
| 3 | Inclusion of elements of *life cycle analysis* in teaching | 65 | 56 |
| 4 | (a) Participation in the maintenance and improvement of the local environment | 47 | 53 |
|  | (b) Considered that active involvement in environmental maintenance and improvement is an important part of environmental education | 85 | 69 |
| 5 | Environmental education should raise political awareness | 4 | 18 |
| 6 | Main personal motivation for involvement in environmental education: |  |  |
|  | (a) care of wildlife and their habitats | 43 | 34 |
|  | (b) reduction of impact on lifestyles on the environment | 42 | 31 |
|  | (c) to follow a holistic approach with a possible paradigm shift in outlook | 15 | 23 |

These results show a progression compared with earlier studies related to teachers' attitudes to environment education (Gayford, 1987 and Gayford, 1993). This study suggests that informed teachers in primary schools as well as in secondary schools are beginning to think more holistically and to relate their teaching to world views rather than simply to follow prescribed guidelines in the National Curriculum. They have an awareness of some of the major issues related to the environment and this has affected the environmental education they provide. They are also prepared to explore ways of integrating broader issues and aspects related to attitudes and behaviour into their regular teaching. There is further evidence in the literature of ways in which teachers are approaching environmental education in less fragmented ways. The significance of the *hidden curriculum*, a term which describes the assumptions implicit in all aspects of school life and which includes things which are not clearly stated compared to aspects of the timetabled curriculum, should not be underestimated, since these things are still effectively learned by students. The potential for using the management of schools and other institutions as models of environmental efficiency, in which students are involved in planning, monitoring and evaluating effectiveness, has hardly began to be realised, but already there are some suggested approaches (Baczala, 1992). From the results of the brief survey there is still a marked reluctance for teachers to embrace some of the political emphases advocated by many environmentalists. This is hardly surprising considering the long tradition of not only political neutrality of schools but also non-political debate.

The reasons for wishing to include environmental education in the curriculum of schools, higher education courses and as part of general public education is clear to most people. There are many more problems over the content, the approaches to be used and the nature of the outcomes that are desired. Much of this chapter has been an exploration of the continuing debate about these issues rather than a justification for environmental education *per se*. Part of the problem to quote Sterling (1991) is that:

> Environmental education is a broad approach to education. Its eclectic nature, paradoxically, has always been its strength and its weakness. The former, because it has allowed environmental education to challenge narrowly-based educational approaches, yet also the latter because environmental education has always sat uneasily with traditional modes of educational thinking and institutional organisations.

Environmental education seems to be unavoidably linked to the process of change in whatever educational context it is being considered.

Current structures within formal educational systems do not encourage its development, but the situation is continually changing both from the perspective of the environment and the pressing issues that it presents. Also within education there is change in the purpose that society demands that it fulfils.

# Bibliography

Ajzen, I. (1988) *Attitudes, Personality and Behaviour*. Milton Keynes: Open University Press.

Baczala, K. (1992) *Towards a school policy for environmental education - environmental audit*. Wolverhampton: National Association for Environmental Education.

Berry, R.J. (1993) Ethics, attitudes and environmental understanding for all. *Field Studies: the Journal of the Field Studies Council* **8** pp. 245--255.

Bowe, R., Ball, S. and Gold, A. (1992) *Reforming Education and Changing Schools*. London: Routledge.

Caduto, M.J. (1985) *A Guide on Environmental Values*. Environmental Education Series **13** Paris: UNESCO.

Costanzo, M., Archer, D., and Pettigrew, T. (1986) Energy conservation behaviour: the difficult path from information to action. *American Psychologist* **41** p. 521-528.

Cotgrove, S. (1982) *Catastrophe or Cornucopia*. Chichester: Wiley.

The Council and the Ministers of Education Meeting within the Council (1988) Resolution on environmental education. *Official Journal of the European Communities*, No. C177/8.

Department of the Environment (1994) *Grants for Education Support and Training 1993-94*. London: DFE, July 1992.

Dorion, C. (1993) *Planning and Evaluation of Environmental Education for secondary Education*. Surrey: WWF, UK.

Ebbutt, D. (1992) *Ordering the Elements: the Management of Environmental Education across the Curriculum*. Surrey: WWF, UK.

Fien, J. (1993) Ideology critique and environmental education. in J. Fien (ed.) *Education for the Environment - critical curriculum theorising and environmental education*. Australia: Deakin University.

Fien, J. (1995) Teaching for a Sustainable World: the Environmental and Development Education Project for Teacher Education. *Environmental Education Research* **1** (1) pp. 21-33.

Fishbein, M. and Ajzen, I. (1975) *Belief, attitude, intention and behaviour: an introduction to theory and research*. Reading, Mass: Addison-Wesley.

Gayford, C.G. (1986) Environmental Education and the Secondary School Curriculum. *Journal of Curriculum Studies* **18** (2) pp. 147-158.

Gayford, C.G. (1987) *Environmental Education: Experiences and Attitudes; a survey of teachers, youth leaders, school pupils and students.* Report submitted to the DoE as part of the NATO CCMS Education and Training in relation to Environmental Problems Project, Reading: Council for Environmental Education.

Gayford, C.G. (1991) Environmental Education: a question of emphasis in the School Curriculum. *Cambridge Journal of Education* **21** (1) pp. 73-79.

Gayford, C.G. (1993) A Study in the Training of Teachers in Environmental Education on England and Wales. *European Journal of Teacher Education* **16** (3) pp. 271-279.

Gayford, C.G. and Dorion, C. (1993) Planning and Evaluation of Environmental Education across the Curriculum. A research monograph on Environmental Education in the School Curriculum. *The New Bulmershe Papers.*

Gayford, C.G. (1995) Environmental Education in the Revised National Curriculum. *Environmental Education* **49** pp. 5-6.

Goodson, I. (1993) *School Subjects and Curriculum Change.* Brighton: Falmer Press.

Greig, S., Pike, G. and Selby, D. (1989) *Greenprints.* London: Kogan Page.

Her Majesty's Government (1991) *Our Common Inheritance: Britain's Environmental Strategy.* Cm 1200. London: HMSO.

Hines, J., Hungerford, H. and Tomera, A. (1986) Analysis and synthesis of research on responsible environmental behaviour. *Journal of Environmental Education* **18** (2) pp. 1-18.

Huckle, J. (1993) Environmental Education and Sustainability: a view from critical theory. In J. Fien (ed.) *Environmental education - a pathway to sustainability.* Australia: Deakin University.

IUCN, UNEP and WWF (1980) *World Conservation Strategy.* Gland: International Union for the Conservation of Nature.

IUCN, UNEP and WWF (1991) *Caring for the Earth.* Gland: International Union for the Conservation of Nature.

Layton, D. (1972) Science as general education. *Trends in General Education* **25** pp. 11-15.

Local Government Management Board (1993) *Local Agenda 21: A Guide for Local Authorities in the UK.* London: LGMB.

Meadows, D.H., Meadows, D.L., Randers, J. and Behrens, W.W. (1972) *Limits to Growth: a report for the Club of Rome's Project on the Predicament of Mankind.* London: Pan Books.

Mintel (1994) *The Green Conscience.* London: Mintel Marketing.

MORI (1987) *Public attitudes towards nature conservation: report of a survey for the Nature Conservancy Council*. London: MORI

National Curriculum Council (1990a) *Curriculum Guidance No. 7: Environmental Education*. York: National Curriculum Council.

National Curriculum Council (1990b) *Curriculum Guidance No.3: the whole curriculum*. York: National Curriculum Council.

Neil, P. and Palmer, J. (1994) *The Handbook of Environmental Education*. London: Routledge.

Office for Standards in Education (1993) *Handbook for the Inspection of Schools*. 2nd ed. London: HMSO.

Orr, D. (1992) *Ecological Literacy - Education and the Transition to a Postmodern World*. London: SUNY Press.

O'Riordan, T. (1981) Environmentalism and Education. *Journal of Geography in Higher Education* 5 (1) pp. 3-17.

Redclift, M. (1993) Values, Education and the Global Environment. *Annual Review of Environmental Education* 6 pp. 42-43.

Redclift, M. (1994) Reflections on the Sustainable Development Debate. *The International Journal of Sustainable Development and World Ecology* 1 (1) pp. 3-21.

Robottom, I. and Hart, P. (1993) Paradigms and the ideology of environmental education research. In I. Robottom and P. Hart (eds.) *Research in Environmental Education - Engaging the Debate*. Australia: Deakin University.

Royal Society of Arts (1970) *The Countryside in 1970: Third Conference*. Birmingham: Kynoch Press.

Schleicher, K. (1989) Beyond the environmental education: the need for ecological awareness. *International Review of Education* 35 pp. 257--281.

Schools Council (1974) *Project Environment: Education for the Environment*. London: Longman.

Schools Curriculum and Assessment Authority (1994) *The National Curriculum and its Assessment: Final Report*. London: SCAA.

Smyth, J.C. (1995) Environment and Education: a view of a changing scene. *Environmental Education Research* 1 (1) pp. 3-20.

Sterling, S. (1990) Environment, Development Education - towards an holistic view. In J. Abrahams, C. Lacey and R. Williams (eds.) *Deception, Demonstration and Debate*. London: WWF/Kogan Page.

Sterling, S. (1992) Mapping Environmental Education. In W.L. Filho and J.A. Palmer (eds.) *Key Issues in Environmental Education*. England: Horton.

UNESCO-UNEP (1976) International Environmental Workshop 'The Belgrade Charter'. A global framework for environmental education, *Connect* 1 (1) pp. 1-3.

UNESCO-UNEP (1978) *Intergovernmental Conference on Environmental Education, Tbilisi, USSR. Final Report*. Paris: UNESCO.

United Nations (1992) *UN Conference on Environment and Development: Agenda 21 Rio Declaration*. Paris: UNESCO.

Witherspoon, S. and Martin, J. (1992) What do we mean by green? <u>In</u> R. Sowell, R. Brook, G. Prior and B. Taylor (eds.) *British Social Attitudes, the Ninth Report*. Aldershot: Dartmouth.

World Commission on Environment and Development (1987) *Our Common Future*, the Brundtland Report. Oxford: Oxford University Press.

# 2 Children's attitudes to the environment

*Cedric Cullingford*

## Abstract

This paper, based on lengthy semi-structured interviews with children aged 6-9, explores the way in which children understand their visual and symbolic environment. Having established how even the very youngest children are interpreting the places around them, from their homes to the experience of the outside world, it goes on to explore several themes that emerge from the rich evidence presented. The world children experience offers clear contrasts between the rich and the poor, and children have to make sense of their relationship with both extremes. They are personal witnesses to social deprivation as well as pollution and they are made aware of the universal scale of such problems through the media, especially television. The chapter explores the tensions which affect children, between town and country, security and insecurity, the convenience and dangers of transport, and the developed and developing world. It also analyses how children find their own way of making sense of their experience of the environment.

## Introduction

Children's awareness of the environment and their analysis of it is developed far earlier than their experience of school. By the time geographical concepts have been presented to them they will have had years of experience in forming opinions about the place in which they live and its relationship to the environment of other people. Long before they will have formed their attitudes towards the conservation of animals or the ozone layer they will have become aware of the way in which the environment affects them. This chapter is not about environmental education as a subject or about the way that children, in what Egan calls their 'romantic' stage, become concerned with the universe (Egan, 1978). Instead it is concerned with the ways in which children respond to and analyse both their immediate and more distant environments. Issues such as pollution and traffic do emerge but they do so not because they are seen as a 'subject', a matter for debate or opinion, but because they are a significant factor in the everyday experience of children. The research from which the findings emerge was a large-scale study of the development of social attitudes. The specific subjects that were mentioned were offered by the children, and not suggested by the researchers.

## The research

Most previous studies of children's attitudes have been small-scale and have relied either on word associations or on pictures. In either case, the information to be gathered was pre-selected and did not arise from children's interests.

This study was based on lengthy interviews. In order to find out what children thought and how they acquired the information, the interviewees were placed in circumstances in which they felt free to talk, responding to a series of open questions. The interviewer was not connected in any way to their school and the children were not aware of what the interviewer wanted to know. They did not, therefore, try to guess what they were supposed to say. The result is a large amount of material, for it was possible to pursue answers in depth, to let the children explore other ideas and to return more than once to similar questions. By creating the right circumstances for this qualitative ethnographic study, the interviewees were able to talk freely, openly and honestly about their attitudes and feelings as well as their knowledge.

After a lengthy piloting process, the subjects of these interviews were 160 boys and girls aged 6-9. They were selected with the schools' co-operation as being representative of a variety of different backgrounds. Some of the children came from private schools. Others came from inner-city schools, defined as low socio-economic circumstances by the DHSS. There were children from rural areas as well as towns. Every effort was made to ensure that the children were representative; that ethnic minorities were also included. The interviews therefore present sophisticated and complex material rather than simplified answers as in a MORI survey.

The interviews were analysed at a number of levels. At one level was the concern to find salient features that demonstrated shared themes, which were validated by internal cross-referencing. At another, any inconsistencies were explored as well as features that showed particular factors of age, gender or class, or indeed other features such as experience of travel, which can be so influential.

## The context

Intelligent perception of the world in which we live begins early. It starts with the understanding of immediate social relations, with the ability not only to respond to others but to understand their different needs (Dunn, 1988). Long before school, young children understand sophisticated notions such as truth and falsehood, and are also making causal inferences which demonstrate analysis of their physical as well as social surroundings (Chandler, Fritz and Hala, 1989; Das Gupta and Bryant, 1989). Their 'gaze' is not limited to the obvious or the immediate. They are aware of the distinctions between places, since objects hidden from them remain just as real (Baillargeon and de Vos, 1991). They also develop conceptual insights about natural growth (Rosengren et al, 1991). All these abilities are manifested in infants, some at a few months old.

Young children, therefore, do not merely react to their circumstances in a passive way. They bring intelligence and intuition to bear and need to interpret where they live as well as to communicate. This is not the place to summarise all the research that has demonstrated the abilities of young children, but the consistency of the findings does have important implications. As this chapter indicates, the views that children express show their need to interpret for themselves their physical and emotional environment and to do so long before anyone thinks of imposing an interpretation on them. Children not only perceive but are aware of the conditions that affect perceptibility. They understand the different points of view of people, and the relationship of the individual to place. Thus they understand the distinction between the deictic and intrinsic space; they need to in order to make sense of the world. They also, very early on, develop a memory for location and the concept of a point of view (Deloache and Brown, 1983; Cox, 1991). Far from being limited by egocentricity, as in the mythology associated with Piaget, they are actively making a perception of the world that is affected by both primary and secondary experience; by what they observe for themselves and by the information presented to them through media like television.

It therefore follows that, without using the term, children develop their own individual notions of culture. Any understanding of the relationship between people and the conditions in which they live is bound to demand an explanation of differences, of contrasts, between countries and between people. It is not just inter-personal matters that are understood but socio-historical ones (Haste, 1987). Furthermore they understand the distinction between those things that all people have in common and the cultures that distinguish the members of one group or category of people from another (Hofstede, 1991). As we will see, both the strengths and the limitations of culture are explored (Bourdieu, 1984). The environment is, after all, a political and a social issue as well as a fact. The way in which children interpret it affects them deeply; they define themselves and their futures in relation to it.

## The findings

The quotations given here illuminate the consistent findings, subject to content analysis, which demonstrate the basic attitude sets, and qualitative analysis, which reveals both the styles of thinking and the sources of influence. Whilst they have their individual tone they do highlight the shared experiences of children whether they live in town or the country. There are no simple contrasts in the attitudes between children according to their socio-economic status but within their accounts. Whether they are talking about micro- or macro-environments, there is a strong sense of consistent and shared experience, as if their world view were formed out of a common train of information. Of course there are differences; each individual case is unique. But just as they share a common humanity so they share a series of attitudes, both prejudices and necessary stereotypes, that reveal the basis of a cultural outlook.

Whilst this is not the place to describe children's attitudes to their own homes, or to parents and siblings, the way that they do so is a basis for the way they construct their understanding of the environment. At the core of their perception is a sense of contrast. The world appears to them to be clearly divided between the rich and the poor, both in their home surroundings and in the wider world. They see images, in the street and on television, that demonstrate vividly the differences between those that have and those that have not. For them there is a constant tension between the two. Their own immediate experience, their micro-environment informs, and is informed by, their vision of the world beyond. They see the contrasts between rich and poor. At the same time they accept it as an immutable fact and resent it.

Hofstede's (1980) demarcation lines of cultural values, like the individual principle versus the collective, does not take into account some of the complex and equivocal, if consistent, attitudes that individuals share. Rather than make a choice between one point of view and another, between one category or typology and another, people express themselves through the acceptance of tension. Attitudes to the rich, for example, reveal the constant relationship between jealousy, and possible admiration, on the one hand and despite, or possible antipathy, on the other. Because there is a tension between a person's circumstances and the experience of others, as seen for instance on television, there is bound to be an equivocal attitude to this measure of the social world. Children are aware of what riches mean, both the acquisition of possessions, which relates to them, and the symbolic power of ownership:

A posh house with us wearing loads of posh clothes with loads of money. And a swimming pool in the garden. That's what I'd describe as rich.
*(girl 8)*

A car with a swimming pool in it. A cadillac. A big mansion. Private placers. I've seen what I think is a rich person, driving around in a Ferrari F40. They would have big cars .....
*(boy 8)*

There is a tension here about the recognition of status as expressed in luxury, and the power to have possession of things. Two phrases give a hint at what all the children delineate; the idea of the rich as being 'posh', which is not a compliment, and the personal desire for 'private places'. What the children consistently long for is space, both within the home and outside. The real advantage the rich have is just that. But at the same time they are held to be snobs, as if the display of wealth were something the children themselves would wish to avoid.

Rich, yeah, but I'm being greedy, you're being greedy if you want to be rich. I do want to be rich but I don't want to be greedy...
*(girl 8)*

If I was rich I could get the things I want but some people might not like me if I'm rich...
*(boy 8)*

The immediate environment, that of home and school, is overlaid with a wider social system. The desire for personal space, the freedom to move is more than a symbolic value even if sometimes expressed in symbolic terms - for example, a large home in the country. On the other hand the world that experienced especially through the visual medium of television is one in which possessions are often flaunted. Just as in school where one of the undercurrents of survival is not to stand out or to be too 'different', so the rich are suspect for being so noticeable. The 'correct' line to take is that no-one should be too rich since that is greedy. At the same time children fully understand the advantages. The reasons for this is that they also witness the alternative: the poor.

Whilst children describe many tensions in their homes - often to do with lack of personal space and quarrelling with siblings - there is a consistent acceptance of their lot. Home is after all where they are and where their friends are. Other places might be better but home is what they are accustomed to. There is an almost laconic acceptance of what Giddens (1990) terms 'ontological security'. For him this is the social basis for self-identity, although it should be pointed out that the children in this research are much more relative in their sense of themselves. They all can see the potential advantage, however unrealistic, of having been born somewhere else - in the countryside, for instance, or in a bigger house or in the United States. Their *own* environment is not, therefore, assumed to be the best. Sometimes they are personally and immediately conscious of this fact.

> I'm quite poor already in my family, I don't have much money and nor does my mum. When we go home we're not allowed to get a taxi or anything to eat. We just have to walk home and when we get home I only have a piece of bread or something out of the fridge or something. We hardly ever go shopping and, er, thinking of being poor, I don't really think much of being poor.                                                    *(boy 8)*

The children do not have to live in straightened circumstances to be aware of the contrast in the world between the rich and the poor. Even those from private schools contrast themselves with those who are very rich. But just as children observe displays of wealth so they observe, both in the street and in images of the news, the dire consequences of being poor. They all have similar stories to tell, observations that deeply inform the way in which they understand the realities of their environment.

> Sad people, unhappy. 'Cos they haven't got enough things. The old people. They can't get about as much as us. They're old. Most of them are old and they have torn clothes and sad faces. Wearing rags.                    *(girl 8)*

> People who carry their homes in carrier bags. They're just cardboard boxes. Just down the road from my house is an old lady. She normally walks past. And she wears plastic bags on her feet for shoes. Because she's hardly got any money.                                                    *(boy 8)*

The tales the children tell of the poor and the homeless, of beggars and 'down and outs' are not generalised. They all derive from personal experience. They start with "down my road ...", "Once I ...", "I've seen ...", "When I went to ...". A central part of their personal experience of the environment is the bleakness of city streets. It is partly for this reason that there is a contrasting longing for the countryside.

The children not only witness but understand their locality. They recognise not just the social factors which underlie the city but the connection between spaces and the way they are used. These are both real and symbolic landmarks for them (Siegel and White, 1975); they are spatially aware (Spencer, Blades and Morsley, 1989). This research shows how such awareness affects them. All the time children need to attune themselves both to the contrasts in the environment and to the tensions between their own circumstances and those of others, between the public and the private (cf. Habermas, 1989).

One of the contrasts in the environment which affects children in the shaping of their social understanding is that between town and country. The town clearly has its conveniences. There are friends to play with and places to play in. There are shops and schools nearby. But towns are seen by all the children to be threatening places. In contrast, the countryside symbolises freedom and unconstrained pleasure; a vast park to play in. Parents might have warned their children to be careful of strangers wherever they are, whether in the town or country (it is not a phrase the children often repeat), but children normally associate only towns with any sense of threat. Bullying, for example, is not confined to schools and school playgrounds. Many children complain that even walking along the street exposes them to some kind of threat.

> I don't like living here because I don't like walking down to school and all the way back.                                              *(girl 6)*

> Where I live some of the people are very, well, quite aggressive or mean.
> *(boy 9)*

The closer the people are together the more children assume there will be danger.

It is, however, not just bullying which makes children fearful of city streets. They have seen the very poor and might have pitied them. There is also, for those who live in inner-city areas, a strong sense of being threatened, even in their own homes. Just as they talk about the bullies of their own age who are in the parks or in the streets, so they observe older people, especially when drunk.

> There's too many drunk people ... there's this shelter and there's a bus stop there and, like loads and loads of drunk people. It's horrible to see it like that and they've just gone like crazy...
> *(girl 8)*

The sense of insecurity also reaches into their homes. The awareness of robbery is not just a theoretical one, reported as news, but affects children personally.

> I want to live somewhere where you haven't got a fire escape leading up to your balcony. Not very safe when I had the robbery ... safer in school because lots of people are there.
> *(boy 8)*

Not all children have personal experience of being robbed, but they all mention burglaries. They assume that one of the disadvantages of being rich is the inevitable danger of attracting thieves. The town is, in fact, perceived as a dangerous place, not only in the streets, but even to the extent that the crowd of neighbours can make them feel uncomfortable in their own homes.

> With my mum I'm in a flat and sometimes it's a bit scary at night and when you go down in the morning 'cos sometimes I think people are hiding against the walls and stuff ... sometimes you think, like, someone's gonna get you.
> *(boy 8)*

There was a time when it was felt that children had a strong sense of security, a type of 'optimism'. This is not detectable in the research reported here, confirming a far more bleak vision of society (Cullingford, 1992). Children very early understand the concept of loneliness (Cassidy and Asher, 1992). They do so because of their experience of it, in the relationships, or lack of them, with other people, both strangers and siblings. Children are aware of lonely places, those parts of school, for example, in which they feel insecure (Cullingford, 1991; Titman, 1994). Sometimes these lonely places include their own bedrooms (Hart, 1979). They are also aware of the impact that physical factors, like living in a flat, like sharing a bedroom, have on their lives, all bound up with cultural, social and personal factors (Chawla, 1986). The impact of the environment, in every sense, is an extremely significant factor in children's sense of self. They do not see themselves in isolation, or well-wadded by ignorance. The human 'gaze' that they manifest takes in the threats, the injustice and the stupidities of life as much as the parochial securities.

Looking at towns with such a close scrutiny makes children analyse in particular their limitations, not only in terms of personal threat but in terms of environmental issues. To all the children one of the problems with towns is the pollution. This takes two forms. One is the everyday sight of litter, and the other is the fumes especially from cars.

I don't like all the factories and people dumping rubbish. *(boy 9)*

When the cars go 'round they leave lots of gas in the air. *(girl 8)*

It could be argued that the concept of 'pollution' is one of the few issues that are brought to children's attention in school. The term itself is not one that they would generally use outside an educational context. But the way they talk about it suggests nothing theoretical. They have a personal animosity to the fumes from traffic, to the litter left in the streets, the glass from broken bottles or the discarded cans. It is out of their personal experience that they feel so strongly about it. There is, after all, no hint in their testimonies of concern about larger issues like the ozone layer. It is through their own observations that they make a connection with greater environmental problems like acid rain.

I don't like them stick trees because they haven't got leaves on them. It doesn't make it look nice without leaves on. *(girl 8)*

The pollution that cars produce is, however, just the final straw. All the children complain about the traffic. They dislike the noise it makes and feel personally threatened.

The thing that I don't really like is how much traffic there is. And there's no traffic lights around to cross the road. It must make things a bit awkward 'cos when we're in a rush we try to cross the road and there's no crossings around and there's lots of cars zooming through. So we can't really cross.
*(boy 7)*

This adds to the consistent picture of the town, and it is the more powerful for being personally experienced. There might be school campaigns against litter, but to the children it is a real and everyday issue as they cite their experience of pollution from dogs, offensive to them, or people who clearly do not care about litter. Environmental issues are strong, but the theoretical concerns, like dealing with the question of overcrowding, emerge from personal experience.

Because we've got the highest record of polluting the atmosphere with cars and things. This country might get over-crowded. 'Cos it's quite a small country and there are lots of people living here. And people might have to start getting shipped away to other countries. *(boy 8)*

> There was a busy road and you had to cross quite a few roads and there were drunks there, too, that lived across the road. Every Sunday and Saturday morning we always get woken up by the noise of drilling things 'cos next door there's a man and he keeps on drilling and making lots of noise. *(girl 8)*

In contrast to this distaste for one aspect of town life, shared by those who live there as well as those who do not, the countryside is held up as being an ideal. All children like places of freedom and security and associate this with fields and space (Hart, 19797). The reason for this has a lot to do with proxemics, how people deal with or construct their personal space against that of others. The sense of being cramped at home leads to the association of riches with larger rooms and larger homes. The juxtaposition of people and traffic leads to the view that in the countryside they can feel free. To some this is a contrast that is personally expressed, to others one that remains theoretical, but held as strongly, as 'existentially' as if they were actually there (Ralph, 1976). The countryside is not, however, thought of as some purely romantic idyll. The reasons for its significance are more pragmatic. First there is the absence of those things which are disliked.

> In the countryside ... it's peaceful. There's no traffic or anything.
> *(boy 8)*

There is that significant factor of having room.

> There would be more places to play in and things like that in the country.
> *(boys 8)*

The results of these kinds of attitudes is that what children seem to suggest they like is houses which have large gardens. The countryside is associated not only with space in terms of woods and fields, but with larger interiors. It is both a pragmatic point of view and a romanticised one; pragmatic for those who are aware of what it is like to live in flats and romantic because the countryside is associated with the rich.

> I like to live in houses that are in the country, like nice big houses, because I like to run around a lot in the country... *(girl 9)*

Whilst there are sometimes hints of the perfect country cottage, with a thatched roof,

> They got lots of roses ... and there's all sorts of bits of flowers.
> *(boy 7)*

the overriding picture which emerges is more akin to a suburban idyll:

> In a cottage, in the countryside, it's nice and quiet and all the homes are nice. They've been nicely built. They're nice and the right shape. And they're all comfy inside...

> I'd like to change the world ... into small houses, like cottages.

*(girl 8)*

Children's views about the environment are not confined to the parochial. The information that shapes their world is derived not just from personal observation and experience and certainly not from school, but from secondary information. They form a view of the world that derives forcibly from television and is reinforced by anecdotes and opinions shared with their families and peer groups. The same perceptions of contrast form the outline structure of their view of other countries, divided into the rich and poor, the attractive ones and those that are to be avoided. It is well established that there are hierarchies of preferences between other countries. People subconsciously acquire collective favourites and least favourites (Gould and White, 1974). It is also well established that 'world-views' are formed wherever people live, that within small communities certain strong assumptions are shared (Rapport, 1993). One cannot fully separate the views expressed about an immediate environment and the more extensive ones. One 'loop of thought' affects another.

This can have disturbing results. All people have 'mental maps'. These, whilst not conveyable in graphic form, except as a kind of pointed joke, create a series of prejudices and images of places. What is disturbing is that when it comes to other countries there is a sense of the immutable, the overreaching inevitability of prejudice. The everyday might be disturbing, but its very threat implies the possibility of change, that it does not have to be like that. When it comes to other countries, one senses an acceptance that the world will always have the same tensions. The sense of the inevitable in the macrocosm can then inform their views of their more immediate surroundings.

Children's maps of the world centre on the essential contrast between the developed and the developing countries. Under the nuances of small prejudices, the eddies of stereotypes, lies the vast coastal shelf that places the rich against the poor. On the one hand there is the United States, symbol par excellence of all that is glamorous. It has possessions, it is up to date, it controls the media, it has theme parks - it is presented as one vast theme park in itself, where friendliness and being rich completely obscure any undercurrent of doubt, despite the attempts to use the underworld of Miami, for example, as a location for thrillers. On the other hand we are presented with the equally powerful image of Africa. Those many affecting pleas for help for the poor and the starving, for those suffering in drought and war, all so clearly presented in advertisements and on television news, convey a very clear picture of Africa as a whole.

> They were black. They had flies all around them. Some of them had wounds.                                                          *(girl 8)*

> I've seen Africa where they have to get water out of puddles. They have cloths on a bit of rags. They live in little houses made of bits they find around, like wood.                                                        *(boy 7)*

That children should be aware of all this is no surprise. The problem is that the images become generalised and immutable. This is the way the world *is*; the contrast is between the cultures conveyed through those images, and those everyday possessions the children take for granted and which represent what they think is normal.

> ... things like plants and three piece suites and television like that. And transistor radios and personal stereos and things. They have not got proper houses at all. Sticks and bits of material stuck together.              *(girl 9)*

The whole of Africa therefore becomes a place to be avoided. The problem is that there is no sense of the possibility of change or difference. No development is mentioned, such as high rise housing or traffic. Not only are the conditions poor, but the implication is that that is how they will always be.

We do not need to labour over the contrast of the United States. The message is clear

> It's good because there's lots of places. It's big. It's got big houses. Big cars. Better houses. Better because most of them are bigger and they've got different styles. There's better films that you can watch. There's bigger playgrounds. Lots of things to do.                                    *(boy 10)*

Lots of things to do, like Disneyland, and lots of things to possess; this is the image presented by the United States. It explains why children think of it as a favourite holiday destination, and as a place which is better to live in than their own country. The awareness of other countries is bolstered by the possibility of travel abroad, an experience which is open to many (Wiegand, 1991). When the opportunity is taken to be a tourist, the awareness of other ways of living adds another dimension to the children's cultural relativism, the sense of choices that can be made in everyday matters such as the food eaten in restaurants (Cullingford, 1995).

The experience of other countries, either personal or taken from secondary sources, adds to children's growing awareness of their environment. One source of information that is very rarely mentioned by them is that of school. The way in which children develop their understanding is therefore not structured by theory. Both of the contrasts between riches and poverty and the sense of relative values derive from the ways in which children make consistent sense of their own experiences. They are therefore aware of environmental issues, such as drought, but more aware of them as matters to be responded to with missionary instincts than as matters that can be dealt with by political will and environmental planning. Issues such as sustainability pass them by. The world is presented to them without explanation.

One subject that demonstrates how children view their environment in a way that is both personal and imbued with self-constructed theory is the weather. They do not know about the weather in terms of global distinction between man-made change and natural causes (Gelman and Kremer, 1991). But the weather is something that matters to them in an everyday sense. The pattern of thinking suggests that they would like the weather to be hotter, but the price to be paid for that can be drought as in Africa. Holidays abroad are associated with better weather and with swimming pools. About their own climate as well as others the children are very equivocal:

> If I lived somewhere like Miami then you would probably be so hot you couldn't even move, or, like, you were so sweaty. That's what I wouldn't like about staying in somewhere hot. And, well, it's, like, the right temperature. It's just partly the weather and it's almost, like, most of the time it's just grey weather. And not very, you know, bright. If you wanted just the right heat then this is the best place to go. But, it's not really very attractive. Not really a good place. Well, if there was more colourful things. If there was more bright, if there was more sun.
>
> There can be places where there are farmers and then when there's good growing that can be happier. Then there's hot places where people are happy. *(boy 7)*

## Conclusions

The evidence presented by the children is complex and would justify far more space than a chapter. It is difficult to summarise succinctly the consistent opinions the children give of themselves in relation to their environment and their attitudes to the environment itself. What is clear is that children are not just aware of their environment, but influenced by it. The big issue is how it affects them, in terms of space and place, in terms of threats and opportunities. The views expressed here, towards the town and country, towards traffic and pollution, towards good and bad climates represent the basis of what they will think for the rest of their lives. These attitudes emerge from their own interpretation rather than theoretical contrasts imposed on them.

There is a balance to be struck between the two extremes of attitudes. One is that the world is a place full of contrasts, between the rich and the poor, between wealthy nations and those in which people suffer from famine. The other is the children's sense of relativism. They do not think that they live in the best of all possible worlds. They are aware of riches and more attractive countries. They know about the threats that are presented by society. There is a sense that they are helpless to change things and must accept them as they are (see Cullingford, 1992). After all they feel they have no choice but to fit into things as they are. This implies that whilst they complain about pollution they do not talk about it as an issue that needs to be tackled. They see litter as a nuisance but do not talk about campaigns or policies to eradicate it.

There are three levels to children's response to the world; there is the individual and at the other extreme the collective shared fact of humanity. In between there is all the cultural 'baggage' of stereotypes and prejudices. It is this middle ground, the definitions that children make of their own preferences and styles of living that is being explored here. The environment, defined as widely as here, is then both a shared experience and a way of defining differences. It is both a supreme attraction and a threat.

The environment is not seen by children as an 'issue'. Perhaps later they will grieve over the loss of rain-forests, and be angered by the destruction of natural habitats and the loss of species. But the environment is important to them long before it becomes academic. Of course it is possible to elicit views from them on green issues, but the point about this research was that it explored children's attitudes without imposing subjects on them. The children themselves created their terms, and definitions. It is they who recognise the consequences of natural phenomena but feel these to be inevitable. They live in the immediacy of the everyday, but do not find it easy.

The way that children talk about the environment, both physical and human, shows it to be an important subject to them. It also raises many political issues that young children are capable of addressing, not in terms of party politics but in terms that would help them make sense of the world and their place in it. It is clear that these issues are being addressed by children in their own ways, and, it seems, not being addressed by schools. It would surely help the value systems and understanding of children if they were.

# Bibliography

Baillargeon, R. and De Vos, J. (1991) Object Permanence in Young Infants: Further Evidence. *Child Development* **62** (6) pp. 1227-1256.

Bourdieu, P. (1984) *Distinction: A social critique of the judgement of taste.* London: Routledge.

Cassidy, J. and Asher, S. (1992) Loneliness and Peer Relations in Young Children. *Child Development* **63** (2) pp. 350-365.

Chawla, L. (1986) The Ecology of Environmental Memory. *Children's Environments Quarterly* **3** (4).

Chandler, M., Fritz, A. and Hala, S. (1989) Small-scale deceit: Deception as a Marker of 2, 3 and 4 year olds theories of Mind. *Child Development* **60** (6) pp. 1263-1277.

Cox, M. (1981) *The Child's Point of View.* Hemel Hempstead: Harvester Wheatsheaf.

Cullingford, C. (1991) *The Inner World of the School.* London: Cassell.

Cullingford, C. (1992) *Children and Society.* London: Cassell.

Cullingford, C. (1995) Children's Attitudes to Holidays Overseas. *Journal of Tourism Management* **16** (2) pp. 121-127.

Das Gupta, P. and Bryant, P. (1989) Young Children's Causal Inferences. *Child Development* **60** (5) pp. 1138-1146.

Dunn, J. (1988) *The Beginnings of Social Understanding.* Oxford: Basil Blackwell.

Egan, K. (1986) *Individual Development and the Curriculum.* London: Hutchinson.

Gelman, S. and Kremer, K. (1991) Understanding Natural Causes: Children's explanations of how objects and their properties originate. *Child Development* **62** (2) pp. 396-414.

Giddens, A. (1990) *The Consequences of Modernity.* Cambridge: Polity Press.

Gould, P. and White, R. (1974) *Mental Maps.* Harmondsworth: Penguin.

Greaves, E. Stanistreet, M., Boyes, E. and Williams, T. (1993) Children's Ideas About Rainforests. *Journal of Biological Education* **27** (3) pp. 189-194.

Habermas, J. (1989) *The Structural Transformation of the Public Sphere: an enquiry into a category of bourgeois culture.* Cambridge: Polity Press.

Hart, R. (19797) *Children's Experience of Place.* New York: Irvington.

Haste, H. (1987) Growing into rules. In Bruner, J. and Haste, H. (eds.) *Making Sense*. London: Methuen.

Hofstede, G. (1980) *Culture's Consequences: International Differences in Work-Related Values*. London: Sage.

Hofstede, G. (1991) *Cultures and Organisations: Software of the Mind*. London: McGraw-Hill.

Rapport, N. (1993) *Diverse World-Views in an English Village*. Edinburgh: University Press.

Ralph, E. (1976) *Place and Placelessness*. London: Pion.

Rosengren, K., Gelman, S., Kalish, C. and McCormick, M. (1991) As Time Goes By: Children's early understanding of growth in animals. *Child Development* **62** (6) pp. 1302-1320.

Siegel, A. and White, S. (1975) The development of spatial representations of large-scale environments. In Reece, H. (ed.) *Advances in Child Development and Behaviour* **10** New York: Academic Press.

Spencer, C., Blades, M. and Morsley, K. (1989) *The Child in the Physical Environment*. Chichester: John Wiley.

Titman, W. (1994) *Special Places, Special People: the Hidden Curriculum of School Playgrounds*. London: World Wide Fund for Nature.

Wiegand, P. 91991) Does Travel Broaden the Mind? *Education 3-13*, pp. 54-58.

# 3 Young people's ideas about global environmental issues

*Martin Stanisstreet and Edward Boyes*

## Abstract

Few would now doubt that global environmental problems will require exacting solutions, including changes in individual life-style and international cooperation. Thus, education about such issues will assume an increasing importance. Such education will be most effective if based on an appreciation of the preconceptions of those to be taught. In this way, sound ideas can be re-enforced, amplified and extended, and misconceptions can be addressed. This paper provides an overview of the results of a series of studies of children's ideas about environmental problems such as global warming and ozone layer depletion, their causes and consequences. The results suggest that although children are aware of the consequences of global environmental problems and of the range of pollutants which cause them, their thinking is over-generalised. Children tend to imagine that all pollutants contribute to all environmental problems. We suggest that it would be helpful to assist children to disentangle their ideas by stressing, initially at least, the separate causes of different environmental problems. Although direct experiential learning might not be possible here, children do show a natural enthusiasm for 'the environment' which may make them receptive to further exploration of the various causes and consequences of global environmental degradation.

# Introduction

Just in time I read the book
Such a revelation we must give back what we took
Or the Earth will roar like a wounded beast
The mountains will come crashing from the valleys to the seas.

(de Burgh, 1979)

Today's youngsters are the 'environmental generation'. For previous generations, whose major concerns were wars of global or potentially global magnitude, the possibility of nuclear devastation or world starvation, the 'environment' as we now perceive it on a global level was hardly an issue. Damage to Scandinavian forests by acid rain, destruction of tropical rainforest by land clearance, worldwide climate change resulting from an exacerbation of global warming by the greenhouse effect, or depletion of stratospheric ozone with the consequent increased exposure of living things to solar ultraviolet radiation were issues which were not on the popular agenda or at the forefront of public attention. Neither were reduction in species biodiversity by habitat destruction, excess use of insecticides or artificial fertilisers. In contrast, the teenagers and 'twenty-somethings' of today have been raised when global environmental issues, usually in terms of problems or anticipated problems, have had a high profile in the popular media (Sachsman, 1995). Thus, young people are aware of a variety of ways in which the integrity and stability of the environment is under threat.

This generation also comprises those who will have to make important decisions about personal lifestyle and the organisation of communities if they are to avoid further, possibly irreversible, global environmental degradation and consequent wide ranging effects on the structures of society (Houghton, Jenkins and Ephraums, 1990; Tickell, 1991). The solutions to these problems are likely to be difficult for a variety of interlocking political, social and practical reasons (Stanisstreet and Boyes, 1990; Stanisstreet and Boyes, 1994). Because the problems are global in dimension, they will require international cooperation or at least agreement.

... resources such as these that exist outside the market, that are owned in common, or by the state, or by nobody, tend to be the ones that are vulnerable, while those primary products whose exploitation is privately controlled are not in danger of exhaustion.

(McRae, 1994)

Thus, those problems which are the responsibility of everybody are those which are the responsibility of nobody. Furthermore, some of these decisions may be costly in that they may require reduction of personal consumption and acceptance of restrictive legislation. For such decisions to be acceptable it will be necessary for citizens to have more than a general awareness of the environment and some of the problems it faces; they will need at least some appreciation of the causes of environmental degradation and some realisation of the consequences of the failure to act. Thus, although environmental education alone may not be sufficient to induce changes in attitudes and modifications of behaviour, it does have an important role in ensuring that such decisions are informed decisions, based at least to some degree on consent rather than imposition.

Children start to form their perceptions of the world early, before their formal education begins. These initial perceptions will be based on their personal observations and experiences of their local environment, and media coverage of more global issues (Cullingford, 1995). These perceptions will not remain as isolated ideas in the minds of pupils. Rather, they will be constructed and incorporated into mental maps which make sense to the child (Driver, 1983). Furthermore, such frameworks contain elements which are not congruent with expert understanding (Driver, Squires, Rushworth and Wood-Robinson, 1994). Moreover, being personally constructed, such conceptual frameworks are resistant to alteration (Ausubel, 1963). If new observations or given ideas do not fit readily into the framework, it is the idea rather than the framework which might be adjusted. In this way, erroneous interpretations can be perpetuated and even strengthened by the pre-existing conceptual framework. Education, therefore, becomes more than simply supplying the learner with the facts and ideas. Rather, it becomes aimed at helping the learner to adjust her or his own alternative ideas, and to re-enforce and extend orthodox ideas and conceptual frameworks. Given this, it is important for educators to have an appreciation of the probable ideas and ways of thinking that they may encounter in their pupils.

The aim of our research programme is to explore children's ideas, their preconceptions and misconceptions, about major environmental issues. For this, we have used semi-structured recorded interviews and open-form questionnaires to elicit the range of children's alternative ideas. These ideas, together with ideas expressing current expert understanding have been incorporated into a series of precoded questionnaires to determine the prevalence of ideas held by children of different ages. The results have been explored using a variety of descriptive, analytical and exploratory statistical techniques. For most of the studies we have explored the ideas of secondary school pupils; the results discussed below are for such pupils, unless specified otherwise.

However, in some cases our studies have been extended both to primary children and undergraduate students, including trainee teachers.

## Children's ideas about the consequences of environmental problems

One set of studies in America (Boyes, Chuckran and Stanisstreet, 1993), England (Boyes and Stanisstreet, 1993) and Portugal (Chagas, Boyes and Stanisstreet, 1995) explored secondary school children's ideas about the possible *consequences* of an increase in global warming caused by exacerbation of the greenhouse effect by atmospheric pollutants (referred to below for brevity as the 'greenhouse effect' or 'global warming'). The results of studies in different countries were generally consistent, suggesting that gaps in understanding and misconceptions might be widespread. A subsequent study examined British pupils' ideas about the consequences of depletion of the stratospheric ozone layer (Boyes and Stanisstreet, 1994a). The results showed that some orthodox ideas about these issues were already established in the youngest group. For example, the ideas that the greenhouse effect will cause changes in weather patterns and increased global warming were already well known to pupils aged 11/12 years, as was the notion that ozone layer degradation would result in an increased incidence of skin cancer. Other ideas appeared to be inaugurated in children over the period of their secondary schooling, although the extent to which this is a result of formal education cannot be determined. For instance, the appreciation that the greenhouse effect may cause flooding was in this category. In a complementary manner, some misconceptions were seen in fewer of the older than younger children. For example, supposed consequences of the greenhouse effect or ozone layer depletion, increased risk of unsafe drinking water and aquatic pollution which would poison fish, were less prevalent in older pupils, although a few of even the oldest group, aged 15/16 years, retained these ideas. More important from an educational stance, some misconceptions about the consequences of global environmental problems were retained by many of even the oldest group. For example, many of the oldest children thought that the greenhouse effect caused skin cancer, hinting at a confusion between the consequences of the greenhouse effect and those of ozone layer depletion.

# Children's ideas about the causes of environmental problems

We have also explored children's ideas about the *causes* of environmental problems. Here too the results revealed some misconceptions which are corrected during the period of secondary schooling but others which persist in many children. Even young, primary school children are aware of, and have formed attitudes to, 'physical', 'concrete' forms of pollution such as refuse (Cullingford, 1995). Many such children appeared to extend and apply their thinking, in that they believed that such waste materials were responsible for global warming (Francis, Boyes, Qualter and Stanisstreet, 1993). Notions of this sort, however, that rubbish in rivers or litter in the streets were connected with the greenhouse effect, were reduced in older pupils (Boyes and Stanisstreet, 1993). Some types of pollutant, however, were mistakenly perceived by even older children as causing ozone layer depletion (Boyes and Stanisstreet, 1994a). Factory smoke, car exhaust emissions and even rainforest destruction were seen by many of the older children in this light. Thus, although older pupils were gaining some discrimination between 'physical', visible littering and atmospheric problems, even these pupils were still confusing some causes of different global environmental problems.

In a more recent study which took the approach of seeking children's ideas about the role of one specific source of environmental problems, car exhaust, the same general picture emerged. Not only were car exhaust seen, correctly, as contributing to the greenhouse effect and acid rain, they were also envisaged by many primary school children as damaging the ozone layer, polluting the sea, destroying rainforests and endangering rare species (Leeson, Stanisstreet and Boyes, 1995). Some of these erroneous ideas, particularly the notion that car exhaust emissions damaged the ozone layer, persisted in a proportion of even the older secondary school children (Leeson, Stanisstreet and Boyes, in preparation).

# Themes in children's thinking

As discussed in the Introduction above, it is probable that children's ideas about the environment, including their non-orthodox ideas, are expressions of more general underlying conceptual frameworks. An appreciation of such patterns of thinking could be useful to educators, so that educational strategies can be designed to address not just specific misconceptions, but also insecure conceptualisations. Insight into the nature and composition of such frameworks, might be gained by seeking themes which are common to several individual ideas. Factor analysis is an exploratory statistical tool which reveals connections between individual items within questionnaires, based on the responses, and groups item within a series of 'factors' (Child, 1979). For example, based on the responses to the questionnaire about the greenhouse effect, such analysis grouped items which were related not to global warming, but rather to ozone layer degradation. The items implied that children might be thinking along the lines that it is the greenhouse effect, exacerbated by chlorofluorocarbon pollutants (CFCs) in the atmosphere, which allows increased solar ultraviolet radiation to penetrate to the Earth, and causes an increase in the incidence of skin cancer. This suggests that children have a tendency not only to confuse the consequences of different global environmental perturbations, and the various causes of such problems, but also the problems themselves. Interestingly, a factor containing similar ideas was isolated by analysis of the responses of a group of university undergraduate students, suggesting that this way of thinking persists in a section of the adult population in higher education (Boyes and Stanisstreet, 1992).

The composition of ideas in this particular factor also draws attention to the possibility that children may hold covert 'double' misconceptions which might not be revealed by more straightforward analyses. CFCs are indeed greenhouse gases. However, their inclusion in a factor which primarily embraces ideas about ozone layer destruction suggests that children do not necessarily appreciate that CFCs contribute to the greenhouse effect, but affirm the widely-appreciated association between CFCs and ozone layer damage, and then confuse this with the greenhouse effect. In general then, a demonstration of correct individual ideas about rather 'abstract' environmental phenomena does not necessarily imply sound underlying conceptualisation.

Another theme to emerge from such analyses of children's ideas about the greenhouse effect is that of 'biological consequences'. Here, there seems to be a link in children's thinking between the greenhouse effect and illness or poisoning of humans and other animals. Interestingly, a similar theme emerged in a separate study of children's notions about ozone layer depletion, adding weight to the suggestion that one way in which children may conceptualise global environmental pollution problems is in terms of their biological consequences. It is possible that terminology plays a role here. Examination of thesauri shows that synonyms offered for 'pollute' are 'contaminate', 'infect' and 'poison'; these have implicit biological connections in terms of poisoned or contaminated foodstuffs and infected organisms. Although many adults would make more subtle differentiation between the usage of these words, children may not, and this may influence their thinking. Later we will revisit the notion of vocabulary as a possible contribution to children's confusion.

## What models do children employ?

More recently, we have started to attempt to dissect some of the reasoning which children might be using in their personal explanations of global environmental issues and to determine which mental models are prevalent. Questionnaires were devised which offered respondents alternative 'routes' of reasoning. For example, one study was designed to address the confusions, revealed by previous studies, between the causes of the greenhouse effect and ozone layer depletion (Boyes and Stanisstreet, in preparation). Here, we concentrated on 13/14 year old school children. The results confirm the suggestion that there is direct confusion in the minds of children between two major environmental problems. More than one third of these pupils thought that the greenhouse effect damages the ozone layer. Only a small proportion of the children appeared to think that this happened by the greenhouse effect causing changes in the world's climate, which in turn damages the ozone layer. Rather, the dominant model used by children seemed to be the notion that the greenhouse effect makes pollutants such as smoke rise, perhaps because it is known that hot air rises, and they believe that these pollutants damage the ozone layer.

Even more of the school children, more than three quarters, thought that holes in the ozone layer actually cause the greenhouse effect. About a fifth apparently pictured rays from the sun approaching the Earth through holes in the ozone layer, and then being 'unable to find' the holes to get back out again. We suspect that this model may have its origin in diagrams illustrating the greenhouse effect where 'rays' as arrows are shown approaching Earth, 'bouncing back' and then becoming entrapped by the Earth's atmosphere. A greater proportion of the children, however, seemed to employ a more direct model in which holes in the ozone layer are envisaged simply as allowing more 'heat rays' or UV rays from the sun to penetrate the atmosphere and reach the Earth, thus warming it. Younger school pupils may even express this idea in terms of ozone holes letting in too much 'sun' (Plunkett and Skamp, 1994).

We have also used studies of children's ideas about a specific source of pollutants, cars, to attempt to dissect their thinking. Cars offer a familiar but potentially complex example of pollution, because car exhaust emissions are a cocktail of different pollutants which contribute to different environmental problems. For example, oxides of nitrogen contribute to acid rain and carbon dioxide is a greenhouse gas. School children's thinking here is also apparently too generalised. For example, more than one third of children aged 13/14 years think, erroneously, that cars contribute to rainforest destruction or to species extinction. Even more, over 80%, envisage car emissions as damaging the ozone layer (Leeson, Stanisstreet and Boyes, in preparation).

We have recently completed a study of some 1600 14/15 year old school children to explore some of the reasoning underlying their views of the links between vehicles and three environmental problems, the greenhouse effect, acid rain and ozone layer degradation. The questionnaire used was of a graphical nature, with arrows representing causal links between ideas. On each arrow were boxes labelled 'Yes', 'Don't know' and 'No'; pupils were asked to tick one box. The questionnaire was designed to explore specific 'routes' of reasoning. So, it probed whether the pupils thought that car exhausts contained certain components (carbon dioxide, CFCs, sulphur dioxide, nitrogen oxides, water vapour, 'acid gases' and heat), and whether each of these constituents contributed to the three environmental problems (the greenhouse effect, acid rain and ozone layer degradation). Thus, it revealed the mechanisms by which children might think that cars damage the environment.

Most of the children realise that cars exacerbated the greenhouse effect. The way in which the majority of these pupils might be reasoning was, correctly, that carbon dioxide was responsible - more than half appreciated both that car exhausts contain carbon dioxide and that carbon dioxide made the greenhouse effect worse. Although three quarters of these pupils thought that CFCs are greenhouse gases (probably in many cases for the incorrect reasoning as discussed previously), only a quarter were under the misapprehension that CFCs are a product of car exhausts, so few thought that cars made the greenhouse effect worse by this mechanism. About a quarter of the children realised that car exhausts contain oxides of nitrogen and about a third appreciated that these gases contribute to global warming. However, only a tenth held both of these ideas, so only a small proportion might realise that this is another mechanism by which car exhausts might make the greenhouse effect worse.

About half of the pupils appreciated that cars caused acid rain. One quarter of these pupils thought that cars emitted sulphur dioxide, and appreciated that sulphur dioxide contributes to acid rain. Such children might well be misinformed about the link between vehicle emissions and acid rain by this route for, although sulphur dioxide does make a major contribution to acid rain, the proportion of the total atmospheric load of sulphur dioxide originating from cars is minor. In those children who connected car exhausts with acid rain, the most popular 'route' appeared to be the idea of carbon dioxide; nearly half realised that car exhausts contain carbon dioxide and also thought that carbon dioxide caused acid rain.

Finally, more than three quarters of the children thought, erroneously, that car emissions damage the ozone layer. Within this group of children, the most common conceptual 'route' was again apparently via carbon dioxide; nearly half of the subset of children both realised that car exhausts contain carbon dioxide and thought that carbon dioxide damaged the ozone layer. In summary, it appears that many children of this age realise that carbon dioxide is a component of vehicle exhausts, but that this knowledge is so dominant that it is used in an uncritical way, such that it is assumed that carbon dioxide is responsible for all of the global environmental problems with which cars are, in one case erroneously, associated.

# Persistence of alternative models in the adult population

We have also undertaken preliminary work using the same questionnaire with a group of Year 2 university students taking an Ecology course. Although this group of undergraduates had not been taught specifically about the issues studied here, we might expect them to be concerned and informed about environmental matters in general. Despite this, we found that some of the undergraduates retained misconceptions. For example, about one third thought that cars were responsible for ozone layer depletion, although some of these offered no 'route' by which this might happen. The fact that even some of this well-motivated group retained some misconceptions leads us to think that such ideas are likely to be present in a proportion of the adult, decision-making population. We anticipate some dangers here. If motorists think in a very general way about the environmental impacts of cars, they may be inclined to imagine that vehicles designed to use unleaded petrol and fitted with catalytic converters, both 'environmentally friendly', are environmentally benign. If so, even environmentally sympathetic adults may use their vehicles in an unrestricted manner.

One opportunity for correcting such misconceptions and for encouraging children to think about global environmental issues in a more detailed and precise way is by introducing such issues as learning examples in the formal, in-school setting. Unfortunately, studies of the ideas of trainee primary teachers about these environmental issues cast some doubt on the security of their knowledge base. This group of respondents had a good knowledge of the nature and location of the ozone layer and were well aware that CFCs, the gases used as refrigerants, propellants for spray cans and in the manufacture of expanded plastics, all degrade the ozone layer. However, some misconceptions persisted; many thought that other pollutants such as radioactivity, car exhausts and factory smoke endangered the ozone layer. More surprisingly, nearly one quarter held the somewhat naive view that holes in the ozone layer would allow air to 'escape' from the atmosphere into space (Boyes, Chambers and Stanisstreet, 1995). Interviews with Australian teachers suggests that this situation, the retention of misconceptions about issues related to the ozone layer and its imagined direct linkage with other environmental problems, may be a more general problem (Plunkett and Skamp, 1994). Initial analysis of the results of a recent study with a similar group of respondents in the UK, trainee primary teachers, concerning their ideas about vehicle emissions supports this general contention. Even in this group there are some misconceptions about the environmental impact of vehicle exhausts, and some lack of understanding about the mechanisms of those actions (Hillman, Stanisstreet and Boyes, in preparation). Clearly, there is a danger that the classroom may become a setting in which, rather than children's ideas being challenged, they may be perpetuated or even re-enforced.

## Why are environmental problems difficult for children?

As we explored pupils' ideas, a number of interlocking reasons for the conceptual difficulty of global environmental issues occurred to us. Firstly, and ironically in view of the fact that these issues are of global magnitude, these problems are imperceptible to individuals. The exhaust gases from most vehicles are invisible, the intangible emissions might not be readily appreciated as pollutants (Brody, 1992). Similarly, we cannot immediately sense global warming, the acidity of acid rain or the consequences of ozone layer depletion. Thus, children's learning cannot be experiential. Secondly, these problems are associated with a degree of uncertainty. Experts do not agree on the extent of the problems, and their comments may reflect this. So, children may receive confusing messages; environmental lobby groups may be tempted to deny uncertainty or even to exaggerate the problems, whereas those with an interest in short-term sociopolitical stability may minimise them. Thirdly, and partly connected with this uncertainty, many of the phenomena and their predicted consequences are stochastic events. Thus, a comprehension of risk and chance is required, and the notion of probability is known to be difficult for children. Next, these environmental problems are long-term, chronic problems and, as such, are more difficult to appreciate than acute, catastrophic events. Furthermore, young children in particular have poor 'foresight' and prefer short-term pleasure despite long-term risks. Finally, these issues are multidisciplinary and require an understanding of a range of traditional, 'curriculum' sciences at quite complex levels.

In addition, the high profile of environmental issues, the fact that they feature often in the popular media, may itself cause problems because children will gain much of their information from out-of-school sources. Even if the information given by these sources is accurate and balanced, there is no opportunity for children to interact with colleagues or peers to test that they have not misunderstood or misinterpreted the information. Furthermore, is there a danger that environmental problems suffer from over-exposure, that children develop 'environmental fatigue' in the same way that people, faced with constant request for support for good causes, develop 'charity fatigue'?

## How might children be helped to mature their thinking about global environmental issues?

Thus, we are faced with the prospect of education about important but complex and difficult ideas. As we explored children's notions, both scientifically conventional and unorthodox, and the ways pupils might be thinking about global environmental problems, ideas occurred to us which might help children to mature their thinking. Teaching requires not only the provision and explanation of new ideas, but also the development, integration, changing and differentiation of pre-existing ideas (Driver, Squires, Rushworth and Wood-Robinson, 1994). In the case of children's thinking about global environmental problems, it appears that the last strategy, the disentanglement and codification of their pre-existing ideas, is especially important.

We wonder if the *vocabulary* used to communicate environmental issues to children might itself be a source of confusion. The term 'environment' has a perplexing range of legitimate uses. It may be used in an immediate, a local, an international or a global dimension. It may concentrate on the animate or inanimate, the natural or the constructed, the physical or social. To say that the 'environment' is endangered is a very imprecise statement. Whilst formal definitions do not make exciting learning or teaching, it might help to specify what is meant by 'environment' in particular learning contexts.

In the same way, perhaps, use of the term 'pollution' might cause confusion by 'funnelling' children's thinking, somewhat like the sand is funnelled through the constriction in an old-fashioned hourglass (Figure 3.1). This model illustrates that children are aware of a range of 'inputs', sources of pollutants such as factory chimneys, car exhausts and so on. They are also aware of a spectrum of 'outputs', the various environmental problems such as ozone layer damage and acid rain. But the sources are seen as giving pollution in general, rather than the mixture of pollutants which produce specific environmental problems. If children employ this model, they may not intuitively envisage different pollutants contributing to different environmental problems.

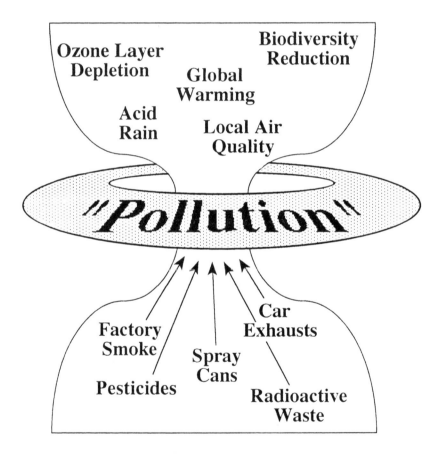

**Figure 3.1 Illustrations of how children's thinking about the consequences and causes of global environmental problems might be confused by the term 'pollution'**

One practical way of helping children to challenge their own rather over-simple models might be to use the term 'pollutant(s)' rather than the more abstract, collective term 'pollution' when discussing environmental insults. In this way, vocabulary can be used to stress the distinction between a *description,* that 'pollution' is a collective term leading to environmental degradation in general, and *mechanisms,* that individual pollutants contribute to specific environmental problems.

In cases of ozone layer damage there seems to be confusion even at the 'output' stage, with a direct conflation of the greenhouse effect and ozone layer depletion in the minds of many children. The two phenomena do have some common characteristics; both are of global dimension and relatively recent origin, and both are imperceptible to individuals. They even have a partially common cause, in that CFCs both damage the ozone layer and act as greenhouse gases. Thus, teachers may need to counteract the instinctive but erroneous fusion of these two problems in pupil's thinking. Perhaps a differentiation between physical and biological consequences might help children to separate these two environmental problems. Thus, children might learn that the major effects of ozone layer depletion are biological, since UV radiation affects animals and plants, whereas the major primary consequences of an enhanced greenhouse effect are physical, deriving from the warming of the planet. The former ideas, that radiation endangers biological systems, appears fairly well established in pupils' minds (Boyes and Stanisstreet, 1994b). Also, at least some repercussions of the latter idea, the physical warming of the Earth, such as flooding and ice-cap melting are 'concrete', or at least easy enough to imagine.

So, is education about major environmental issues a lost cause? The children themselves give us more optimism. Children have a natural enthusiasm and concern for the environment - they do not need persuading that environmental issues are important or that the science of environmental issues is 'relevant'.

Who should be educated (about pollution)?
Children mostly, I think, because when they grow up they might know what pollution does ... and they might all just help.                    (girl, 10)

Similarly, cars appeal to children and appear to feature in their thinking early. In addition, most pupils will have direct, everyday experience of cars. Linking these two subjects, cars and environment. might be a useful way in which to start to address some of the alternative ideas revealed by our studies, especially since children readily see human-made artifacts as sources of pollutants (Ali, 1991), and cars are a prime example of such artifacts.

Furthermore, some of the approaches we have used here in a somewhat summative manner, particularly probes which explore possible mental 'routes' of reasoning, might be useful teaching tools in helping pupils to challenge their own conceptual frameworks. This might be done using short questionnaires or, more simply in the classroom setting, as informal discussions. For example, exploration of the idea, already established in principle in children, that exhaust emissions are a cocktail of different pollutants might be used to persuade them to start to dissect their rather general model of pollution, wherein all sources of pollution result in all consequences of pollution, and to think in terms of a series of separate pollutants.

Once the overall principle of distinction between different environmental problems is established, older children might be progressively introduced to the complexities of the situation; the formation of secondary pollutants from primary pollutants, and the primary, secondary and higher-order effects of specific environmental problems. This might lead in turn to a more mature appreciation of the interdependence web of different elements of the global ecosystem.

## Acknowledgements

We wish to thank our colleagues, Debbie Batterham, Isabel Chagas, David Chuckran, Matthew Hillman, Emma Leeson and the graduate students who contributed to this research programme, the teachers who gave of their time to assist us, the school pupils who answered the questionnaires, and the Ford of Britain Trust and Vauxhall Motors Ltd for financial support.

## Bibliography

Ali, I.M. (1991) How do English pupils understand pollution? *Environmental Education and Information* 10 pp. 203-220.

Ausubel, D. (1963) *Educational Psychology: A Cognitive View.* New York: Holt, Rinehardt and Winston.

Boyes, E. Chambers, W. and Stanisstreet, M. (1995) Trainee primary teacher's ideas about the ozone layer. *Environmental Education Research* (in press).

Boyes, E. Chuckran, D. and Stanisstreet, M. (1993) How do High School students perceive global climatic change: what are its manifestations? What are its origins? What corrective actions can be taken? *Journal of Science Education and Technology* 2 pp.541-557.

Boyes, E. and Stanisstreet, M. (1992) Students' perceptions of global warming. *International Journal of Environmental Studies* **42** pp. 287--300.

Boyes, E. and Stanisstreet, M. (1993) The 'Greenhouse Effect': children's perceptions of causes, consequences and cures. *International Journal of Science Education* **15** pp. 531-552.

Boyes, E. and Stanisstreet, M. (1994a) The idea of Secondary School children concerning ozone layer damage. *Global Environmental Change* **4** pp. 317-330.

Boyes, E. and Stanisstreet, M. (1994b) Children's ideas about radioactivity and radiation: sources, modes of travel, uses and dangers. *Research in Science and Technology Education* **12** pp. 145-160.

Brody, M.J. (1992) Student science knowledge related to ecological crises. Paper presented to the American Education Research Association (AERA), San Francisco.

Chagas, I., Boyes, E. and Stanisstreet, M. (1995) Ideas and misconceptions of Portuguese school students about global climatic change. *Química* (in press).

Child, D. (1979) *The Essentials of Factor Analysis.* London: Hilt, Rinehart and Winston.

Cullingford, C. (1995) *Children's attitudes to their local environment.* In Harris, G. and Blackwell, C. (eds.) Monitoring Change in Education, Vol. 2: Environmental Issues in Education pp. 21-36. Aldershot: Ashgate.

De Burgh, C. (1979) Just in Time. On: *'Crusader',* Compact Disc No. CDMID 113, A and M Records Ltd, London.

Driver, R. (1983) *The Pupil as Scientist.* Multon Keynes: Open University Press.

Driver, R., Squires, A., Rushworth, P. and Wood-Robinson, V. (1994) *Making Sense of Secondary Science: Research in Children's Ideas.* London and New York: Routledge Press.

Francis, C., Boyes, E., Qualter, A. and Stanisstreet, M. 91993) Ideas of elementary students about reducing the 'Greenhouse Effect'. *Science Education* **77** pp. 375-392.

Houghton, J.T., Jenkins, G.J. and Ephraums, J.J. (1990) *Climate Change: The Intergovernmental Panel on Climate Change Scientific Assessment.* Cambridge: University Press.

Leeson, E., Stanisstreet, M. and Boyes, E. (1995) Primary children's ideas about cars and the environment. *Education 3-13* (in press).

McRae, H. (1994) *The World in 2020. Power, Culture and Prosperity: A vision of the Future.* London: Harper Collins Publishers.

Plunkett, S. and Skamp, K. (1994) The ozone layer and hole: children's conceptions. Paper presented to the Australian Science Education Research Association Conference, Hobart, Tasmania, July.

Sachsman, D.B. (1995) *Communicating Environmental Issues on the 21st Century.* Paper presented to Environmental Issues for the 21st Century: An International Interdisciplinary Conference, Lehman College, City University of New York, USA.

Stanisstreet, M. and Boyes, E. (1990) Human influences and influencing humans: Attainment Target 5 of the National Curriculum. *School Science Review* **72** pp. 144-145.

Stanisstreet, M. and Boyes, E. (1994) Environment education: problems and possibilities. *Revista de Educaçao* **4** pp. 101-112.

Tickell, C. 91991) The quality of life: What quality? Whose life? Address to the British Association, reported in the Independent Newspaper, 27 August, p. 3.

# 4 Environmental education, the National Curriculum and the way ahead

*Liz Lakin*

## Abstract

This paper outlines the history of environmental education within the English and Welsh education system, from inception to its early role in the National Curriculum as a 'cross-curricular theme'. This is explored further within the 'New Orders', with emphasis being given to progressive marginalisation as its current place in the National Curriculum has evolved. The Scottish and Irish Curricula are also examined.

Early in 1993 the Association for Science Education (ASE) recognised the need for a policy statement outlining its commitment to the promotion of environmental education within member schools. A task group was established to address the policy statement, with a view to implementation. Several key areas have been highlighted during the group's initial year of office. These include the need to recognise and publish examples of 'good practice', to look 'in-house' and audit ASE headquarters from an environmental standpoint, to address the poor provision with initial teacher training for the promotion of environmental education and to establish, in conjunction with other interested bodies, criteria for the effective evaluation of environmental resource material.

The application and promotion of environmental education within education institutions and its future within the National Curriculum is considered.

# Introduction

The current pedagogic concept of 'environmental education' is based on the internationally accepted definition outlining a process:

> ... of recognising values and clarifying concepts in order to develop skills and attitudes necessary to understand and appreciate the inter-relatedness among man, his culture and his biophysical surroundings.
>
> (IUCN, 1970)

and is the result of a series of developments in both time and space. Starting in the early seventies as *nature* or *rural* studies, and later *environmental studies*, the rural environment was still seen as the prime focus for the study in schools, and science-based approaches dominated. Where environmental education ventured into the urban domain, it was approached from a geographical, historical and sociological basis. In geography the prevailing emphasis on quantitative analysis made it very difficult to introduce qualitative studies which emphasised appraisal, valuing and judgement-making.

Art teachers were content to use the environment as a source of stimulus for art-making activities. The area of *critical studies* had not yet acquired its current significance.

The first major development occurred in the early 1970s when the notion of *urban studies* was taken on board. The *urban studies* movement was inspired by planners, architects and educators and was concerned that the *social issues* and the *non-academic child* should be the focus of an education which empowered. Curriculum development was underway. The involvement of architects and planners in environmental education acted as a catalyst in bringing together teachers from a range of subject areas to work on cross-curricular studies. The outcome had far-reaching consequences, with the rural-urban imbalance being adjusted in favour of the majority who lived in urban surroundings. The supremacy of knowledge-based studies was challenged by a greater focus on the approaches of experience, attitudes and values, on local issues and on encouraging people generally to become involved with the political processes associated with their local environment. Changes in Advanced Level Geography and Design syllabuses also reinforced the need to address the issue of environmental design. Some syllabuses were attempting to introduce cross-curricular approaches, involving English, geography, history, science, social studies and art and design, and requiring both objective and subjective study, focusing on environmental and social issues. Schools however found it difficult to accommodate this new approach as it required working relationships and attitudes different from those they were used to. It was not until the late 1980s that a surge of public interest in the environment 'kick-started' the situation. The mood was for a more holistic and biocentric understanding of the environment which was supported by a theoretical entitlement to an environmental education through the newly established National Curriculum.

# Environmental education in the English and Welsh National Curriculum

Environmental education was first introduced into the English and Welsh National Curriculum as one of the five *cross curricular themes*. These themes

> ... aim to promote discussion of values and beliefs, extend knowledge and understanding, encourage practical activities and decision making and further the interrelationship between the individual and the community.
>
> (ASE, 1993)

As can be seen from Figure 4.1, it is a complex area of study with many facets requiring coordinated contributions from a number of curriculum areas. Curriculum Guidance 7: Environmental Education (NCC, 1990) provided guidelines for the promotion of environmental education, outlining the aims of environmental education in England and Wales as being to:

- provide opportunities to acquire the knowledge, values and attitudes, commitment and skills to protect and improve the environment.

- encourage pupils to examine and interpret the environment from a variety of perspectives.

- arouse pupils' awareness and curiosity about the environment and encourage active participation in resolving environmental problems.
  (NCC, 1990)

With these aims in mind the purposes of environmental education may be summarised according to the generally accepted 'three strand' or 'tripartite' model:

Firstly, learning **about** the environment through development of knowledge and understanding, enquiry methods, values, opinions and judgements. This component of environmental education is probably the most straightforward to address. Education about the environment

TO33263

| Objectives of environmental education | English | Mathematics | Science | Geography |
|---|---|---|---|---|
| Knowledge (natural processes) | Assembling information from various sources to prepare debate, e.g. flooding of a valley | Compare data, i.e. regional variation in rainfall in Britain | Natural processes of purification management issues, e.g. sewage out-fall into sea | Water cycle |
| Skills (communi-cation) | Conduct debate | Graphs diagrams | Newspaper article for environment column of local paper | Role play siting of dam |
| Attitudes (appreciate, care, concern) | Impact of floods/dams on local area | Use of water and land use. Water as a resource - political dimension | Impact on tourism, health, other living things | Management of catchment and transport-ation. Visual concerns |

| | History | Technology | Art      Music | PE |
|---|---|---|---|---|
| Knowledge (natural processes) | Pollution in Industrial Revolution | Water power | Art and Music inspired by e.g. gorges | Understand river processes (currents, erosion, deposition) as related to e.g. canoeing |
| Skills (communi-cation) | Prepare investiga-tive report | Working models | Own      Own work      work | Produce own safety guide-lines or code of practice, e.g. video |
| Attitudes (appreciate, care, concern) | Domestic consump-tion of water. Then & now | Environmental impact - upstream and downstream | Destruction of inspirational environments | Code of conduct. Respect for environment |

**Figure 4.1 Environmental education in the National Curriculum**
Source: Chosenhill School, Gloucestershire (1993)

encompasses a body of knowledge and understanding which can be identified within the core and foundation subjects. Curriculum Guidance 7 suggests that a basic knowledge and understanding of the environment can be developed through the following topics:

- Climate
- Soil, rocks and minerals
- Water
- Energy
- Plants and animals
- People and communities
- Buildings, industrialisation and waste.

Secondly, learning **for** the environment, through the promotion of quality, sustainable life-styles and interactions with the environment, equality of access to resources and control of the environment and a personal and public action to attain these ends. In this context, Curriculum Guidance 7 states that

> pupils are already actively involved in activities which affect the environment, for example they are already inhabitants, consumers, road users and followers of leisure pursuits. As children, these activities are likely to take place within a relatively narrow range of social contexts - home and family, school, neighbourhood and peer group. In this respect the school can be viewed as a dynamic resource. It could enable young people to exercise a degree of control over the environment. It could encourage them to form environmentally friendly habits that could be sustained into adulthood.
>
> (NCC, 1990)

Thirdly, learning **in** or **through** the environment by the inclusion of regular first hand experience of nearby localities, visits to a range of localities further afield and the use of secondary sources of information about more distant environments.

Since its introduction in 1991, debate over the National Curriculum has been ongoing. Teachers, parents and governors have not been satisfied and the need to revise the Curriculum has been seen as paramount. This has been implemented by the Schools Curriculum and Assessment Authority (SCAA), led by Sir Ron Dearing (SCAA, 1994). The process was extensive and rapid, beginning with the Draft Report in December 1993, followed by the Draft Orders for each subject in the Spring of 1994. Proof copies were distributed to schools and other institutions before the end of 1994 and Final Orders were distributed to schools early in the 1995 (SCAA, 1995). It soon became apparent that the emphasis was on core subjects and the *cross-curricular themes* were slipping from view. It is now clear that these will be a matter for individual schools - using the 20% discretionary time now made available. As the government does not wish to be over-prescriptive, the existing guidance documentation is all that will be available.

The New Orders do, however, provide a framework for environmental education across the whole curriculum. Emphasis is placed on the need for young people to experience different types of environments. The use of fieldwork and school grounds is given particular importance. Within each subject area, knowledge and understanding is emphasised, but so too are other aspects equally important to environmental education. For example, within the Science curriculum, the notion of care and sensitivity towards living things and the environment are emphasised at all Key Stages. Key Stage 2 focuses on protecting the environment and investigating the role of various components within that environment which ensure its stability. At Key Stage 3 there is mention of the use of *fieldwork*, with reference to the collection of realistic data and the problems associated with this. The impact of science and technology on the environment is also considered. Our insatiable demand for energy and the notion of energy conservation, in terms of renewable and non-renewable sources is included. The effects of burning fossil fuels and acid deposition are also referred to, particularly with respect to impact on the environment.

At Key Stage 4 the scope widens. The power and limitations of science in addressing environmental issues, including ethical dilemmas are involved. In the programmes of study such terms as *quality of life, competing priorities* and the mechanics of *decision-making* when industrial, economic, social and environmental issues are to be considered, are included. The notion of *value judgements* is apparent here. Ideas of *managing the working environment* and *minimising risks* to the environment, concepts that industries are having to pay attention to, now appear within this Key Stage. The whole Science curriculum still offers a framework within which much environmental education may be promoted.

Within Geography, the emphasis is even greater. In thematic studies pupils are required to investigate the *quality of the environment* within a locality which can be national or international. At Key Stages 1, 2 and 3 pupils are required to make value judgements about the environment and discuss how the quality of the environment can be sustained and improved. Human impact is introduced at Key Stage 2, in relation to the *changing environment*. This is developed further at Key Stage 3, by considering the issues arising from people's interaction with their environment. Pupils are required to investigate management strategies within specific case studies. This develops more complex ideas concerning conflicts of interest and sustainable development. Unfortunately Geography is not compulsory at Key Stage 4: a matter of concern for those who consider that the development of positive attitudes and a deeper understanding of the pressures upon the environment are important at this stage in a pupil's development.

Design and Technology contains important references to the environment in the sections on *Health and Safety* in Key Stages 2 and 3. The impact, in terms of quality of manufacture and use upon the environment, is raised at Key Stage 3. Conflicts of interest and environmental issues in relation to product design, quality and health and safety are all emphasised at Key Stage 4.

In the curricula for Modern Foreign Languages, Art and Music there are references to the use of the environment as a context for teaching the subjects. There are also opportunities in English and Mathematics, but these are not mandatory. Within the general requirements for Physical Education, Key Stages 1-4, there is important reference to the development of positive attitudes to others and the environment. The inclusion of the environment in all of these curricula supports Gayford's view that:

> The overall impression is that the new Orders provide a good deal more scope for environmental education than was expected from earlier drafts.
> (Gayford, 1995)

The main criticism, however is that much is still left to individuals to determine how, when and where environmental education will be promoted. It has been suggested that the available 20% of curriculum time could be devoted to the *cross-curricular themes*. This is only a suggestion, and in reality there are many other demands on this time.

## Scottish National Curriculum

The proposed 5-14 Scottish Curriculum is separated into five areas: Mathematics, English Language, Expressive Arts, Religious and Moral Education and Environmental Studies. The framework for Environmental Studies consists of Science, Social Subjects, Technology, Health Education and Information Technology.

> The environment ... encompasses all the social, physical and cultural conditions which influence, or have influenced, the lives of the individual and the community and which shape or have been shaped by, the actions,

artifacts and institutions of successive generations. At a more immediate level, this definition includes everyday curricular experiences through which the pupil's knowledge of the environment develops.

(SOED, 1993)

The Scottish National Guidelines summarise the aims of Environmental Studies as follows:

Pupils should:

- achieve knowledge and understanding of the environment, as defined above;

- develop skills which will enable them to interact effectively with the environment;

- progressively recognise the knowledge, understanding and skills associated with Science, Social Subjects and Technology;

- develop knowledge, understanding, skills and attitudes associated with Health Education;

- develop knowledge and understanding of, and the capacity to use, Information Technology;

- develop informed attitudes and values relating to the care and conservation of the environment.

(SOED, 1993)

It is the final element that echoes the true ethos of environmental education. Being primarily concerned with people's interaction with their environment, it seeks to develop awareness within a framework of global environmental principles. The approach, however is not prescriptive, encouraging the study of environmental 'success stories', for example the return of Osprey to the Scottish Highlands, as well as key problem areas. Importance is placed firmly on the *whole school* ethos being consonant with the development of responsible attitudes towards the environment.

# Northern Ireland National Curriculum

The formal Northern Ireland National Curriculum consists of contributory subjects and cross-curricular themes. Aspects of environmental education have been written into the programmes of study and attainment targets for many of the contributory subjects of the curriculum. These include English, Mathematics, Science, Technology and Design, Geography, History, Music and Religious Education at Key Stage 1 and 2; English, Mathematics, Science, Technology and Design, Home Economics, Geography, Business Studies, History, Art and Design, Physical Education and Drama at Key Stages 3 and 4. The various ways in which environmental education has been included, either as part of a specific requirement within the programme of study, or as a potential context of study, has been summarised and exemplified by the Northern Ireland Curriculum Council within their guidelines for teachers. Some of the objectives of the educational (cross-curricular) themes seek to address issues related to the environment:

> Education for mutual understanding highlights specifically the need to know about global interdependence and the impact that environmental change can have at a range of scales ...
> Economic awareness highlights the needs for pupils to appreciate that individuals, as consumers, and those in the business community, have a responsibility to take account of environmental issues in both a local and international context.
>
> (NICC, 1994)

# The Association for Science Education and environmental education

As can be seen from the above summaries, a framework exists within which environmental education can be promoted. This in itself is not sufficient. It must be emphasised to all those engaged in the formal education process that environmental education has an important part to play. The government indicates that teachers are to use their professional discretion in adopting the cross curricular approach when it is appropriate to do so. They are to decide when and how environmental education is to be included. From informal discussion with Association for Science Education (ASE) members, it has become apparent that there exists a mixed response to this approach. This emanates from the early days of the National Curriculum and is indeed still present today.

In January 1993 the ASE launched its policy statement on environmental education. The policy statement outlines the purposes of environmental education and the special contribution of science education. It includes the development of:

a)  an understanding of:
- natural processes in the environment

- human dependency on these
- ways that human activities can replace them.

b) an ability to:
- appreciate the nature of scientific evidence
- recognise and be critical of scientifically weak arguments
- evaluate uncertainty and degrees of risk.

c) skills in problem solving, research and communication.

d) care and concern for living things and the environment.

(ASE, 1993)

Many of these it may be noted, now appear in the Science Orders of the National Curriculum for England and Wales. The policy statement urges its members to ensure that their education institution develops a coherent approach towards environmental education. It proposes schemes of work for science education in accordance with the principles of effective environmental education and encourages the production and implementation of a whole-school policy for environmental education. The document concludes by listing seven strands which the Association aims to follow in order to promote environmental education.

The ASE established the Environmental Education Task Group in 1994 to address issues raised by the policy statement. The Task Group's membership spans a broad spectrum, including a Secondary School Science Teacher, Industrial Education Liaison Officer, Field Centre Ecologist, Primary Science Advisor and a member of the ASE Publications committee. It was decided by the Task Group to concentrate on specific aspects of the policy statement, namely:

- evaluation of current resources and initiatives
- liaising with other organisations
- identification of areas of good practice.

The Final Report of the inaugural year of office of the Environmental Education Task Group was presented to Council in October 1994. The report was accepted and a new remit was formulated for the Task Group. This outlined a three-phase action plan addressing the following issues:

- the needs of members with regards to the promotion of environmental education

- the promotion of sound environmental practice with ASE headquarters

■   environmental education within initial teacher training.

At the Annual meeting at Lancaster, January 1995, the Task Group launched a survey of the current status of environmental education within ASE member institutions, with specific reference being given to the following areas: resources, the experience of teaching staff, methods of delivery and pupil/student response to environmental education programmes.

The results of the survey confirmed that evidence of good practice was apparent, but all too often teachers and educators were confronted by a host of bureaucratic and administrative barriers. Generally, there was a lack of available schemes of work for environmental education; of more concern was evidence of the decreasing use of residential field centres as a result of changes to the National Curriculum.

The findings supported those of the research project conducted by National Foundation for Educational Research (NFER) in 1993 entitled 'Environmental Education: Teaching approaches and students attitudes' and those of the Royal Society for the Protect of Birds (RSPB) survey in 1991 entitled 'Environmental Education in England'.

However, the survey raised many more questions than it answered, and generated many suggestions for further development and action research. These include:

■   a consideration of the place of environmental education as part of the whole curriculum and ethos of the school: could this be reflected in the revised framework for inspection of schools?

■   how INSET can be developed for environmental education.

■   how schools/colleges can involve pupils in developing their grounds to enhance teaching and learning, and how they can take action for the environment. (Groups such as *Learning through Landscapes* and the *GroundWork Trust* are already taking a lead in this field).

■   the need for a management system for recycling in schools/colleges. (The *Tidy Britain Group* is addressing this in certain areas).

■   what is the depth of knowledge and understanding of pupils with a good awareness of and positive attitude to environmental issues?

A more general consensus regarding the promotion of environmental education highlighted the following areas which need addressing:

- the need for a series of case studies depicting ASE member institutions successful (and at times not so successful) experiences.

- established guidelines to assist in the promotion of environmental education in an easy to use format which could be presented to senior management to elicit support.

- a balanced evaluation of available resource material, with indicators of suitable usage, accessibility and cost.

These findings were supported at a Department of Education/Department of Environment Conference in February 1995 which identified that one of the most pressing needs was for teachers to receive help in identifying suitable materials and resources for teaching about the environment. It was felt that although there is a wealth of available materials, not all are of good quality, and they are aimed at a variety of age groups and on a variety of topics (DoE/DFE, 1995).

Although Scotland is seemingly ahead of England and Wales with regard to the promotion of environmental education, this is not necessarily the case. The Government's review of education from 5-14, carried out by the Scottish Consultative Council on the Curriculum (SCCC, 1991) offers opportunities across the curriculum and specifically in environmental studies for the promotion of environmental education. Some excellent resource material has been disseminated to schools to assist in this promotion, yet it is not obligatory for schools to adopt this system and indeed many do not. In addition, the document 'Learning for Life' funded by Scottish Natural Heritage, presents a national strategy for environmental education in Scotland and is a superb resource which is still awaiting Government response (SEEC, 1993). Enthusiasm for environmental education runs high in Scotland, but this enthusiasm is being tested to the extreme.

## Development of the environmental audit training pack

The Environmental Education Task Group has recognised a need to encourage ASE members to take a more environmental approach to teaching within their respective institutions. However, it is appreciated that there are other pressures on teachers from a variety of sources and hence the time required to develop material, or indeed to encourage members of staff to become more aware, is difficult to find. There is a need for guidance from a lead body, and this role could be taken by the ASE. It is obvious that if members are to look to ASE for a lead, then

ASE should, as stated in the policy statement, adopt environmentally sound practices.

A training package based on the British Standard for Environmental Management - BS7750 has been developed. The package covers everything from defining the responsibility of staff and the organisation of business functions to buying goods in a more environmentally conscious way. The principle of BS7750 is 'REDUCE, RECYCLE, REUSE'. In addition to the training pack, the Task Group has developed an environmental audit for use in schools. The audit is activity-based and asks pupils to investigate a variety of subjects and analyse their environmental effects. This will not only help the school to become more environmentally friendly, but could save a great deal of money. More importantly, it encourages pupils to become more environmentally aware.

## Support for initial teacher training

Several members of the Task Group are addressing the initial teacher training aspect of the remit, developing a package which promotes environmental education within education institutions. The package will be of a self study format, which can be used at two levels: a foundation level aimed at the acquisition of basic scientific concepts relating to environmental issues, and a more advanced level expanding these concepts, in both depth and application. Although aimed primarily for use in initial teacher training, the package lends itself for use in INSET with practising teachers. The proposed outline of the package is:

*Introduction* - will cover the following areas:

- definition of environmental education
- the need for environmental education, with reference to Agenda 21
- global and local issues
- the position of environmental education within the National Curriculum

*Main body of package/module* - composed of two main areas:

Theoretical analysis: examination of the issues concerned

- physical issues such as the greenhouse effect, ozone depletion, acid rain, water quality, air quality, noise pollution, mineral extraction, rock depletion, peat extraction and human population growth.

- agricultural issues such as biodiversity, intensive farming, set-aside, use of genetic engineering and the effect of fertilisers, pesticides and herbicides.
- leisure and tourism
- political, economic and industrial issues, including BS7750 and European standards of environmental monitoring.
- energy, to include the laws of thermodynamics, global and local demand, electricity generation - alternative methods.

Practical application: (in the classroom, in everyday life)

- environmental policy
- environmental audits
- reuse, reduce, recycle
- use of school grounds
- creating links with industry.

Interest has been expressed in the package by several bodies including Higher Education institutions and industry. Two modules will be on trial in Gloucestershire in late 1995.

## The way ahead

It can be seen that there is a need for the work of the Environmental Education Task Group to continue. Once the local trials of the initial teacher training package are complete, it will become available nationally, together with further guidelines and evidence of good practice. However, effective environmental education cannot be confined to the classroom. The school has an important part to play in the promotion of environmental education in the neighbourhood and the local community; this can be effected by a planned sequence of environmental experiences:

which may help develop the idea of 'acting locally and thinking globally' (United Nations, 1992) promoted by many Local Agenda 21 initiatives.

Each local authority is encouraged to adopt an individual Local Agenda 21 by 1996. This is a strategy for sustainable development at the local level involving partnerships with other sectors, such as business, community and voluntary groups. As seen in Figure 4.2, schools can also be involved, and can help promote learning about the environment including:

- raising awareness about environmental education and action;
- helping to identify local environmental issues, and the methods and resources to tackle them;
- providing good access to information and advice about the local environment;
- providing ideas/support in moving towards self-sustaining action;
- training volunteers - which takes account of a range of motives and abilities;
- securing resources to trigger action and support projects.

(After SEEC, 1993)

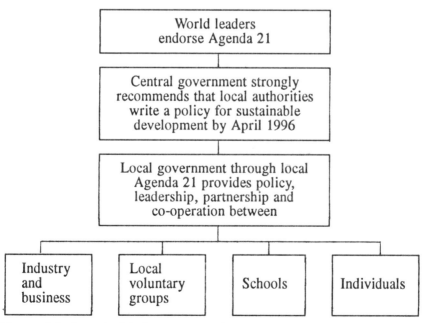

**Figure 4.2 Agenda 21: Implementation and responsibilities**
Source: Somerset Education Consultants (1995)

Many local authorities are well advanced in the development of their Local Agenda 21. The Grampian Regional Council in Scotland has outlined a policy proposal - the *Environmental Charter Action Programme* (Grampian Regional Council, 1994). Part of the charter focuses on environmental education and seeks to identify key policy issues; it also describes a comprehensive development strategy for environmental education in the Grampian Region (see Figure 4.3).

In Somerset, the County Council's policy on sustainable development is complemented by a paper put forward by the Somerset Education Consultancy Group for environmental education in Somerset schools. It aims to

> ... support schools wishing to make their unique contribution by helping pupils to understand the concept of sustainable development and to play their part in making it a reality.
>
> (Somerset Education Consultants, 1995)

The policy outlines proposals to meet the aims of Agenda 21 and provides exemplar material enabling schools to put the policy into practice. Many other county councils recognise the school system as the only means of providing environmental education for everyone which will go some way towards achieving the aspirations of Agenda 21. Most local authority policies identify key areas of good practice:

- the development of a whole-school policy on environmental education
- an environmental audit of the school and its grounds
- the appointment of a member of staff with overall responsibility for environmental education
- the identification of development targets for environmental education and a time scale for that development.

The Council for Environmental Education (CEE, 1995) has recently published a document encouraging schools to include an environmental policy within their school development plans. Entitled *Develop an environmental policy: a call to action to schools*, it outlines the need for such a policy and includes a checklist of issues which could be raised and activities which could be carried out by staff and pupils. The purpose of an environmental audit is to involve all members of the school in examining every aspect of the school environment. The aim is to identify areas for improvement and to plan for change. The audit will also bring to light areas where possible financial saving could be made.

| Areas for development | 1993-94 |
|---|---|
| 1. Policy (Action 71) | Policy formulation and dissemination. Establish Regional Steering Group. |
| 2. Curriculum advice and guidance | Produce Regional Guidelines: (various) |
| 3. Learning and support materials (Actions 72, 74) | Progress existing developments in collaboration with external agencies (site specific packages). Complete Directories. |
| 4. Staff development and training | Policy and development programme formal launch. (Conference) Specific training for school co-ordinators. Subject based training through wider in-service programme based on developments under 1 and 2 above. |
| 5. Communications | Further development on REEF network. Production of regular newsletter. |
| 6. Environmental audit | Establish inter-disciplinary task group to prepare proposals for environmental audit and audit training. |
| | **1994-95** |
| 1. Policy (Action 71) | Progress Policy and Development Programme. |
| 2. Curriculum advice and guidance | Establish pilot project using regional and national guidelines. |
| 3. Learning and support materials (Actions 72, 74) | Ongoing (long-term programme). Update Directories and Database |
| 4. Staff development and training | Ongoing curriculum-related in-service: Initiate training for environmental audit. |
| 5. Communications | Ongoing |
| 6. Environmental audit | Initiate establishment audits. Establish consultancy service. |

**Figure 4.3 Provisional environmental education development programme for Grampian Regional Council 1993-95**
Source: Grampian Regional Council (1994)

Ideally all pupils should be involved in the audit as part of their curriculum. Areas of study could include:

- energy and energy efficiency
- school's purchasing policy
- school grounds - development of conservation area
- building and materials
- waste
- school lunches
- transport
- resources
- cleaning

In order for most of the above to be realised, there is a need for recognition by schools, the community and local and central government that environmental education is a national priority area. Comprehensive and pro-active guidelines on aspects of environmental education need to be formulated. As shown by the examples mentioned previously, it is being addressed in some localities, but there is a need to go further still. Specific grants for in-service training need to be made available, and further pilot studies need to be carried out, together with the inclusion of environmental education as a component of all pre-service teacher training. Within the infra-structure of education institutions at all levels, environmental issues must be addressed, perhaps through the OFSTED inspection process. As schools move into a new era of management and inspection, environmental education has implications for all aspects of school life. Future school inspectors will be seeking to evaluate:

> ... pupil's attitudes to people, property, work, school, the community and the environment ..... the range of, and pupils responses to, opportunities to exercise responsibility and initiative; ... the values, beliefs and attitudes which the school promotes and demonstrates ... the conditions, appearance and use of buildings and the whole school site. ... the appropriateness of fieldwork, visits and other practical geographical activity.
>
> (OFSTED, 1993)

The role of the Association for Science Education, in particular the Environmental Education Task Group, is to support and develop the changing role of environmental education both as part of science education and as part of the whole curriculum of schools and colleges. As a result, our general understanding of the world in which we live will improve and we will be able to take positive steps towards a sustainable future - a future which meets the needs of the present *without* compromising the ability of future generations to meet their own needs.

The final word comes from Chief Seattle, Chief of the Ogwamish:

Whatever befalls the earth
befalls the sons of the earth.
If men spit upon the ground,
they spit upon themselves.
This we know: the earth does not belong
to man; man belongs to the earth.

This we know.
All things are connected.

Man did not weave the web of life;
he is merely a strand in it.
Whatever he does to the web
he does to himself

Source: NICC (1993)

# Bibliography

ASE (1993) *Environmental Education Policy Statement*. Hatfield, Herts: Association for Science Education.

CEE (1995) *Develop an environmental policy: a call to action for schools*. Reading: Council for Environmental Education.

DoE/DFE (1995) *Education and the environment: the way forward*. Conference report, February 1995. London: Department for Education.

Gayford, C. (1995) Environmental education in the revised National Curriculum. *Environmental Education* 40 pp. 5-6.

Grampian Regional Council (1994) *Environmental Charter Action Programme*. Aberdeen: Grampian Regional Council.

IUCN (1970) Conference Report. Nevada, USA: International Union for the Conservation of Nature.

Lakin, L. (1995) A possible solution from the ASE Environmental Education Task Group. *Education in Science* 163 pp. 9-10.

NCC (1990) *Curriculum Guidance 7: Environmental Education*. York: National Curriculum Council.

Neil, P. and Palmer, J. (1994) *The Handbook of Environmental Education*. London: Routledge.

NFER (1993) *Environmental Education: teaching approaches and attitudes*. Slough: National Foundation for Educational Research.

NICC (1993) *Environmental Education: a guide for teachers*. Belfast: Northern Ireland Curriculum Council.

OFSTED (1993) *Handbook for the inspection of schools*, 2nd ed. London: HMSO.

RSPB (1991) *Environmental Education in England: report of a survey*. Sandy, Bedfordshire: Royal Society for the Protection of Birds.

SEC (1995) *A Policy for Environmental Education in Somerset*. Taunton: Somerset Education Consultants.

SEEC (1993) *Learning for Life: a National Strategy for Environmental Education in Scotland*. Scottish Environmental Education Council/ Scottish National Heritage. Edinburgh: Scottish Office.

SCAA (1994) *The National Curriculum and its assessment: final report*. London: Schools Curriculum and Assessment Authority.

SCAA (1995) *The National Curriculum Orders*. London: Schools Curriculum and Assessment Authority.

SCCC (1991) *Environmental Studies 5-14: a report of the review and development group on Environmental Studies*. Scottish Consultative Council on the Curriculum. Edinburgh: Scottish Office Education Department.

SOED (1993) *Environmental Studies 5-14*. Edinburgh: Scottish Office Education Department.

United Nations (1992) *UN Conference on Environment an Development, Agenda 21 Rio Declaration*. Paris: UNESCO.

# 5 A multicultural perspective on environmental education

*Paul Oliver*

## Abstract

It is only relatively recently that environmental issues have been discussed to any extent within our education system, yet in a number of other societies, a sensitivity to the environment has for a long time been an intrinsic part of the culture and religion. This paper starts by examining aspects of other cultures which have an implication for the environment, then seeks to argue that these concepts have become integrated into contemporary perceptions of the environment; finally it stresses the importance of cultural traditions in these areas for a pluralist education system. In order to illustrate the issues, examples are drawn from cultures and religions in Africa, India, China, Japan and South-East Asia.

## Introduction

The increasing focus in society upon environmental issues is leading gradually to a reappraisal of the relationship between human beings and their environment. This reappraisal exists on both a practical and conceptual level, and has implications for both the manner in which commercial and industrial activities are conducted and also for the philosophical position we hold about the nature of human existence. The fundamental ideas which are part of this reappraisal include the notion of the impermanence of the living world and of the cyclical nature of existence. In the West for example, since the Industrial Revolution, it has been part of the general ideology that, to all intents and purposes, resources are unlimited. In other words, increases in production based on the consumption of natural resources could continue more or less unchecked. In addition, the assumption has been that the waste products of production could be disposed of within the ecosystem, and that there would be no significant ill-effects. This kind of assumption has been an intrinsic part of thinking in the industrialised West and has been fully integrated into political attitudes, economic structures and education. Only relatively recently has it been challenged.

Perhaps one can argue that in the industrialised countries there has been more of an emphasis upon controlling the environment rather than being part of it. There is now a greater sense of the importance of living in equilibrium with the environment rather than in competition with it. The basis of this chapter is that such ideas have in fact been part of the philosophies of a number of cultures outside the Western industrialised tradition. Such ideas are not only of historical and academic interest, but are starting to have more and more relevance because of the emphasis upon environmental issues. Moreover, the presence in Britain of children and families from other cultures carries with it many implications for the education system, not least of which is the obligation on teachers to understand the cultures of their pupils and students in order to relate to them in a positive way. This chapter starts by exploring some ideas relevant to the environment from other cultures, then shows how these ideas are integrated into contemporary views of the environment, and finally stresses the value for children of being aware of their cultural tradition in this respect.

## Perspectives on the environment from other cultures

The religious tradition of India has had an enormous influence in terms of cultural ideas, not only because of Hinduism, but through the development of Buddhism about five hundred years before the Christian era (BCE). Buddhism became the predominant religion in South-East Asia and Japan, and has greatly influenced Chinese culture. One of the fundamental features of the Indian tradition is the cyclical nature of existence. Hindu, Buddhist and Jain cosmologies all share the same concept of the universe proceeding through a series of never-ending cycles. Each complete cycle of the universe includes a period of evolution and development followed by a period of decline. This is followed in turn by a period of development. Not only is the cyclical nature of existence seen to be the norm on a cosmic scale, but also among life on the micro scale. Living things are born, grow and develop, and then decline. This is seen to be true of plant and animal life, and is true also on the psychological level. Buddhists point out that thoughts arise in the mind, stay for a while, and then gradually disperse. Some people are less adept than others at controlling thought patterns, but the general assertion is that all aspects of the universe are subject to patterns of expansion and contraction, or development and decline. Basham (1977) suggests this when he writes:

> The university is transient. There is no abiding entity anywhere ... Every being or object, however stable and homogeneous it may appear, is in reality transient and composite.

The idea that existence is in a state of flux and that this is the norm has become a very important concept of Buddhism. The concept of *impermanence* is central. In the Buddhist scriptures written in Pali, it is termed *anicca* (pronounced aneecha). Although the notion of the impermanence of life may seem like a self-evident truth, the Buddhist feels that human beings generally live their lives as if things were much more permanent than they are. A Buddhist would probably point out the numerous ways in which human beings try to reassure themselves about the permanence of things and try to shield themselves from the inevitability of ageing and decline. There is the preoccupation with the 'new' in all aspects of life - the new car, new house, and new household appliances. In addition, an entire industry has developed around the impetus to deny the facts of ageing and to try to retain the impression of youth. The cosmetics industry, cosmetic surgery and the youth icons of contemporary media all reinforce the idea that youth is desirable and ageing undesirable. One would not want to deny here that youth and vitality may generally be desirable and that old age and ill-health may in many ways be undesirable. However, the Buddhist would suggest that the problem here is the futile desire to try to make things different from their natural state. There is nothing intrinsically good or bad about the phenomena of youth and ageing. It is simply the way things are. There is no need to perform evaluative judgements about them. A leading Thai Buddhist (Chah, 1982) put it like this:

> When you see this much, you'll be able to know constantly this arising and passing away; and, when your knowing is constant, you'll see that this is really all there is. Everything is just birth and death. It's not as if there is anything which carries on.

For the Buddhist, this is not a particularly bleak or pessimistic view of life. Rather it is an acceptance of reality, of the ebb and flow of existence as it is. Now if the Buddhist perception that many societies strive for a false certainty and permanence to existence is correct, then this does have implications for the environment. If we discard products which show signs of ageing or which are simply no longer fashionable, then this will inevitably result in greater consumption of natural resources.

The concept of impermanence is a useful unifying idea in environmental education. It can be used to indicate on the one hand a universal characteristic of life, but on the other hand it can provide a link with the way in which an economy devoted to satisfying the need for the new and novel can consume resources much more rapidly than necessary. There are echoes of this idea in the advocacy of 'alternative technology' which tries to use natural or recycled sources of energy rather than irreplaceable ones. Quite clearly, we do employ in environmental education concepts which are akin to impermanence, but the latter provides a useful linking mechanism for a number of disparate ideas.

For the Buddhist, one of the results of an understanding of impermanence is that there is compassion for other living things which must pass through the cyclical process of birth, life and death. In the Pali scriptures, this approach is designated by the terms kindness (*metta*) and compassion (*karuna*). Such compassion is not intended to be directed simply at other human beings, for example those who are ill, but to all life forms. The Buddhist, for example, would as far as possible refrain from harming any animal, however small. This approach would also be extended to attitudes towards plants. A devout Buddhist would be unlikely to casually snap off a twig from a bush, or idly pick a flower while on a walk. The point is that any action which needlessly damages another life form would be avoided. Buddhists are nearly always vegetarians and clearly there would be an exception to the above argument in the need to cultivate and gather vegetables. The essential argument, though, remains that the Buddhist ideal is to exist in harmony with the environment, and to take as little as possible from that environment.

This minimalist position in terms of resource consumption is reflected in the Buddhist monastic tradition, where monks and nuns lead a very simple lifestyle conditioned by a desire to consume only resources essential to the maintenance of life. Buddhist monks are allowed very limited possessions, which include only one set of garments and one pair of sandals, and a food bowl. They eat only before noon each day, and then in quantities adequately only to sustain health. The idea of consuming food because it is particularly delicious or marketed to appeal to the palate would be anathema to the monk. This monastic tradition has developed with a philosophy which sees a virtue in the non-consumption of environmental resources. Buddhist monks and nuns are expected to act as exemplars to lay people for whom the material world of constant production and consumption may still hold some considerable attraction.

The idea of impermanence is a theme which can be detected in all aspects of Buddhist philosophy and indeed it is recorded as being the subject of the last utterance of the historical Buddha, Siddhattha Gotama. Just before he died in 483 BCE, in Bihar, India he is noted in the Pali canonical texts (Schumann, 1973) as saying:

> Now, monks, I exhort you: the components of the personality are subject to decay; exert yourselves with diligence.

In Buddhism, monks and nuns, as exemplars of this particular world view, are encouraged to develop a lack of attachment to the material world. The latter is seen as transitory and subject to continuous change. Sumedho (1987) describes some features of life in a Thai monastery. In particular he notes:

> At Wat Pah Pong we had to accept whatever hut we were given, so sometimes you were fortunate, you got a really nice one, and sometimes you got a not very nice one.

The monks were required to develop a dispassionate attitude to the material world by having to accept whatever living accommodation they were allocated, rather than wanting something better or more comfortable. The application of this idea is that it may sometimes be more desirable to learn to accept and adjust to the environment as it is, rather than to try at all costs to change it to suit our particular wishes. One might suggest that this seems a very passive philosophy, unsuited to the needs of modern life. However, a Buddhist would no doubt reply that contemporary attempts to change our environment to create greater and greater levels of personal comfort for people are probably counter-productive and will lead ultimately to a diminution of the very resources which are so valued.

This world view which sees it as desirable to use only those resources which are necessary for the essentials of existence is also found in Hinduism, and its most notable modern exponent has been Mahatma Gandhi. While working as a lawyer in South Africa, Gandhi was much influenced by the writings of Tolstoy, and at different times founded two independent rural communes based on the principle of self-sufficiency. When Gandhi returned to India and became involved in the struggle for Indian independence, these early experiments in living became transformed into a philosophy for Indian education and society, and indeed for the entire world.

Gandhi's view of society and of the dignity of human beings was based very much around the concept of the nobility of the farmer, the craft worker and the small-scale producer. To say that he was antagonistic to modern industrial production is probably unfair, but he certainly advocated the notion of small, self-sufficient communities. His concept of Indian schools was that they should incorporate the idea of self-sufficiency by teaching craft skills with the curriculum and encouraging children to produce either artefacts or agricultural produce which could be sold. As Kumar (1994) wrote:

> Basic education was an embodiment of Gandhi's perception of an ideal society as one consisting of small, self-reliant communities. To him, Indian villages were capable of becoming such communities:

For Gandhi, Indian villages would be self-supporting communities which lived in harmony with their surroundings, with the villagers involved in agriculture or in cottage industries which consumed a minimum of natural resources. Gandhi also wanted to bring about a transition in people, so that they were satisfied with a more modest life-style. Gandhi expressed it like this (Kripalani, 1969):

> The first step towards it is for him who has made this ideal part of his being to bring about the necessary changes in his personal life. He would reduce his wants to a minimum, bearing in mind the poverty of India.

It was an integral part of Gandhi's philosophy of social cooperation that changes in society would take place in parallel with changes in the individual. Village life or school life were seen as opportunities to develop an ethical perspective on life. Brotherton (1992) writes:

> It is a logical part of his picture of the school as a cooperative community linked organically with life outside it. Nothing was to be without an opportunity for teaching mutual respect, service and self-awareness.

The notion of the school curriculum acting as a vehicle for practical education in self-sufficient agriculture and environmental understanding finds a parallel in the work of Julius Nyerere of Tanzania. He advocated a similar idea of schools having their own school farms which would be collaboratively managed by teachers, pupils and community members. In this way theoretical learning of agricultural principles would be completed by practical understanding of the environment, agriculture and agricultural economics. Nyerere suggested that (Hinzen and Hundsdorfer, 1979):

> The possibilities of proper grazing practices, and of terracing and soil conservation methods can all be taught theoretically, at the same time as they are put into practice.

A central concept in a number of Eastern religions, including Hinduism, Buddhism and the Jain religion, is that of non-violence; in a number of ways this notion has had an impact upon environmental issues. One can look to India for the documented origins of the idea, and also for its implementation as a practical policy of government. The doctrine of non-violence (or, in Sanskrit, *ahimsa*) was espoused by the Mauryan emperor Asoka (269-232 BCE). His support for non-violence is known because of a number of extant stone inscriptions found in a range of locations in India (Basham, 1954).

The principles of non-violence can be loosely interpreted as not causing harm to other human beings or animals. However, in many contexts and cultures it is also extended to imply a sensitivity to all life and a respect for the natural environment in general. Asoka, for example, did not participate in the hunting of animals and encouraged the spread of a vegetarian diet. He arranged for trees to be planted alongside roads in order to provide shade and also for wells to be dug. In addition, he encouraged the planting and use of medicinal herbs.

The idea of non-violence has perhaps been carried to an extreme in the Jain religion of India. Smart (1969) describes how devout Jains always strain water before drinking it, in case they should swallow small living organisms. They similarly wear a white gauze mask over their mouths to prevent their inadvertently breathing in small insects. In addition, they make a special attempt to tread very carefully when walking in case they should kill a small living thing, and it is quite common for them to gently sweep the path in front as they walk, for the same reason.

The principle of non-violence has proved to be very effective as a political weapon. Perhaps the best-known advocate in this context was Gandhi himself. In the struggle for Indian independence he consistently employed non-violent demonstrations in conjunction with calm, moral arguments as a means to build up a groundswell of public opinion. It is interesting that contemporary advocates of environmental causes also frequently employ the same principle of non-violent protest as a means of trying to establish the validity of a moral argument.

The themes of the transitory nature of life and of the wisdom of not being attached to worldly existence occur frequently in the painting and poetry of China and Japan. Chinese art, influenced by both Taoism and Buddhism, has a number of recurring themes which are all connected with the environment. Paintings nearly always emphasise the extent and grandeur of nature, with mountains receding into the distance and a lake or river in the foreground. A small figure, often of an old man, sits in contemplation by the water, or in front of a simple hut. The small size and apparent vulnerability of the human figure is contrasted with the scale of the mountains and rocks. The human figure, perhaps bowed and holding a staff, seems transient when compared with the scale of the surrounding countryside. The human is impermanent, while only the process of life continues. Many Chinese paintings leave much of the paper or cloth empty, with the focus of the painting in one corner - a flower, a stand of bamboo, or a figure crossing a stream. The purpose of the paintings is to encourage in the viewer a feeling of serenity and of unity with our natural surroundings. The Taoist painter Shih t'ao (1641-1717 CE) painted a picture of a poet on a mountain top beneath a pine tree, reflecting on the scene around him. The calligraphy in the corner of the painting as translated by Chung-yuan (1975) reads:

What does the old master do here?
By the side of the rock he is hunting for a new verse.
Suddenly a cool breeze blows from the pine tree;
Silently and quietly it purifies his spirit and thought.

The same themes recur in the Japanese poetry form of *Haiku*, which was much inspired by the tradition of Zen Buddhism. Traditionally an abbreviated form of seventeen syllables, the haiku captures a fleeting moment of nature and often hints at the impermanence of existence. The following haiku by Matsuo Basho (1644-1694 CE) translated by Yuasa (1966) illustrates this:

How many columns of clouds
Had risen and crumbled, I wonder
Before the silent moon rose
Over Mount Gassan

The themes which have been discussed above can be traced in a variety of forms across many societies and cultures and have often been interrelated with religious philosophies. They include an awareness of the impermanence of life, the effects which an understanding of this can have for the world-view of human beings and a sense of the importance of a truly non-violent coexistence with the natural environment of which humanity is inevitably an integral part. Although these ideas have some considerable documented history, they are becoming of central importance in the contemporary conception of environmental imperatives.

## Contemporary views of the environment

Munro (1991), in a publication sponsored by, among others, the United Nations Environment Programme, states at the beginning of the introduction:

> We must adopt life styles and development paths that respect and work within nature's limits. We can do this without rejecting the many benefits that modern technology has brought, provided that technology itself works within those limits.

The contemporary understanding of the need to operate 'within nature's limits' reflects the Buddhist and Hindu concept of the cyclical nature of existence. Any serious disregard for the established dynamic equilibrium of the ebb and flow of life may lead to a permanent dissolution of that equilibrium.

One of the most worrying aspects of the current threat to the environmental equilibrium is that this threat comes from a minority of the world population, living in countries with an advanced industrialised economy. The consumption of world resources by this minority is so excessive that it is the prime cause of the current threats to the environment. If the non-industrialised countries were ever to achieve this level of resource consumption, then the damage to the environment could be on an irreversible scale. Lacey (1987) argues however that:

> The rich countries of the world maintain or increase their share of wealth while the poor make little progress and in many cases sink further behind in the unequal race for resources.

The message for Gandhi, to redistribute wealth and to be satisfied with less, seems all too relevant. In several different ways, however, there are important signs of growing awareness in industrialised countries of the need to correct the inequalities in much of the world economy. For example, consumers in the West have become increasingly aware of the power that they can exercise in supporting products which are produced in a manner sensitive to the environment; Ekins (1992) argues that such ethical and preferential consumerism can have considerable economic impact.

There has, in addition, been a growth in organisations which practise what might be called 'alternative trading'. The purpose of such organisations is to encourage relationships with producers in under-developed countries and to encourage markets in industrialised countries. Help is normally provided for the producer in developing low-cost production systems and products which are likely to appeal to the market in a more developed country. At the same time, the organisation explores the market in the industrialised sector, simultaneously publicising the context in which the product is manufactured. The ethical dimension here is to sensitise consumers to the economic background of the producer and to encourage them to support developing countries. The activities of alternative traders can help to establish a regular and reliable income for producers in developing countries.

It can sometimes happen that support of this kind has more benefits for the small-scale producer than aid at the macro level. As Blackwell (1991) argues:

> African rural development suggests that nongovernmental organisations have been more successful than government donors in terms of community involvement. Primarily motivated by humanitarian rather than political or economic concerns, most nongovernmental organisations naturally base their projects on community participation and on local direction.

I have tried so far in this chapter to show that, throughout various cultures and traditions, one can detect a world view which is sensitive to the environment, appreciates the interaction of life forms, supports a non-violent approach to existence and perceives a virtue in the consumption of relatively few natural resources. I have continued to argue that these same perceptions of the world permeate the entire contemporary 'environmental movement'. The question that remains is the extent to which the existence of ideas on the environment from other cultures should permeate the curriculum in Britain. (Incidentally the arguments which follow would apply to any other multiethnic country, besides Britain).

## Environmental issues within a multicultural curriculum

The first point is that it seems to me that the origins of ideas are significant. This is not to say that it is necessarily profitable for different cultures to initiate arguments about a claim on a particular concept.

Rather it may be more positive to acknowledge that, in many cases, ideas may have had multiple origins in different cultures at different times. A simple acknowledgement of this may prevent the development of ethnocentric claims about particular ideas.

In a multicultural society such as Britain it is arguably very supportive for children of a particular ethnic background to be reminded that their cultural tradition has certain ideas or belief systems which are held to be of value in other societies. Sikhs, for instance, have a vegetarian diet, yet are noted for their robust health. They have demonstrated that a vegetarian diet can form the basis for a healthy existence and have been an inspiration to vegetarians in other societies. In addition the Chinese, among other groups, have retained a respect for the cultivation of herbs and their use in medical remedies. This is not to set cultures in competition with each other, but rather to argue that there has been a flow of ideas from country to country and culture to culture for centuries and that this exchange of ideas is something to be applauded. As Young (1993) argues in the case of science teaching:

> A sophisticated anti-racist science curriculum would compare the thought system of our own culture with those of others. It would also show the examples where systems of knowledge have successfully cut across particular cultures - Arabic numbers, acupuncture, herbal remedies.

It is easy to be so ethnocentric about different cultures that we come to believe that our own culture has all the right answers and that we can reasonably assume the moral high ground. Perhaps a rational view would be not to assume that any particular culture has exclusive access to the truth, but that each culture, within its own parameters, seeks to formulate a meaningful understanding of the world and of existence. An interesting perspective on different views of the environment is that in less-industrialised cultures, both in the past and in modern times, there has been a continuous attempt to adjust to the environment and to adapt to its imperatives, while only in societies which are advanced technologically has there been the potential to try to change the environment. Perhaps this is an increasingly relevant point and industrial societies should reflect on whether such attempts are ultimately likely to be counterproductive. So perhaps within our education system the strategy should not be to attempt to rank different societies in terms of apparent successes or failures, but to treat them as a coherent human system in need of objective evaluation. Figueroa (1993) suggests that:

Furthermore, pluralism does not necessarily imply a radical relativism. That would be self-defeating. All cultures are committed to standards of true and false, and of right and wrong - and so to the very concept of truth and rightness. Cultures must be constructively critical of themselves as well as of others.

The study of other cultures is especially important for children in Britain, because it enables them to analyse their own society in terms of a response to environmental issues. For example, a study of the traditional ways of life of the original inhabitants of Australia and of the Kalahari desert demonstrates people living in harmony with the environment, taking very little from it, and indeed moving within the ecosystem so that no permanent damage is done to any particular location. This provides an enormous contrast to the desolation of much of the industrial landscape of Britain. One is obviously not trying to suggest to children that Europeans should revert to the life of wandering hunter-gatherers, but that such study provides lessons of which we should continually be reminding ourselves. The opportunities for young people to re-live these lessons is enormous today, with the proliferation of organisations devoted to the improvement of the environment. Heater (1992) argues that:

> Even in the state participation through interest and pressure groups gives much fuller meaning to the concept of citizenship than the occasional turnout to the polling booth. Opportunities for involvement at the global level, especially on development and environmental issues, are rapidly increasing.

With our present curricula, particularly in science and technology, it is so easy to give the impression to ethnic minority children in our schools that the key advances in knowledge have been achieved in a European context. The view that technological advance *per se* is insufficient to guarantee a high quality of life for coming generations is now gaining ground. It is a positive statement for children coming from other cultures to assert that, in some cases, the insights belonging to those cultures can be of enormous benefit to the industrialised countries of today.

In conclusion, it can perhaps be argued that we should not fall back on a bipolar debate with the forces of technology on the one hand and an apparently idyllic rural lifestyle on the other. Technology and environmental consciousness need not be in opposition. As the OECD (1991) argues:

Policy-makers in many European societies are now aware that questions of technological and economic development are inextricably bound up with the protection and conservation of the natural environment.

Under-developed countries need more technology to improve their standard of living, but, at the same time, technologically advanced countries must re-learn the timeless lessons inherent in the ways of life of people in developing countries. These lessons are often enshrined in religious or moral principles, but reflect truths about ways of living in a natural environment which are as relevant today as when they were first articulated.

# Bibliography

Basham, A.L. (1977) *The Wonder that was India*. New York: Grove.

Blackwell, J.M. et al (1991) *Environment and Development in Africa*. Washington DC: The World Bank.

Brotherton, J. (1992) Worlds Apart? Gandhi's educational message for us. *New Era in Education* 73 (1) pp. 16-19.

Chah, A. (1982) *Bodhinyana*. Ubon Rajathani, Thailand: Wat Pah Nanachat.

Chung-yuan C. (1975) *Creativity and Taoism*. London: Wildwood House.

Ekins, P. (1992) *A New World Order*. London: Routledge.

Figueroa, P. (1993) Cultural diversity, Social reality and Education. In Fyfe, A and Figueroa, P. (eds.) *Education for Cultural Diversity*. London: Routledge.

Heater, D. (1992) Political Education for Global Citizenship. In Lynch, J. et al (eds.) *Cultural Diversity and the Schools, Vol.4*, London: Falmer.

Kripalani, K.J. (ed.) (1969) *All Men are Brothers: Life and Thoughts of Mahatma Gandi*. Paris: UNESCO.

Kumar, K. (1994) Mohandas Karamchand Gandhi. In Morsy, Z. (ed.) *Thinkers on Education, Vol. 2*. Paris: UNESCO.

Lacey, C. (1987) Introduction. In Lacey, C. and Williams, R. (eds.) *Education, Ecology and Development*. London: World Wildlife Fund and Kogan Page.

Munro, D.A. (1991) *Caring for the Earth, A Strategy for Sustainable Living*. Gland: Switzerland, IUCN, UNEP, WWF.

Nyere, J.K. (1979) Education for Self-reliance. In Hinzen, H. and Hundsdorfer, V.H. (eds.) *The Tanzanian Experience: Education for Liberation and Development*. Hamburg: UNESCO.

OECD (1991) *Environment, Schools and Active Learning*. Paris: OECD.

Schumann, H.W. (1973) *Buddhism: An outline of its teaching and schools*. London: Rider.

Smart, N. (1971) *The Religious Experience of Mankind*. London: Collins.

Sumedho, A. (1987) *Cittaviveka*. Hemel Hempstead: Amaravati.

Young, R.M. (1993) Racist Society, Racist Science. In Gill, D. et al (eds.) *Racism and education*. London: Sage.

Yuasa, N. (1966) *Basho: The narrow road to the deep north, and other travel sketches*. Harmondsworth: Penguin.

# 6 Eurosurvey: an analysis of current trends in environmental education in Europe

*Walter Leal Filho*

## Abstract

The provision of information on the results of on-going attempts to promote environmental education in European countries is acknowledged as a significant component of the environmental problem-solving process. The collection of information from those at the receiving end of the teaching system or, in other words, the 'users' of information, such as school children, is seen as an important element in assessing the effectiveness of teaching policies, the extent to which pupils are benefiting from the environmental education provisions in their countries, and as an indicator of any changes in approaches or practices that may be needed.

On the basis of the perceived need for research which may provide insights into environmental education in formal teaching in Europe, the Eurosurvey was undertaken. This paper describes the initial findings of the Eurosurvey, a study on the levels of information and attitudes towards the environment, involving a sample of around 20,000 school children from 16 member countries of the Council of Europe. The study identifies a number of features related to school children's level of awareness of both global and national environmental issues, as well as the contribution of schools and the media as providers of information on environmental matters. This set of data provides a profile of current trends on European environmental education, reflecting the impact of current practices. A set of measures for further improvement are suggested.

## Introduction

The need for information on environmental education practices in European countries is as great as the very need for environmental information. This is seen as particularly important in the present political climate, where there is a noticeable increase in initiatives aimed at the integration of European countries. As stated by Leal Filho (1994c) a reasonable degree of knowledge of environmental education practices in individual countries is a useful tool in catalysing improvements in the way Europeans see, treat and co-exist with the environment.

The literature registers a number of studies which have looked at environmental education within individual countries at various teaching levels. These include works by Jakucs and Lakatus (1990) and Csobod (1995) in Hungary, Episcopopoulou (1991) in Greece, Lob (1994) in Germany, Hens (1995) in Belgium, Moran, Fernandez and Cartea (1995) in Spain and Jerzak and Jerzak in Poland (1995). There are also examples of authors who have devoted a great deal of time and effort in trying to understand trends related to environmental education in the teaching systems of their countries (e.g. Gayford, 1984; Schleicher, 1992) and trying to find ways of addressing them. Finally, there are also registers of attempts to develop environmental education at a country level, through the preparation of national strategies (e.g. Smyth, 1995) and the documentation of them (e.g. Leal Filho, MacDermott and Murphy, 1995).

With particular relevance to field research, it is noticeable that, although there are on the one hand several studies dealing with aspects of environmental education at the national level in European countries, there is not, on the other hand, sufficient research in the field of international environmental education which may enable trends and tendencies to be seen in a wider context. Moreover, there have been relatively few initiatives in this field which look at environmental education in Europe as a whole and which focus on items for integration and co-operation (Leal Filho, 1994a).

Based on this reality, the European Research and Training Centre on Environmental Education (ERTCEE) of the University of Bradford, in liaison with various universities, schools, governmental and non-governmental organisations across Europe, prepared the framework of the Eurosurvey, a study which would attempt to throw more light onto the levels of information and attitudes of European school students towards the environment, as well as their level of information on some basic environmental issues.

The idea of undertaking the 'Eurosurvey: a study of school children's attitudes towards the environment in a sample of member countries of the

Council of Europe' (the study's full title) was born out of the need to look critically at some aspects of environmental education which would be of interest in identifying European trends.

Such research was also seen as a timely effort: data gathered from the study could not only enable a better understanding of trends and patterns seen today in Europe, an important development as stated in Chapter 36 of UNCED's Agenda 21 (Leal Filho, 1994b), but could also prove useful in the preparation of suggestions as to how the improvement of the environmental awareness-raising role of schools may take place, thus reinforcing environmental education in the context of formal teaching. In addition, as it was initiated in the run up to the Maastricht Conference, held in November 1993, which in practice set in motion the economic unification of Europe, the study may be followed up by similar surveys, to be undertaken in a few years time, when progress may be assessed.

## Objectives of the study

The general objective of the Eurosurvey was to assess the levels of information, the opinions and attitudes of a sample of school children from European countries towards the environment, identifying their level of information on current environmental issues and their awareness of current environmental affairs. Specifically, the study aimed to:

a) evaluate children's knowledge of, and familiarity with, national and international environmental problems, especially those seen in modern Europe;
b) demonstrate the extent to which schools act as suppliers of environmental information in comparison with other sources;
c) identify children's participation in outdoor activities and in environmental conservation activities;
d) suggest, based on the aims above, measures that can be adopted in order to improve the role of schools as environmental awareness-raising institutions.

## Methodology

The study was undertaken in the period from May 1992 to December 1994. After careful consideration with regard to the size of the sample, it was decided that the survey would be undertaken by using a sample of 40 schools, selected by collaborators in each of the surveyed countries. The target group were school children from the age range 10-18 years. It was felt that the differences seen in the teaching systems of the sampled countries did not warrant the formal division of the sample into 'primary' and 'secondary' students. Age ranges and not teaching levels - which differ among countries where the age of entry to school varies substantially - were thus seen as the best parameters for data collection across the sampled countries.

The execution of the survey consisted of a postal questionnaire sent to all sampled schools, complemented by interviews and visits to schools in some of the surveyed countries. It was divided into three phases:

Phase 1 consisted of the preparation of a standard questionnaire, in English, which was expected to be distributed to all participant schools. In May 1992 the first draft of a questionnaire was conceived and piloted in a sample of British schools. Changes were made to the original draft, and a final version, suitable for use in schools in Britain, was sent to forty schools in West Yorkshire. While the British chapter of the survey was being undertaken, attempts to extend the study to other European countries were also initiatied. In doing so, it was felt on some occasions that the questionnaire needed to be translated into a particular country's language. In many countries however, the original English version was employed in schools as an exercise in foreign language comprehension, in line with the true interdisciplinary nature of environmental education.

Phase 2 involved the circulation of the questionnaires among a sample of 50 students per school in specific regions in each participant country. The total sampled group was thus expected to consist of 2000 students per country. Such a total was seen as being a large enough sample to enable the draft of a general profile of environmental education in Europe to be prepared. It was acknowledged, however, that on the basis of the experience gathered from similar international surveys and the difficulties involved in undertaking such studies, there would eventually be the need to accept a possible reduction in the total size of the sample.

Phase 3 consisted of the processing and statistical analysis of the data gathered, followed by the preparation of a final report containing the conclusions that could be drawn from the information collected. The survey's findings were officially presented at the *European Seminar on Environmental Education Research*, held in Bradford in March 1995. A summary with all relevant results is expected to be sent to all contributors and to the international media.

The first contact with potential participants from European countries was through a standard letter, sent to over 300 teachers, academics, practitioners, governmental and non-governmental organisations, across Europe, along with a leaflet describing the study's aims and structure.

Upon receiving confirmation of a participant's interest, a second letter was sent, along with the English questionnaire matrix. At that point, the relevant contributors would make a choice on whether they would wish to translate the questionnaire into their home country's language, or whether they would prefer to use an English questionnaire. The questionnaire was translated into German, Galician, Greek, Portuguese, Italian and Polish.

To ensure that an many questionnaires as possible would be returned, especially in the case of questionnaires in English, reminders were send to the collaborators two months after an agreed deadline, and at two-monthly intervals thereafter. A good number of responses were received through this approach.

Table 6.1 Levels of response to the survey country

| Country | Percentage received |
| --- | --- |
| Austria | 85 |
| Cyprus | 70 |
| Denmark | 50 |
| Finland | 50 |
| Germany | 100 |
| Greece | 48 |
| Ireland | 56 |
| Italy | 90 |
| Norway | 68 |
| Poland | 90 |
| Portugal | 25 |
| Spain | 100 |
| Sweden | 49 |
| The Netherlands | 38 |
| UK | 100 |

A total of 2000 questionnaires were distributed to collaborators in each of the sampled countries. Response rates varied significantly among countries, from around 25% (the lowest) to 100% (the highest). By January 1995 responses were received from school children from 13 EU countries (Austria, Denmark, Finland, France, Germany, Greece, Ireland, Italy, Portugal, Spain, Sweden, the Netherlands and the UK), in addition to 3 non-EU nations, namely Norway, Poland and Cyprus. Table 6.1 gives an overview of the entries gathered per country. In total, 21,090 European school children took part in the study, which makes the

Eurosurvey one of the largest comparative environmental education investigations ever undertaken in Europe.

## Limitations of the methodology

In undertaking a study which would aim to gather information from various European countries, a number of methodological and logistical barriers needed to be faced. A set of factors limited the scope of the study and influenced its methodology. The analysis of the 'results and discussion' section should therefore take these into account and needs to be seen in a wider context. As the experiences gathered through the Eurosurvey may prove helpful to similar investigations in the future, it is useful to mention the difficulties encountered and the ways in which they were overcome:

a) *language*: the natural difficulty in providing a data collection instrument which could be easily understood. The questionnaire was translated into various languages or, whenever feasible, the English version was used. The Eurosurvey data collection questionnaire was therefore made available in the following languages:

- English
- Galician
- German
- Greek
- Italian
- Polish
- Portuguese

b) *the culture of co-operation*: was represented by the usual difficulties in gathering active support for research. This problem, well described by Murphy (1994), was overcome by emphasising the benefits of participation in the study and offering the results of each country's analysis to collaborators.

c) *size of the sample*: as surveys have different aims and are performed under varied conditions, there is no consensus as to which sample size is ideal. This issue was dealt with by selecting a specific total of schools, namely forty per country, with a view to increasing the scope of the study and the diversity of answers.

d) *representation of the sample in a European context*: in order for the survey to have a truly European perspective, the survey would need to involve at least 13 countries; 16 countries were surveyed in this first phase and it is hoped that other countries will be surveyed in a second phase.

e) *usefulness to Europe*: the data needed to provide a contribution to the understanding of current trends in European schools. It was decided that, rather than providing a limited national focus, results would be analysed and disseminated in a European context, bearing in mind the study's limitations and scope.

## Environmental education

In order to enable a full understanding of the study's outcomes, some degree of simplification will be applied in this section. To enable an understanding of the depth of the differences found among countries regarding some of the questions posed, namely 'meaning of the word environment', 'sources of information on the environment' and 'levels of concern about the environment', a breakdown of responses per country, is provided. More detailed, comparative analyses of the finding on a nation by nation basis will be described in further publications. In this paper, percentages are given throughout as a measure of response; these refer to the total responses given to a particular question rather than to the total number of respondents of the questionnaire.

Table 6.2  Age range of the sampled school children

| Age | Percentage of pupils surveyed |
|---|---|
| 10-11 | 4 |
| 12 | 7 |
| 13 | 13 |
| 14 | 16 |
| 15 | 23 |
| 16 | 19 |
| 17 | 10 |
| 18 | 8 |
| Total number in sample | 21,090 |

The main findings of the survey are as follows:
The sample was composed of 58% boys and 42% girls. The age range of the pupils surveyed is described in Table 6.2. It can be seen that the majority of students sampled were in the 12-16 years range.

## Travelling to school

The extent to which one uses public transport is seen as relevant in assessing how one's commitment to environmental conservation is translated into action. In this context, pupils were asked to specify the distance they lived from school and the means of transport they use, so that a correlation between these two trends could be made. The majority of the children sampled live near their schools: 46% live up to ½ mile away, and 34% between ½ and 2 miles away. Only 20% of the sampled pupils stated that they live more than 2 miles away from their school. This would indicate that the need for transport is particularly acute for 20% of the surveyed children.

From the questionnaires returned, it was seen that 39% of the children walk to school, while 23% use the bus, 17% use a bicycle, 12% travel by car and 9% travel by train. If compared with the previous question about the distance travelled to school, it is seen that although in principle around 20% of the children would need transport to get to school, in fact approximately 44% of them make use of some type of transport other than a bicycle; it is also seen that although the use of public transport (bus and train) exceeds the use of private cars, figures for the latter are not particularly low taking into account the context.

## Words/statements which best describe the environment

When asked to choose the term which best describes the environment, many school children (37%) replied that it is 'the countryside', for 15% of school children it means 'towns and cities', for 21% it means 'animals and plants', for 8% it means 'rainforests', for 11% of the sample the environment means 'human beings' and 9% of respondents mentioned 'other' things (e.g. oceans, the planet). This seems to indicate that pupils place a higher emphasis on the 'natural environment', that connected with nature, rather than on the 'man-made' aspects as being part of the environment. It was also interesting to note that 'rainforests', eco-systems exotic to Europe, were referred to in pupils' responses.

A breakdown of responses per country can be found in Table 6.3. It can be seen that, in many of the countries surveyed, especially Greece,

Poland and Spain, a great number of the pupils see the expression 'environment' as related to the countryside, while Swedish, Portuguese and Norwegian pupils tend to see it more closely related to animals and plants. Among the pupils who stated that the 'environment' refers to towns and cities, British, Italian and French school children gave the highest percentage of entries. It was also noted that among the pupils who related the environment to tropical rainforests, the German, Swedish and Dutch provided the highest levels of replies. Among the issues mentioned by pupils under the 'others' heading, there are topics such as 'blue skies', roads, traffic, pollution, chemicals, farms and the sea.

**Table 6.3 Statements used to describe the 'environment' by pupils**
(percentage by country)

| Country | Country-side | Animals & plants | Mankind | Towns & cities | Tropical rain-forests | Other |
|---|---|---|---|---|---|---|
| Austria | 41 | 18 | 13 | 15 | 5 | 8 |
| Cyprus | 40 | 19 | 9 | 14 | 4 | 14 |
| Germany | 35 | 16 | 15 | 7 | 19 | 7 |
| Denmark | 30 | 27 | 12 | 15 | 10 | 6 |
| Spain | 43 | 21 | 12 | 10 | 4 | 10 |
| France | 39 | 18 | 8 | 22 | 8 | 5 |
| Gt Britain | 37 | 12 | 13 | 25 | 6 | 7 |
| Greece | 52 | 19 | 7 | 8 | 7 | 7 |
| Italy | 36 | 10 | 14 | 24 | 8 | 8 |
| Ireland | 32 | 24 | 15 | 13 | 5 | 11 |
| Norway | 32 | 28 | 13 | 19 | 2 | 7 |
| Netherlands | 41 | 23 | 6 | 8 | 14 | 8 |
| Portugal | 33 | 32 | 9 | 9 | 6 | 11 |
| Poland | 44 | 24 | 11 | 6 | 5 | 8 |
| Sweden | 16 | 35 | 13 | 12 | 16 | 8 |
| Finland | 38 | 18 | 8 | 12 | 11 | 13 |
| Average | 37 | 21 | 11 | 14 | 8 | 9 |

# Main sources of environmental information

For the majority of the school children surveyed, television and radio are the main sources of environmental information (38% of the responses indicated as such). This was closely followed by the school which featured in 34% of responses, 18% of responses featured friends and family, and newspapers and magazines featured in 10% of the returned questionnaires. This is an interesting trend as, if combined, the total response given to the media (press, television, radio) as sources of environmental information are higher (in excess of 40%) than the mentions made of the school.

**Table 6.4  Sources of environmental information**
(percentage by country)

| Country | Schools | Radio & television | Newspapers magazines | Friends |
|---|---|---|---|---|
| Austria | 28 | 35 | 20 | 17 |
| Cyprus | 25 | 47 | 8 | 20 |
| Germany | 45 | 30 | 5 | 20 |
| Denmark | 26 | 48 | 10 | 16 |
| Spain | 41 | 40 | 2 | 17 |
| France | 39 | 30 | 11 | 20 |
| Gt Britain | 38 | 35 | 5 | 22 |
| Greece | 36 | 24 | 23 | 17 |
| Italy | 25 | 36 | 14 | 25 |
| Ireland | 54 | 29 | 3 | 14 |
| Norway | 37 | 33 | 11 | 19 |
| Netherlands | 37 | 49 | 6 | 8 |
| Portugal | 32 | 46 | 4 | 18 |
| Poland | 33 | 49 | 6 | 12 |
| Sweden | 25 | 37 | 21 | 17 |
| Finland | 19 | 40 | 20 | 21 |
| Average | 34 | 38 | 10 | 18 |

The survey also identified that there are significant differences in responses among pupils in the various countries (see Table 6.4). For example, it was noted that Irish, German, Spanish, French and British pupils are among the ones who obtain most of their information on the environment from schools, while for the Dutch, Polish, Danish, Cypriot and Portuguese children sampled, radio and television are the main providers of environmental information. Among those who use newspapers and magazines in order to obtain information on environmental issues, pupils from Greece, Sweden, Finland and Austria provided the highest percentages of responses, while a considerable amount of the sample children in Italy, Britain, Finland and Cyprus stated that they obtain some information on the environment from members of their family and friends. These trends have many implications which should be the subject of further studies.

## Level of concern about the environment

From the data collected, 62% of the surveyed children indicated that they are 'a lot concerned' about the environment; 31% said that they are 'a little concerned' and 7% registered that they 'have no concern at all'. Although it is not possible to identify precisely why some pupils did not express some degree of concern about the environment, it is encouraging to note that over half are very concerned about environmental issues. In terms of country distribution of these finds (Table 6.5) it is noticeable that Spanish, Cypriot, German and Swedish pupils show most concern for the environment, while a 'little concern' was shown by the majority of Norwegians and a considerable proportion of Portuguese, Italian, Polish and Danish Pupils. Among those who stated that they have no concerns regarding the environment, Finnish children provided the highest levels of responses, followed by Polish and Italian pupils.

**Table 6.5  Level of concern about the environment**
(percentage by country)

| Country | Very concerned | A little concerned | Not concerned |
|---------|----------------|--------------------|---------------|
| Austria | 67 | 30 | 3 |
| Cyprus | 85 | 11 | 4 |
| Germany | 71 | 27 | 2 |
| Denmark | 58 | 33 | 9 |
| Spain | 88 | 8 | 4 |
| France | 69 | 29 | 2 |
| Gt Britain | 59 | 33 | 8 |
| Greece | 67 | 27 | 6 |
| Italy | 41 | 47 | 12 |
| Ireland | 62 | 29 | 9 |
| Norway | 39 | 54 | 7 |
| Netherlands | 67 | 27 | 6 |
| Portugal | 46 | 47 | 7 |
| Poland | 48 | 35 | 17 |
| Sweden | 71 | 26 | 3 |
| Finland | 50 | 30 | 20 |
| Average | 62 | 31 | 7 |

## Awareness of environmental disasters and major environmental issues

Pupils were asked to tick, from a list of environmental disasters, those of which they were aware. On the basis of the replies, the following ranking can be made:

- Exxon Valdiz oil spillage (Alaska) featured in 62% of the responses;
- Chernobyl nuclear plant accident (Ukraine) was indicated in 25% of the entries;
- Bhopal chemical plant incident (India) was mentioned by 7% of the sample.

An interesting feature about this question is that around 6% of the sampled children referred to local or regional environmental disasters (e.g. Tomsk in Russia, mentioned by many Austrian and Swedish children). The fact that the Exxon Valdiz incident and the Chernobyl nuclear disaster are on the top of the list may be because of the wide media coverage given to them and the various articles, television programmes and school materials available on both events.

They were then asked to name three major environmental problems in the world of which they were aware. The most common responses were:

- pollution (51%)
- acid rain (27%)
- greenhouse effect/gases (8%)
- rainforest destruction (5%)

Approximately 9% of the respondent school children provided information on other problems such as 'nuclear waste disposal', 'depletion of the ozone layer' and others. It is perhaps not surprising to see pollution as the main environmental problem, as this term encompasses air, water and soil contamination. It is once again interesting to see rainforest depletion on the list of environmental issues of global concern.

Next, pupils were asked to identify environmental problems of national importance; acid rain was the most common issue mentioned, accounting for 38% of the entries, followed closely with 34% for pollution. The problem of local waste was also fairly well represented, by mention of garbage/litter which featured in 15% of returned questionnaires. Thirteen percent of the sampled school children mentioned various other issues and matters of national/local relevance.

These findings seem to indicate a concrete level of awareness of local environmental issues and in fact show a link between the existence of environmental problems seen as 'global', such as pollution and the extent to which they affect people at the national or local level.

## Involvement in environmental issues

Pupils were then asked to give an approximate frequency (often, sometimes, rarely or never) for which they undertake activities related to the environment. These were: a) discussing environmental issues at school; b) discussing environmental issues at home; c) performing tasks such as recycling; d) performing voluntary work in the environment such as litter picking, cleaning of gardens or pond cleaning and e) whether they undertake fieldwork. Taking into account the various differences between countries, it was seen that the sampled children overall:

OFTEN discuss the 'environment' at school (indicated in over 50% of the returned questionnaires);

OFTEN discuss the 'environment' at home (featured in over 50% of the sample);

SOMETIMES do recycling (indicated by 25% of the sampled school children);

SOMETIMES do voluntary work in the environment (stated by 25% to 50% of the sample);

RARELY or NEVER do school fieldwork (indicated by up to 25% of the pupils).

The fact that pupils frequently discuss environmental issues at school is seen as an encouraging trend; once again differences among countries are inevitable, but the underlying feature is that environmental matters are definitely part of the school routine. It is, on the other hand, interesting to see the extent to which environmental matters are discussed at home, as over half of the sample said they did. The entries received from the Southern European and Mediterranean pupils have significantly contributed to this situation, as in those regions of Europe home debate on environmental matters - along with other issues - are widely seen and are an interesting cultural aspect.

Other questions were posed in the context of the survey, which refer to issues such as energy use and the impact of industrial activities on their health. Although these go beyond the scope of this paper, it is probably worth mentioning that a considerable degree of differentiation was found within countries.

## Conclusion

Although the limitations in both the size of the sample and the methodology used in the Eurosurvey suggest that care should be exercised when interpreting its results and that no particular country should be seen as superior or inferior to the others, a number of issues were clearly identified during its execution regarding the ways European school children, as a whole, see the environment. These are:

a)  the 'countryside' and 'animals and plants' are seen by the majority of pupils as the main expressions related to the theme of 'environment', despite the fact that 'rainforests', 'human beings' and a range of other topics were also seen as associated with it. The plurality of the meanings of terms such as the 'environment' to children, the choice of which certainly depends on one's background and exposure to information (Caduto, 1985), illustrates the diversity of ways in which such an expression is understood by the sample. In the context of pupils' perceptions of the environment, a matter which has received a considerable emphasis since the early days of environmental education (e.g. Trent, 1976), it is interesting to note that the countryside and animals and plants received a considerable amount of emphasis by the sampled pupils, while human beings - in comparative terms - were not perceived as being immediately related to the environment by many of them.

b)  the use of public transport among pupils was not seen as having environmental importance. In addition, despite the fact that many pupils live within a short distance of school, they use some sort of transport to get there. The fact that schools are often within walking distance does not seem to bear much influence on such a trend; here again care in interpreting the data should be exercised. Although on the one hand there seems to be the impression that current trends are satisfactory, simple acts such as being driven to schools - especially older children - have an impact on road use, consumption of fuel, air pollution etc. There is thus a great deal of room for improvements in this area.

c) the media was seen in most cases to be the main source of environmental information for pupils, the school coming in second place. This illustrates the need for a careful consideration of the impact of the media (i.e. television, radio, newspapers, magazines) as providers of information on the environment. Even though the fact that the mass media act as major sources of information on the environment is internationally seen as a welcome trend (Roseberg, 1982; Gunawerdene, 1994), it should be noted that the type of information being provided and the ways it is provided need to be carefully assessed, as well as its suitability to certain groups.

d) a significant amount of the sampled pupils had a great concern for the environment and only a minority was slightly or not concerned at all. This finding clearly shows the emphasis attached to environmental matters by young people, which may be interpreted as a result of the increased attention given to environmental issues as a whole and to environmental problems in particular. The fact that European pupils are so concerned with the environment may be seen as a positive development, especially if this concern is translated into an active contribution towards environmental conservation.

e) pupils have shown a wide awareness about some of the most recent environmental disasters and have referred to other disasters which have occurred near to them, such as the oil spills in the Galician region of Spain in late 1992. This trend may indicate that the mass media have become efficient tools for information dissemination. An interesting finding is the fact that a broad awareness of international environmental disasters was complemented by mention of local disasters.

f) according to the sample, pollution and acid rain were the main issues on a global scale, followed by greenhouse effect/gases and rainforest destruction. With regard to issues of national concern, pollution and acid rain were the items most commonly mentioned. The distribution of these problems across many European countries, the subsequent level of media coverage they get, as well as the emphasis given to them in school activities, help to understand this situation. Had the research been performed elsewhere, as in other recent studies (e.g. Thioune, 1993; Briguglio, 1994; Howell, 1995), these issues would probably give place to other matters such as desertification, uncontrolled land use or the impacts of tourism.

g) there is a noticeably high level of awareness of a country's energy sources. This is an encouraging outcome of the study in the sense that energy use is an important environmental matter which, it seems, is being reasonably well dealt with at school level in most of the surveyed countries. Pupils' awareness of energy sources and of sustainable consumption patterns, which reflect integrated thinking (Miller, 1982) is seen as an important step towards an environmentally aware society.

h) pupils in many countries do not appear to play an especially active role in initiatives such as recycling and fieldwork, despite some exceptions. In addition, the level of discussion of environmental issues both at school and at home is not as high as could have been expected, although the evidence gathered gives reason for optimism. Even though the situation and the challenges in the field of environmental education vary widely between the various educational sectors (Peters, 1992), the fact that initiatives such as recycling are not widely practised by pupils in some countries, while often reflecting a lack of policies in this field, may also indicate that provisions for their implementation are needed. In addition, the current level of use of fieldwork gives the impression that such a technique, perceived as an effective tool for environmental education (Leal Filho, 1994d) does not appear to be efficiently used in European schools as a whole. There is a clear case for improvements on this front.

An aspect of the Eurosurvey which is beyond any doubt is the fact that it has identified some areas where there are similarities in the ways European school children see the environment, as well as the existence of many diverse differences in their perceptions.

## Recommendations

On the basis of the study's findings, the following recommendations are made:

- pupils should be encouraged, whenever possible, to walk to school or at least make use of public transport to get there, rather than use private cars, as is the case at present. If their active participation in the environmental conservation process is to be encouraged, it ought to start with such simple acts; although the present scenario is encouraging, there is scope for improvement.

- as the media provides pupils with vital data on environmental issues, it is important that the environmental education potential of the information provided by television, radio and newspapers is fully utilised.

- schools should review their approaches with a view to identifying why they do not provide as much information on the environment as they should and, more importantly, what they can do to improve their performance. The Eurosurvey also identified the fact that the present diversity of emphasis given to environmental education, although useful, ought to be balanced by pan-European information initiatives on the environment.

- pupils should be encouraged to talk more about environmental issues both at school and at home and, more importantly, be motivated to take an active part in schemes such as recycling and fieldwork. If environmental awareness is to be systematically developed among school children, it is essential that pupils are encouraged to participate.

It is acknowledged that the urgency with which the above recommendations need to be implemented varies from country to country. It is also clear that most of the recommendations above can only be reached by careful research, hence the need for in-depth studies at the national level. It is therefore urged that the relevant authorities in the countries concerned facilitate the execution of research projects to analyse systematically the above trends, the variables involved and viable ways of addressing existing problems.

The Dublin Declaration on the Environment, approved by the Council of Ministers in Dublin, Ireland, in 1990, emphasised the special duty of the European Union towards helping to solve environmental problems and towards promoting sustainable developments (CEC, 1990). The Declaration also emphasised the need to improve public information on environmental matters and the need to respond to the aspirations of young people who need to be made aware of environmental issues. European schools are ideally placed to address information needs, but in order to fulfil their role they need to fully appreciate the value of environmental education and the need for educating pupils **about, through** and **for** the environment.

# Acknowledgements

Over the two and half years in which the study was undertaken, a number of people have provided a valuable contribution towards its execution, which was greatly appreciated. Special thanks are due to Caroline Sharpe, who helped to put the survey on the way and to Veronique Gallo-Khan who assisted with data collection and treatment. Thanks are also due to Zena Murphy and to the many contributors, throughout Europe, who have directly or indirectly assisted with the execution of the Eurosurvey.

# Bibliography

Briguglio, L. 1994) *Tourism and Environment in the Maltese Islands*. Malta: Foundation for International Studies.

Caduto, M.J. (1985) *A Guide on Environmental Values Education*. Paris: UNESCO.

Commission of the European Communities (1990) *The Dublin Declaration on the Environment*. Brussels: CEC.

Csobod, E. (1995) Environmental Education and Training in Hungary. In Leal Filho, W., MacDermott, F.D.J., Murphy, Z. (eds.) *Practices in Environmental Education in Europe*. Bradford: ERTCEE.

Episcopopoulou, C. (1991) Environmental education as an educational experiment in Greek schools. Paper presented at the International Conference on Environmental Education. Manchester: DES.

Fensham P.J. (1978) Stockholm to Tbilisi - the Evolution of Environmental Education. *Prospects* **8** (I) pp. 446-455.

Gayford, C. (1984) Biological fieldwork in a sample of secondary schools in England and Wales. *Review of Environmental Education Development* **14** pp. 11-13.

Gunawerdene, N. (1994) Media and Environment in Sri Lanka. In Leal Filho, W.D.S. (ed.) *Environmental Education in Small Island Developing States*. Vancouver: The Commonwealth of Learning.

Howell, C. (1995) *An environmental education and communication strategy to the Caribbean*. Barbados: CCA.

Jakucs, P. and Lakatus, G. (1990) The ecological aspects of environmental education in Hungary. *Higher Education in Europe* **15** (4) pp. 24-28.

Jerzak, I. and Jerzak, L. (1995) Environmental Education in Polish Schools. In Leal Filho, W. MacDermott, F.D.J., Murphy, Z. (eds.) *Practices in Environmental Education in Europe*. Bradford: ERTCEE.

Leal Filho, W.D.S. (1994a) Cooperazione e lavoro di rete. *Environnement, Europe, Education* **22** pp. 15-16.

Leal Filho, W.D.S. (1994b) An overview of the UNCED process, Agenda 21 and Chapter 36. *Environmental Awareness* **17** pp. 141-146.

Leal Filho, W.D.S. (1994c) European Environmental Futures: a review of past, current and future developments in the field of environmental education in Europe. *Proceedings of the Conference on Environmental Education in Europe (CEEE)*. Jurmala, Latvia 11-15 October.

Leal Filho, W.D.S. (1994d) Field studies in develop and developing countries. In Hale, M. (ed.) *Ecology and Education*. Cambridge: Cambridge University Press.

Leal Filho, W.D.S., MacDermott, F.J., Murphy, Z (eds.) (1995) *Practices of Environmental Education in European Countries*. Bradford: ERTCEE.

Lob. R. (1994) Environmental Education in Germany. In Leal Filho, W. and Hale, M. (eds.) *Trends in Environmental Education Worldwide*. London: London Guildhall University Press.

Miller, A. (1982) Integrative Thinking as a Goal to Environmental Education. *Journal of Environmental Education* **12** (4) pp. 3-8.

Moran, C., Fernandez, M. and Cartea, P.M. (1995) Promoting Environmental Education in Spain: a Historical Perspective and Present Trends. In Leal Filho, W., MacDermott, F.D.J., Murphy, Z. (eds.) *Practices in Environmental Education in Europe*. Bradford: ERTCEE.

Murphy, Z. (1994) *Networks and Environmental Education in the Commonwealth*. Unpublished MPhil Thesis. Bradford: University of Bradford.

Peters, J.A. (1992) The Netherlands: environmental education as an essential tool to help bring about sustainable development. *Proceedings of the Conference on Environmental Education in Europe, 8-14 November 1992*. Hogeschool Rotterdam and Omstreken and Nooredelijke Hogeschool Leeuwarden.

Rosenberg, V. (1982) Information Policies of Developing Countries: the Case of Brazil. *Journal of the American Society for Information Science* **33** (4) pp. 203-207.

Schleicher, K. (ed.) (1992a) *Lernorte in der Umwelterziehung*. Hamburg: Kramer.

Smyth, J. (1995) A National Environmental Education Strategy for Scotland. In Leal Filho, W., MacDermott, F.D.J., Murphy, Z. (eds.) *Practices in Environmental Education in Europe*. Bradford: ERTCEE.

Thioune, O. (1993) The ENDA Micro Project Approach. In Schneider, H. (ed.) *Environmental education: an alternative approach to sustainable development*. Paris: OECD.

Trent. J.H. (1976) Changes and Trends in Environmental Education in 1972-1975. *Journal of Environmental Education* **7** (31) pp. 51-60.

# 7 Support systems in environmental education

*Chris Gayford*

## Abstract

Support systems for environmental education in the UK are varied and provided by a range of organisations to both the formal and non-formal sectors. Central and local government, industry and non-government organisations all play an important part. Cooperative initiatives between these different agencies have frequently resulted in excellent examples of support.

Networking, by which expertise and information is made more widely available, is an essential feature of many support systems and the increasing sophistication of information technology is rapidly increasing their scope and value. The provision of support via resources, handbooks and training is a further way in which change in environmental education practice is being brought about.

The role of non-government organisations has become central to the whole support process in recent years. Their flexibility and ability to relate to grassroots local community activities has been instrumental, coupled with a growing professionalism.

## Introduction

The nature of support for environmental education should be viewed in relation to three main purposes. All of them have implications for both the formal and non-formal sectors and all are inter-related. These purposes are: campaigning, provision of information and resources and research. The first two are closely associated with teaching and learning, and the other with the development of new educational approaches and improvements to provision. In considering the support that is being provided, its nature and where it is coming from, this article will review the major players and the principles upon which they operate, as well as the type of support that they are able to offer. An element in making the support more effective and more generally available is the process of networking. The importance of, and need for, this is repeatedly emphasised (see for example the Council for Environmental Education, (CEE), 1992 and 1995). Throughout this article reference will be made to different types of networks and the ways in which they enhance the support provided.

Environmental education has been described as a learning process that takes place between three main groups. Smyth (1995) identifies these groups as those who:

■ promote and support environmental education. They include administrators, curriculum developers, environmentalists and local activists.

■ deliver environmental education in formal or non-formal contexts. These include school and college teachers, youth and community workers, a variety of people working for voluntary organisations as well as some working in the media.

■ receive environmental education. These include school and college students as well as the public in the varied contexts in which they are educated. This third group includes the whole population in whatever way they may be sub-divided.

There are a number of routes through which people are influenced over environmental matters; these include schools, higher and further education, community and other informal educational influences, professional training, the mass media and the cultural context in which we live, including religion and the arts (the World Wide Fund for Nature (WWF), 1993).

To fit into this complex matrix, support systems for environmental education must adapt to a rapidly changing situation. To give some understanding of how this operates it will be necessary to be selective rather than attempting to be comprehensive. Instead of giving a lengthy catalogue of support systems, agencies and organisations, the different types that exist will be discussed together with selected examples to illustrate the range. Emphasis will be on support within the UK, but some of the international organisations which are part of the scene will be included to give a wider perspective and to show how networking between countries may operate. Also the agreements reached by some of these international organisations often affect our own ways of working in Britain. There is no attempt to include the great variety of support systems that exist elsewhere in the world or to include the activities of certain organisations in this country, for example the British Council, whose main purpose is to relate to situations in other countries. The various support systems that will be discussed here target the three groups mentioned previously and it is the interaction that occurs between the support systems and the users that will form the main focus for the discussion.

It is necessary also to consider who it is that is providing support. These may be categorised under a number of headings, such as:

- Central and local government.

- Non-government organisations (NGOs), otherwise referred to as voluntary organisations. These cover a broad spectrum and include WWF, Friends of the Earth, the CEE and the National Association for Environmental Education (NAEE).

- International agencies such as the Organisation for Economic Cooperation and Development (OECD), UNESCO and the United Nations Environment Programme (UNEP).

- Academic institutions and research bodies.

- The media.

- Commercial and industrial organisations.

Examples from most of these categories will be considered in this paper but not all; the contributions of academic institutions and research bodies, as well as the media, are omitted.

Even taking into account all of the ideas about support for environmental education that have been introduced so far, there are still problems with how the term support may be interpreted. There is a sense in which all agencies and organisations involved with environmental education, or even those concerned with the protection of the environment, tend also to provide some kind of support for the promotion of the educational processes that underpin their concerns. It is the intention in this paper to identify some of the different ways that support agencies function, some of the issues that arise and to point to some possible directions for growth.

## Support from central and local government

There exists at present a mismatch between what is stated and promoted at a high level by different government departments with a responsibility for the environment and environmental education (Gayford and Dillon, 1995). On one hand the Department of the Environment (DoE) appears to be supportive of environmental education, both in the recommendations that are being made and in the initiatives that are being set up. In contrast the Department for Education and Employment (DFEE) has not promoted environmental education in an explicit way, apparently finding the ideas and methodologies in conflict with current thinking about the school curriculum and its assessment. There has also been little direct involvement from the DFEE with environmental education in non-formal contexts. Consequently most of the support from central government has come from the DoE, rather than the DFEE. In influential reports (DoE, 1992 and 1994) the case for support for environmental education is clearly made.

The 'Environmental Action Fund' was set up in 1990 in direct response to *This Common Inheritance*, the Government White Paper on the environment (DoE, 1990), in which the importance of education in helping to maintain and improve the national environment was emphasised. The fund was conceived with the purpose of providing finances for environmental NGOs to develop initiatives which would support environmental education. Among the projects funded from this source was the *Environmental Education Information Needs Project* which was managed by the CEE (Matthews and Stephens, 1992) with the purpose of enquiring into the information requirements and other needs of teachers in the formal education system and youth service. Also, following the United Nations Rio Summit in 1992, the DoE set up the 'Local Projects Fund' in 1993, which was particularly aimed at action by local groups. The emphasis was on the encouragement of local activities which would support the concept of sustainability, and although local, may well have global consequences.

The *British Government Panel on Sustainable Development* in their first report (1995) makes it clear that they endorse the views expressed in the Government White Paper, *Sustainable Development: The UK Strategy* (DoE, 1994) that

> education and training are crucial to the achievement of sustainable development ..... The influence of education and training thus applies across the boundaries of the voluntary, public and private sectors

The Panel also considers that it is important for the Government to develop a comprehensive strategy for environmental education and training to cover both formal and informal education. Environmental education is seen as transcending the boundaries of formal education and the variety of different interest groups have essential roles to play. In order to achieve this strategy the wide range of related activities of official and voluntary bodies, industry and commerce and local communities should be encouraged and networked to optimise expertise. The need for a 'round table' to bring together the main sectors, both voluntary and statutory, to encourage cooperation and build consensus will be one way of helping to bring about the desired changes. The recommendations of the Panel go even further in suggesting that the Government should establish a comprehensive database, with local applications, to draw attention to the many resources available, including written material, lectures and facilities on offer from official and voluntary bodies and others. Attention was also drawn to the significance of the *Toyne Committee Report* (DFE, 1992a) which relates to institutions of further and higher education, recommending that they should develop strategies for environmental education and for 'greening' their own management. Finally the Panel recommended that universities and higher education institutions in Britain should subscribe to the *Talloires Declaration* (Tufts University, 1990). This is an international initiative for institutions of this type and it covers interdisciplinary work on education, research, policy formation and information exchange. It encourages universities to contribute to a more sustainable future by becoming responsible for the management of their own environmental affairs, as well as by cooperating with international institutions, governments, industry and the general public. These and the other initiatives discussed all presuppose the establishment or improvement of existing networks of support agencies, which as yet, does not seem to have been sufficiently forthcoming.

Coming out of *Agenda 21* (United Nations, 1992) was the strong recommendation that each nation which was a signatory should set up *Local Agenda 21* initiatives (Local Government Management Board, 1993). These should focus on local communities to facilitate and support action for environmental improvement and protection. Work should include cooperation with other local organisations, industry and commerce, and should draw together the activities of formal and informal education agencies. These initiatives are seen as a way of emphasising the concept of 'acting locally and thinking globally'. The role of the NGOs was seen as vital in shaping and implementing participatory democracy, an essential network in the establishment of a sense of common purpose, as well as a major source of support in the form of expertise and knowledge.

The contribution of the Department of Education and Employment has tended to be related to the National Curriculum. The revised statutory curriculum following the *Dearing Report* (Schools Curriculum and Assessment Authority, 1994) was more encouraging to the spirit of education *for* the environment (see National Curriculum Council, 1990a) than had been previously feared (Gayford, 1995). However, the notion of the cross-curricular themes as outlined in *Curriculum Guidance 3: The Whole Curriculum* (National Curriculum Council, 1990b) has all but disappeared in an attempt to make the curriculum more manageable for schools. There is also little support through the Framework and Handbook of Inspection (Office of Standards in Education, 1993) where there is no significant acknowledgement of environmental education. Nor is there much support through the Grants for Education, Support and Training (GEST) In-service training programmes (DFE, 1992b), managed mainly by local education authorities, which constitute a major contribution to the professional development of teachers.

The contribution of central government has tended to operate at the overall policy level with some emphasis on encouraging other support agencies to cooperate and network their activities. Sometimes this encouragement is in more tangible forms whereby grants are given to NGOs to part-finance their work. Grants are given, for instance, to the Council for Environmental Education (CEE) to coordinate the activities of many of the organisations which relate to environmental education. The DFEE, for instance, provides funds for youth work to the same organisation and also to *Learning Through Landscapes* particularly to promote the work of the organisation on the educational use of school grounds (see for example WWF/Learning Through Landscapes, 1994). Local government often facilitates local networks with other organisations operating in the area. This may be, for instance, through the *Local Agenda 21* initiatives and centres that have appeared in recent years.

Many local governments provide some form of advisory service to schools on environmental education, usually financed through the education authority in a variety of ways. The advisers are essentially experts in the field and frequently operate a local network. However, the situation here is rapidly changing since more environmental education advisers than in previous years combine this function with other responsibilities, such as geography or humanities education. Other education authorities employ environmental education advisers on a consultancy basis in which they undertake work along with other kinds of paid employment (Ellis, 1992). Many teachers, in particular localities, have organised their own informal networks to support each other (Gayford and Dorion, 1992).

# The role of non-government organisations (NGOs)

Traditional definitions of NGOs describe them as non-party-political, non-profit making, usually grassroots organisations. According to statistics provided by the National Council for Voluntary Organisations (1993) about one in two adults in the UK were involved in some form of volunteering and these organisations employed between 100,000 and 500,000 people on a part-time or full-time basis.

The role of the NGOs in the support of environmental education, in both the formal and non-formal sectors, has been central for many years (Neal, 1992). They support practice through the provision of materials, research and curriculum development and also by providing political support through lobbying at all levels. The NGOs are seen as having an innovative role, often being the first and only organisations to identify and address problems and deficiencies in provision (Martin, 1989; Greig *et al*, 1989). The growing professionalism of many of the NGOs is now widely acknowledged and welcomed. It is of interest to note that in recent studies of the extent to which different sources of information about the environment are trusted by the public, the NGOs had a high standing relative to other informed sources, especially compared with information disseminated by industry or government (Frewer and Shepherd, 1994). NGOs by their nature are often able to offer an independent voice from government. Recent developments have resulted in government consulting NGOs more frequently over environmental and environmental education matters.

The NGOs that provide support for environmental education include some of the large campaigning charities such as the World Wide Fund for Nature which has branches world-wide. Some other large charities, such as Oxfam and Save the Children, which have traditionally had a rather different remit, have begun to take an interest in environmental issues, particularly since recently explicit links have been established between environment and development (see the World Commission on Environment and Development, 1987; United Nations, 1992). Other NGOs such as the Friends of the Earth and Greenpeace, with a concern for the environment, find that it has been necessary to take an interest in environmental education in order to enhance their campaigning effectiveness. Still other environmental NGOs, for example the Royal Society for the Protection of Birds (RSPB) or the Tidy Britain Group, which both began as what might be described as 'single issue' organisations, have found the need to extend their activities to include wider environmental issues and to develop a strong educational supporting role. Several of these organisations undertake baseline research to support their own activities and to identify the nature of support that is required by practitioners (see for example The RSPB, 1991 and Dorion, 1993 on behalf of the WWF). NGOs also support environmental education by producing information bulletins, such as the Council for Environmental Education (CEE) *Newssheet* or the International Centre for Conservation Education (ICCE) *Greenletter*. The amount of curriculum development (e.g. Tidy Britain Group, 1985; WWF, 1988), or training materials (e.g. the CEE *Earthworks* training project for face to face youth workers, 1990 and WWF *Reaching out*, a training project for teachers in schools, 1995) produced by the NGOs are further examples of a significant part of their support for environmental education in many different contexts.

However, despite their significant contribution in supporting environmental education, the NGOs are subject to the limitations experienced by similar organisations operating in parallel fields. Lemaresquier (1987) identifies a series of elements which appear to be common to most NGOs:

a) The income of the organisation insufficiently covers the running costs; consequently the organisation spends much of the time on activities that are not directly concerned with their central purpose. There is a degree of self-exploitation which is used to compensate for this and tends to carry the organisation. The fact that they seem to survive and appear autonomous, providing an alternative to statutory bodies at a low level of operation means that there is little opportunity for change within or incentive for change outside.

b) Most of the funders prefer to finance projects for a maximum of three years. This usually results in fragmented programmes of work making strategic planning difficult. Continually the NGO is involved in making applications to funders. It is also difficult for the organisation to respond to the needs of users of their service.

c) Most funders prefer to finance work that is innovative. This pressure results in difficulties in consolidating existing work.

d) Most funders do not wish to finance the service provided by the NGO but prefer to finance a product such as a project, course, publication or a conference. Consequently strategic processes such as publicity, lobbying and research are neglected.

Among the most international of all environmental NGOs is the International Union for the Conservation of Nature (IUCN), now often referred to as the World Conservation Union. Again, this is an organisation whose central remit is directly concerned with the environment but it has been repeatedly shown that to achieve their aim there must be a significant public education programme. The IUCN headquarters for education is in Gland, Switzerland, and is small in comparison with its purpose. There are limited funds and some of these are used to support and facilitate projects. Once more all of this is symptomatic of the problems faced by NGOs, even prestigious international organisations. A good deal of the activity of the IUCN is involved with experts, putting them in touch with projects or in networking in other ways. IUCN also networks and cooperates with some of the other large NGOs such as the WWF or with some of the international agencies such as UNESCO and UNEP (see for example IUCN/UNEP/WWF, 1980 and 1991 also IUCN-UNESCO, 1994).

One of the greatest challenges currently facing the environmental education NGOs is how they will achieve greater impact while maintaining their traditional strengths of flexibility, innovation and attachment to their values and principles (Edwards and Hulme, 1992). The NGOs have a somewhat ambiguous role as intermediaries between established or official authority as represented by government agencies, and social movements, groups and individuals. Levels of state funding have implications for the position of the NGOs in contesting government activities, representing alternative views and supporting such activities as environmental education (Farrington and Bebbington, 1993). Also since NGOs are dependent on external funding they are often forced into a competitive situation with each other making cooperation more difficult. However, attempts have been made recently to make NGOs collaborate more effectively in their support of environmental education through such international initiatives as NGONET (The Environmental Education Network Newsletter, 1993), which is an environment and development information service for NGOs using CD-ROM. It was initially based on the United Nations Conference on Environment and Development (UNCED) archives and it is now being extended by the contributions of experts worldwide. There are other examples of networks using the internet, providing opportunities to link with even more extensive information networks.

# The international agencies

Included amongst these are organisations such as the Organisation for Economic Cooperation and Development (OECD), UNESCO and the United Nations Environment Programme (UNEP). Their roles in the past have been to bring together governments and government agencies and NGOs, calling on the expertise of a wide variety of individuals working in the field. UNESCO, directly arising from its commitment to education, has been instrumental in supporting environmental education for many years; a significant landmark was the intergovernmental conference in Tbilisi in 1977 (UNESCO-UNEP, 1978). Here many of the basic principles of environmental education for the general public and environmental professionals were established. Subsequent work of UNESCO has been to produce handbooks (e.g. Sharma and Tan, 1990), to initiate studies in particular aspects related to environmental education (such as UNESCO-UNEP, 1988) or to gather together experts to debate and disseminate information (e.g. UNESCO, 1991). UNESCO has also been given responsibilities for reporting on some of the follow-up activities to *Agenda 21*. One of these tasks is promoting education, public awareness and training. To achieve this it offers pilot projects, technical assistance and the development of methodology, bringing together educators and media specialists, as well as cooperating with the private sector.

Another international organisation that exemplifies the contribution of this type of body to the support of environmental education is the Organisation for Economic Cooperation and Development (OECD). Through its Centre for Educational Research and Innovation (CERI) in Paris *The Environment and School Initiatives* (ENSI) was set up (see OECD, 1991). Coordinators from 19 participating countries, mainly in Europe but also extending to Australia, identified networks of schools involved in environmental initiatives. Pedagogical support experts were appointed to work closely with the schools and to monitor and evaluate the projects. Training was considered to be an essential part of the project with action research as an important element which enabled participants to be involved in evaluating their own practice. An important principle of the project was the idea of international networking. This was conceived as not simply linking people electronically, but finding efficient ways of exchanging information, experiences and outcomes. In doing this it was intended to help others to set up projects and to work on issues of common interest, even sharing resources. Emphasis is on active learning rather than the straightforward transmission of knowledge (Posch, 1991).

# Industry and commerce

The Confederation of British Industries (CBI) has had a longstanding interest in environmental education. In 1989 they published an action plan on the environment for the 1990s and set up an Environment Management Unit to implement it. In order to achieve their aims, the plan was circulated to many of their members. This initiative sprang from a desire for companies to compete for 'greenness' and their own confusion over the mass of information that was available at that time. Through their initiative the CBI set out to address many of the major environmental issues of the day that were likely to have a direct effect on industry; these included waste law amendments, integrated pollution control and environmental labelling. While their intention was essentially to educate those in industry there was a significant spill-over into public education about products, production and waste disposal.

Marsden (1991) who was then Head of Educational Affairs for BP, writing at a similar time about the support that industry can give to environmental education, considered that industry could help enrich the curriculum, offering up to date expertise and knowledge in specific areas, as well as in some cases providing resources. Many of the large industrial corporations such as ESSO, Unilever and BP have had a longstanding interest in education. However, it would over-simplify the situation if they were thought to be only concerned with good public relations. There have been many highly supportive initiatives that have been developed through partnerships between industry and other organisations. Examples include the cooperative partnership between the NGOs, the Groundwork Trust and ESSO in the production of *Greenlink* (1990). This is an initiative that brings together companies and schools in partnerships which provide the pupils with environmental education experience. PowerGen and National Power in conjunction with the CEE have assisted in the development of INSET materials which support school teachers in providing environmental education in the context of their own subject specialism of the National Curriculum (see for example CEE 1992 and 1994). There are many more examples of good practice supported by industrial expertise and finance.

# A study of teachers' needs for support in environmental education

A study was carried out by the author in early 1995 among 85 school teachers which enquired into the support that they most needed. The teachers were all closely involved in environmental education and included those from both primary and secondary schools. The data was collected whilst they were attending in-service training courses. Information was collected on a number of issues as follows:

1   The support that teachers feel is most needed. Here teachers were given an open-ended question and asked simply to list the ways that they would wish to be given additional support. They were also asked to indicate two or three of these as their priorities.

2   Use of the services of Local Government, NGOs and Industry. Here the teachers were asked
   i)   to indicate which of these organisations they used to support their work
   ii)  the importance they placed on these contributions (this was based on a three point scale, with 3 for very important, 2 for quite important and 1 for low level of importance).

3   Their access to and use of experts on environmental issues. Here the teachers were asked
   i)   to give some indication of whether they had access to experts and
   ii)  how much they used such experts.
   The latter was answered on a three point scale (3 = frequently, i.e. more than three times a year, 2 = sometimes, i.e. less than 3 times a year, 1 = never).

4   Their estimation of the availability to them of
   i)   suitable resources
   ii)  appropriate time
   iii) support from the senior management team of the school.
   In each case they were asked to estimate on a three point scale, in which 3 was good, 2 was moderate and 1 was poor.

5   The style of coordination of environmental education in their school. The teachers were given this as an open-ended question.

The results are summarised in Tables 7.1 and 7.2. In terms of the support that the teachers felt they most needed (Table 7.1), there was a high level of agreement that they wanted information about pre-evaluated materials (with 88% seeing this as a priority). It was clear that it was not simply a matter of requiring more resources. What is needed is assistance in finding their way through the great variety of resources that are already available. There was general consensus that teachers frequently have not the time nor the expertise to evaluate materials and that they need help in this. Coordination was seen to be a significant factor both from the point of view of coordination within the school which would help to effectively target and disseminate information once it had arrived (with 49% identifying this as a priority), and also coordination of the distribution of information from the various organisations that were offering services. Since a good deal of education *in* the environment (see National Curriculum Council, 1990a) required local knowledge and contacts this was felt to be one aspect where additional support would be welcome (36% considered this to be a priority).

**Table 7.1  Types of support needed by teachers**

| Types of support needed | % listed | % high priority |
|---|---|---|
| Training for environmental education | 98 | 96 |
| Pre-evaluated lists of materials | 94 | 88 |
| Dissemination of examples of good practice | 85 | 44 |
| Coordination of environmental education in the school | 76 | 49 |
| Local information, materials and contacts | 68 | 36 |
| Coordination of the distribution of information from support agencies | 46 | 14 |
| Assistance with networking | 38 | 6 |
| Specifically targeted materials | 31 | 19 |
| Guidance on how to evaluate materials | 28 | 18 |
| Use of information technology in environmental education contexts | 25 | 11 |

Training was also identified as being an area where teachers overwhelmingly felt that they needed further support (with 96% stating that this is a priority). This was not simply a matter of telling them how to teach, but included providing examples and models of good practice, opportunities to use innovative methodologies, including the use of information technology in environmental education contexts (11% reporting this as a priority).

**Table 7.2   Responses of teachers to Questions 2-5**

|  |  | % using the service | level of importance (mean score) |
|---|---|---|---|
| Q2 | Use of services from: |  |  |
|  | i)   Local government | 84 | 2.2 |
|  | ii)  NGOs | 88 | 2.6 |
|  | iii) Industry | 75 | 1.1 |
| Q3 | % who had: |  |  |
|  | i)   Access to outside experts |  | 85.0 |
|  | ii)  Level of use of outside experts (mean score) |  | 1.3 |
| Q4 | Mean score for availability of: |  |  |
|  | i)   Suitable resources |  | 1.2 |
|  | ii)  Reasonable time allocation |  | 0.6 |
|  | iii) Support from senior management team of the school |  | 0.4 |
| Q5 | Style of coordination of environmental education in the school (% in each category): |  |  |
|  | i)   Senior management team |  | 7.0 |
|  | ii)  Head of a Department or a deputy |  | 65.0 |
|  | iii) A junior member of staff |  | 28.0 |

NB.  In each case mean score relates to a maximum score of 3.

The replies to the question about the use of support from outside agencies, such as local government, NGOs and industry (Question 2 and Table 7.2), showed that while teachers use outside organisations to a large extent, there was a considerable difference in the importance that they attached to the support that they were given. NGOs were clearly seen as highly significant, with WWF, RSPB and the National Association for Environmental Education (NAEE) being amongst the most frequently mentioned. The local authority was considered to be of almost equal importance. The contribution of industry, while not negligible, was seen to be of considerably less importance.

In Question 3, the majority of teachers felt that they have a reasonable degree of access to outside experts but, while they acknowledged their potential contribution, at present the teachers make little use of this facility. In response to Question 4, it was clear that nearly all of the teachers felt inadequately supported in terms of the resources that were available, the time that was allocated and the general support from the senior management team of the school. The style of coordination in the school seemed to be of three main types with the head or deputy in one of the departments, usually geography, having this role (65% of responses). In 28% of cases this role was taken on by an even more junior member of staff and in only 7% of the replies was this function performed by a member of the school senior management team.

Many of the teachers made additional comments which indicate that they felt that there was inadequate incentive and support for environmental education in schools from the Department for Education and Employment and OFSTED and that this made it difficult for the senior management of the school to give environmental education anything more than qualified support.

These results perhaps do not provide any surprising insights but they do seem to confirm many of the suppositions that exist among those involved in environmental education about the feelings and needs of teachers. They also indicate some possible areas for development by support agencies.

# In conclusion

Traditionally the formal system, particularly schools, has been viewed as the most appropriate target for environmental education; consequently support services and systems have turned most of their attention towards them, although we now see the need to support environmental education in a broader context than this. As a result there are many examples of materials and projects directed to the perceived needs of schools. The overall situation has therefore become one in which there is no lack of resources and materials, but a deficiency of evaluation or other mechanisms for making it easier for hard-pressed teachers or non-formal educators to use them (CEE, 1992). However, in England, Wales and Northern Ireland, since the implementation of the National Curriculum, the ability and willingness of schools to include environmental education as part of the general entitlement of all pupils has become less clear. This is particularly the case when considering the different interpretations and purposes given to environmental education by the various support agencies. Recently the essential political implications of much of education *for* the environment has been put forward as an important barrier to establishing environmental education in schools (Fien, 1993). This is also likely to be a significant factor affecting the level of support from government sources. It would be incorrect to suggest that the revised National Curriculum (Schools Curriculum and Assessment Authority, 1995) does not provide opportunities for environmental education but the level of encouragement and therefore official support is still small. Schools themselves frequently report a high level of motivation in this area but feel rather unsupported (Saunders *et al*, 1995). Overall the situation in schools is often characterised by partial diffusion and implementation of ideas and values. A few enthusiastic pioneers adopt new ideas and find difficulty in involving other colleagues (Gayford, 1986). The support structures, including resources and other teaching materials, professional development, advisory services and systematic research are all inadequate (Skilbeck, 1993). The need for this type of support for school teachers is articulated also as a result of studies by the CEE (1992) and Lakin (1995).

There has been no shortage of official statements from international conferences or government bodies supporting the need for environmental education but these have not been followed through with the provision of appropriate infrastructure for support and development. The lack of a unified voice from policy makers and those who operate the public purse has been apparent, including the problematic absence of consensus about what is to be achieved. Inadequate coordination within institutions and between organisations has also characterised the support that is being offered from many different sources.

The role of support systems should be to facilitate an enabling process rather than creating an organisation as an end in itself. Centralisation has significant disadvantages; the emphasis should therefore be on providing support for grassroots organisations. Environmental education is about action and participation, consequently the support process should concentrate on overcoming barriers to these activities by promoting communication, networking, information and opportunities for education and training (Elkins, 1992).

However, the picture with regard to the support systems for environmental education is not all negative; despite complexity and change the major players are becoming more professional and cooperating more frequently and effectively. Networking is increasing both in the amount and the sophistication with which it is being used. From the point of view of putting experts in contact with those in need, and making information more widely available to those who require help, it has an important part to play. As with any network, whether it is based on people or information technology, the system will only be as effective as those who provide the input, who take into account the needs and expertise of the audience, and who disseminate the information constructively.

# Bibliography

Confederation of British Industries (1989) *Action Plan for the 1990s*. London: CBI.

Council for Environmental Education (1990) *Earthworks*. Reading: CEE.

Council for Environmental Education (1992) *INSET 5-16: Environmental Education for Science*. Harlow: Longman.

Council for Environmental Education (1994) *INSET 5-16: Environmental Education for Geography*. Reading: CEE.

Council for Environmental Education (1995) *Good Practice: Criteria and Case Studies*. Reading: CEE.

Department for Education (1992a) *Environmental Responsibility: An Agenda for Further and Higher Education*. Committee on Environmental Education in Further and Higher Education (Chairman Peter Toyne) London: HMSO.

Department for Education (1992b) *Grants for Education Support and Training 1993-94*. London: DFE.

Department of the Environment (1990) *This Common Inheritance: Britain's Environmental Strategy*. CM 1200, London: HMSO.

Department for the Environment (1994) *Sustainable Development: The UK Strategy*, Cm 2426. London: HMSO.

Department for the Environment (1995) *British Government Panel on Sustainable Development: First Report*. London: DoE.

Edwards, M. and Hulme, D. (1992) *Making a Difference: NGOs and Development in a Changing World*. London: Earthscan.

Elkins, P. (1992) *'A New World Order', Grassroots Movement for Social Change*. London: Routledge.

Ellis, J.C. (1992) Giving and receiving - the contribution of environmental organisations to education in schools. *Annual Review of Environmental Education* 5 pp. 17-18.

Environmental Education Network (1993) NGONET - Environment and Development information for non-government organisations, *Environmental Education - NET News* 3 (2) p. 20.

ESSO/Groundwork Trust (1990) *Greenlink*. Birmingham: Groundwork Foundation.

Farrington, J. and Bebbington, A. (1993) *Reluctant Partners*. London: Routledge.

Fien, J. (1993) Ideology critique and environmental education. In J. Fien (ed.) *Education for the Environment - critical curriculum theorising and environmental education*. Australia: Deakin University.

Frewer, L.J. and Shepherd, R. (1994) Attributing information to different sources: effects on the perceived relevance of information and on attitude formation. In *Public Understanding of Science* 3 pp. 385--401, London: IOP Publishing Ltd and The Science Museum.

Gayford, C.G. (1986) Environmental Education and the Secondary School Curriculum. *Journal of Curriculum Studies* 18 (2) pp. 147-158.

Gayford, C.G. (1995) Environmental Education in the Revised National Curriculum. *Environmental Education* 49 pp. 5-6.

Gayford, C.G. and Dillon, P.J. (1995) Policy and the Practice of Environmental Education in England: a dilemma for teachers. *Environmental Education Research* 1 (2) p. 173-185.

Gayford, C.G. and Dorion, C. (1992) Local Support System for Teachers and the Implementation of Environmental Education in the Primary School Curriculum. *Cambridge Journal of Education* 22 (2) pp. 193-199.

Greig, S., Pike, G. and Selby, D. (1989) *Greenprints*. London: Kogan Page.

International Union for the Conservation of Nature (1994) *National Strategies for Environmental and Development Education in Europe: Report of an IUCN-Unesco Meeting*. Gland: International Union for the Conservation of Nature.

IUCN, UNEP and WWF (1980) *World Conservation Strategy*. Gland: International Union for the Conservation of Nature.

IUCN, UNEP and WWF (1991) *Caring for the Earth*. Gland: International Union for the Conservation of Nature.

Lakin, L. (1995) A possible solution from the ASE Environmental Education Task Group. *Education in Science* 163 pp. 9-10.

Lemaresquier, T. (1987) Prospects for Development Education: Some strategic issues facing European NGOs. *World Development* 15 pp. 3-8.

Local Government Management Board (1993) *Local Agenda 21: A Guide for Local Authorities in the UK*. London: LGMB.

Martin, P. (1989) *Roads to salvation or roads to nowhere? - the non-governmental organisations and environmental education* (unpublished paper). Surrey: WWF UK.

Marsden, C. (1991) *Why industry should be involved - International Conference on Environmental Education*. London: DES.

Matthews, G. and Stephens, D. (1992) *Environmental information needs. A report of a survey of environmental information needs in schools and youth work*. Reading: Council for Environmental Education.

National Council for Voluntary Organisations (1993) *Facts and Figures on the Voluntary Sector. Information briefing No. 1*. London: NCVO.

National Curriculum Council (1990a) *Curriculum Guidance No. 7: Environmental Education*. York: National Curriculum Council.

National Curriculum Council (1990b) *Curriculum Guidance No. 3: the whole curriculum*. York: National Curriculum Council.

Neal, P. (1992) Non-governmental organisations - their role in environmental education. In W.L. Filho and J.A. Palmer (eds.) *Key Issues in Environmental Education*. London: WWF/Kogan Page.

Organisation for Economic and Cooperation and Development (1991) Environmental and Schools Initiatives (ENSI) *News No. 1*. Paris: OECD/CERI.

Posch, P. (1991) Environment and school initiatives: background and basic premises of the project. In *OECD Environment, Schools and Active Learning*. Paris: OECD.

Royal Society for the Protection of Birds (1991) *Environmental Education in England - Report of a survey*. Bedfordshire: RSPB.

Saunders, L., Hewitt, D. and MacDonald, A. (1995) *Education for Life - the cross-curricular themes in primary and secondary schools*. NFER: Slough.

Schools Curriculum and Assessment Authority (1994) *The National Curriculum and its Assessment: Final Report*. London: SCAA.

Schools Curriculum and Assessment Authority (1995) *The National Curriculum Orders*. London: SCAA.

Sharma, R.C. and Tan, M.C. (1990) *A Sourcebook in Environmental Education for Secondary Schools*. Paris: UNESCO.

Skilbeck, M. (1993) *The Way Ahead*, Occasional Paper No. 16. Wolverhampton: NAEE.

Smyth, J.C. (1995) Environment and Education: a view of a changing scene. *Environmental Education Research* 1 (1) pp. 3-20.

Tidy Britain Group (1985) *Materials and the Environment*. Brighton: Tidy Britain Group.

Tufts University (1990) *University Presidents for a Sustainable Future: The Talloires Declaration*. Tufts University European Centre.

UNESCO (1991) *International consultation meeting in the Development of Networks in Environmental Education*. Paris: UNESCO.

UNESCO-UNEP (1978) *Intergovernmental Conference on Environmental Education, Tbilisi, USSR, Final Report*. Paris: UNESCO.

UNESCO-UNEP (1988) *An Environmental Education Approach to Training Elementary Teachers: A Teacher Education Programme*. Environmental Education Series No. 27. Paris: UNESCO.

United Nations (1992) *UN Conference on Environment and Development. Agenda 21 Rio Declaration, Forest Principles*. Paris: UNESCO.

World Commission on Environment and Development (1987) *Our Common Future*. The Brundtland Report. Oxford: Oxford University Press.

World Wide Fund for Nature (1988) *What we consume*. Surrey: Richmond Publishers.

World Wide Fund for Nature (1993) *Education Policy Paper*. Surrey: WWF UK.

World Wide Fund for Nature/Learning Through Landscapes (1994) *The Hidden Curriculum of School Grounds*. Surrey: WWF UK.

World Wide Fund for Nature, UK (1995) *Reaching Out: a professional development programme for delivering environmental education and education for sustainability*. Surrey: WWF UK.

# 8 The changing role of fieldwork: use of a wetlands area as a teaching and learning resource

*Pam Green, Linda Platten and George Raper*

## Abstract

The paper illustrates how a partnership between the University of Warwick and the National Rivers Authority developed a wetlands site for educational use. Review, revision and development of fieldwork teaching programmes from Key Stage 1 to post-graduate level are discussed. Future plans for monitoring the site, processing data on the use of the site and promoting concern for the environment are outlined. Mention is made of the enthusiasm and interest shown by the public which has further widened the educational activities.

## Introduction

In 1991, as part of the 25th Anniversary celebrations at the University of Warwick, a collaborative venture with the National Rivers Authority saw the development of a wetlands area. The site, extending over six acres of the University campus, is bordered by a medieval woodland on its eastern edge, the remnants of an old hedgerow on the western side and a well established ornamental lake to the north. A fast flowing stream runs through the area. (See Figure 8.1)

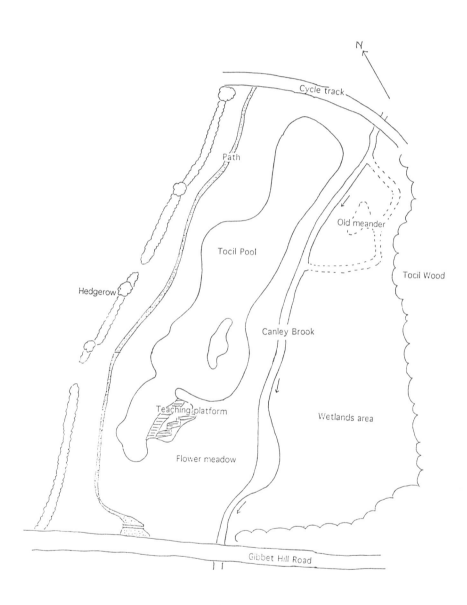

**Figure 8.1   Tocil pool and wetlands (not to scale)**

# Purpose and development of the site

The area identified for this development had proved unsuitable for sports facilities, for buildings, or as a car park and was of no special ecological interest. The university was keen to improve this site and consulted the National Rivers Authority who at the time were improving a nearby site. Plans were subsequently agreed for a joint development of the six acres, primarily for educational purposes, and financing of the venture was eventually achieved through contributions from the University Parent Fund and substantial backing from the National Rivers Authority. Subsequent construction was undertaken by the National Rivers Authority. During the excavation work, several problems were encountered in connection with the removal of underlying heavy clay from the flood plain during a very wet season. This had to be deposited on a site across a busy road. Further development included the widening of the stream to form a small bay, and alongside this, tiered semi-circular reed beds were excavated with great precision to allow 100 mm increments between habitat bands. A wide range of marginal habitat plants was subsequently planted.

A small meander was dug out and planted as a marshy backwater, creating another habitat and restoring the water table to a phragmites reedbed which had been rapidly drying out. On the flood plain, swatches of wetland meadow wildflower seeds were sown to provide succession of colour and flowering. The final construction phase was the teaching area. Pond dipping platforms were erected with reeds planted around them and board walks were designed to run between the reeds, so that children could appreciate their scale and character. A small ramped 'beach' allows people in wheelchairs access to the water.

Finally the pool was filled ..... and emptied, several times! Tile drains had unknowingly been intercepted. Once remedied, the pool held water extremely well, so well that several exceptionally high waters in the spring caused the dipping platforms to rise and these have now been anchored with sheet piling. The project was finally launched in July 1991 completing the Anniversary celebrations - in deluging rain!

A planned mowing regime alongside the pathway and around the pool provides for mown enclaves and tall wildflower peripheries. Pollarded willows border the pool and stream, giving expression to the flood plain character of the landscape. All the managed plantings have proved successful and the pool now continues a wildlife corridor from the established lake to the adjacent woodland and, whilst primarily providing educational facilities, the development has proved to be an attractive amenity within the landscape. We now have an area of very special ecological significance. A stimulating environment has been created, promoting conservation and enhancement of the water area (Green and Platten, 1995).

## Educational opportunities

The creation of these new features has provided a wealth of educational opportunities particularly for environmental studies. Initially, fieldwork studies by geography and biology students at the University produced essential information about early colonisation of the site. These exercises were important and the opportunities for such traditional studies continue. It was necessary, however, to fulfil the intention of the National Rivers Authority and ensure that educational use of site should be as wide as possible. After several revisions of the National Curriculum, environmental education requirements are scattered across the subject orders, but are recognisable at all key stages (DES, 1991a; DES, 1991b; DFE, 1995a; DFE 1995b). The importance of field studies for all children from five to sixteen was emphasised even in the early stages of the development of the National Curriculum, as the following extract shows:

> The emphasis of environmental education should be on enquiry and investigation by the pupils themselves, including direct experience. Fieldwork has an important part to play in both primary and secondary schools. It provides opportunity for drawing on the environment as a stimulus to learning, at the same time developing awareness and curiosity about the environment.                                    (NCC, 1990)

It is essential therefore to seize every opportunity to promote investigative studies in the environment. While acknowledging the value of the well intentioned nature study activities of the past, it is crucial that fieldwork is rigorously planned to ensure progression both in skills and conceptual understanding. With this in mind a wide variety of programmes has been developed.

During the four year period since its establishment, the site has accommodated many different groups. Children of infant and junior age, middle and secondary school pupils and university students have all increased their knowledge and understanding by working here. Practising teachers, through regular in-service courses, have been introduced to a wide range of approaches to teaching in the environment.

# Early fieldwork development

Initially, local schools were invited to bring children to work with student teachers in specific subject areas, mainly biology and geography. In order to prevent over use and damage in the early stages of development, the numbers participating in any form of field study were restricted. At this time subject tutors made positive efforts to strengthen cross curricular links by collaboratively planning course programmes in order to realise the full potential of the site for all students in initial teacher training. Some individual students undertook small scale investigative projects within their academic studies, contributing to our knowledge of the early colonisation. As the habitats have continued to develop successfully the educational use has been extended, thus fulfilling the original aims of the University - National Rivers Authority partnership. Figure 8.2 indicates the widening use of the site over these four years.

# Current fieldwork programmes

Groups of children work either with student teachers or with their own teachers. If the latter they work independently of the university on their own school programme of study. For the youngest groups of infant children, from schools in Warwickshire and the nearby towns of Coventry and Solihull, coming to the wetlands is a very special and different experience. We encourage emphasis to be placed on response to the environment. These young children in particular need the opportunity to develop their sense of place, to use their senses and appreciate the diversity of their surroundings. Earth walk activities are a very important part of their work, enabling them to begin to see the variety of life around them, both plant and animal, and to enjoy being in the countryside. They are able to observe pond life and compare flowing and still water habitats. As part of this fieldwork simple mapping and route following skills can be developed. These topics can be structured and linked to form an environmental investigation which, at Key Stage 1, is part of the requirement for geography in the National Curriculum.

At Key Stage 2, whilst experiential work is still important, teachers are encouraged to introduce a more rigorous investigative approach as part of fieldwork progression. Investigations involving accurate observation, recording and hypothesis testing, pollution studies, simple surveying and map making have been undertaken. The emphasis here is to help children to make links between habitats and the kinds of plant and animal life they support to develop their understanding of the environment. Children have worked on food chains and webs and the

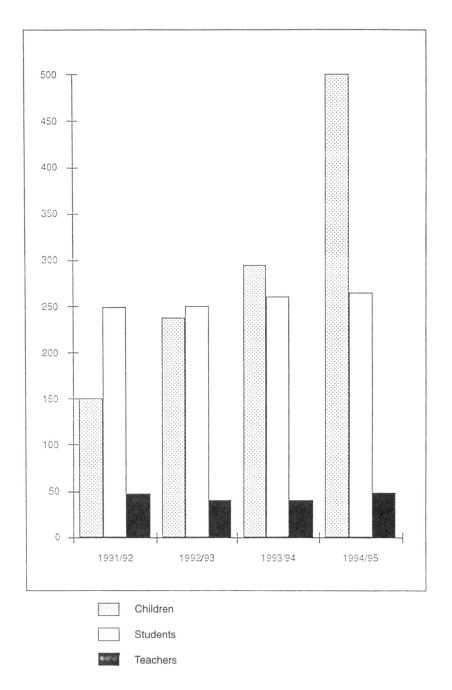

**Figure 8.2   Graph to show the increased usage of the wetlands
facility over the past 5 years**

effects of seasonal change. They have learned about the natural cycles of growth and decay, and gained better understanding of how elements of the water cycle fit together. Through such experiences and study, children are encouraged to develop and express their own feelings towards the environment and above all to deepen their respect for all the other living things in their environment.

Currently a small research programme to follow up schools' use of the site is being undertaken. The development and use of school grounds, the ways in which fieldwork has been extended and enriched through use of the wetlands and the extent to which National Curriculum needs have been met are of particular interest.

## Teacher development programmes

In England and Wales the implementation of the National Curriculum has involved all teachers in reviewing their planning to ensure that all the requirements are adequately met. The wetland site has provided an excellent opportunity for developing cross subject links, particularly in science and geography, increasing environmental awareness and understanding at the same time. Figure 8.3 shows the range of activities undertaken.

Science and geography have been linked in a variety of ways. Through focusing on the study of weather and its effects within a small area, on soils and how they are formed, and on water in the environment, for example, teachers have been encouraged to work in a cross curricular way and plan fieldwork tasks which emphasise the basic inter-relationships which are fundamental to our understanding of the natural environment. After some basic work on micro-climates around the university site, some groups have then used these techniques to investigate the effect of local weather conditions on the numbers and location of minibeasts found at Tocil Pool and Canley Brook on a particular day. Other teacher groups have investigated differences in soil profile in the woodland and by the pool and tried to relate this both to the underlying rock type and to the nature of the vegetation cover. Study of the stream flow and the nature of the stream bed and banks has been used to highlight the way in which water erodes, transports and deposits soil and rock and to emphasise the difference between erosion and weathering. These processes, basic to the understanding of physical geography, can then be related to aspects of the water cycle which forms part of the science curriculum content. To support this work further, funding was provided by the National Rivers Authority for educational

Children 5–8 years

Earthwalk activities using the senses

Pondlife and stream life observation and comparison of flowing and still water habitats

Weather observation and studies of seasonal change

Simple mapping and route following

Similarities and differences between places

Children 8–16 years

Accurate observation, recording, hypothesis testing, data handling

Studies of growth and decay

Plant and animal adaptation

Food chains and webs

Elements of the water cycle

Pollution Studies

Map making and simple surveying

**Figure 8.3   The range of activities at the wetlands site**

equipment and for a teachers' resource pack, 'The Wetlands Experience', which is available for all participating schools (Barker and Platten, 1994).

Such activities have formed the basis of many courses organised at the university for teachers. In some cases such teachers have been pursuing a further course of study for their own professional and academic development, such as that leading to the award of B.Phil (Ed.); for others the work has been undertaken as part of an In-Service Education and Training (INSET) programme for science or geography, most recently developed through Grants for Education, Support and Training (GEST) funding. Some participants have been able to use such work as a building block towards a further qualification and others have been enabled to seek posts of special responsibility as a geography or science co-ordinator.

However, some teachers need a great deal of support in planning fieldwork, and in-service courses have been developed to make full use of the wetlands facilities for teacher development in this respect as well. Such courses have covered curriculum planning and implementation, evaluation and assessment, as well as subject updating and field techniques.

## In-service case study

One such innovative 3-day course was planned in collaboration with Warwickshire LEA for teachers returning to the classroom after an absence (Green and Platten, 1994). Twenty two teacher returners were selected, some of whom were already engaged in supply teaching, others as much as fifteen years away from the classroom. Their previous experiences covered all age phases including infant, junior, middle and two from secondary schools wishing to transfer to middle school, but none were very familiar with the National Curriculum.

The content of the course was chosen with Department for Education concerns in mind regarding the need for development of subject knowledge and skills to teach the programmes of study for both science and geography across Key Stages 1 and 2. Certain parts of both programmes were selected as being those most easily linked in the study of particular places, and specific linking themes such as 'change', 'growth', 'processes' and 'place' were also identified. An important aim was to demonstrate and emphasise the complementary nature of the two disciplines through field experiences.

It was essential to offer opportunity for developing confidence with specific field techniques and to consider organisational aspects of fieldwork, but also important to provide the chance to apply the knowledge gained and skills learned in a teaching situation with children. Day one was therefore used to familiarise the group with National Curriculum requirements and give initial help in making links between subject areas. A variety of structured fieldwork activities was planned which enabled teachers to observe, investigate, collect data and record accurately. Care was taken to select investigations which could be adapted and undertaken in school environments. Small groups worked on these activities, using the wetlands site. They reviewed their findings, relating them to the National Curriculum, and then presented them to the whole group. It was very clear that there was a wide range of individual need and it was important therefore to offer a choice of activity for the follow up work with children on the third day. From the ideas generated from the first day's experience, individuals chose according to their own particular needs and interests and re-grouped on this basis to plan work in detail on day two in readiness for day three.

The need to make use of specialist equipment and employ a variety of recording methods and questioning was specified and the teachers were given a day to reflect on the task, to prepare teaching materials and plan the organisation of the fieldwork session. These fieldwork plans were implemented on day three, each pair of teachers working with a small group of Year 6 children provided by a nearby Warwickshire school. The children were specially selected for their considerable experience in fieldwork so rigorous planning by the teachers was essential if they were to motivate and engage the children in meaningful activities. Figure 3 shows some of the activities which were undertaken.

Teachers, tutors and LEA advisory teachers used the final session on day three to evaluate the course. The teachers identified several benefits, such as experience of new techniques using a range of equipment; the updating of their subject knowledge and reinforcement of this by using it with children straight away; and the development of recording methods. Tutors also felt that some needs had been met effectively in this short course. However, they felt that the course had demonstrated very clearly that more subject updating was necessary if primary teachers are to feel wholly capable of meeting the demands of the National Curriculum and therefore an ongoing and developing programme of teacher in-service provision of this kind was required.

## Programmes for student teachers

Involvement in initial teacher education is an important part of the work of the University. Each year approximately four hundred students embark on training programmes at undergraduate or post graduate certificate level. The wetlands site with its extensive and varied habitats is valuable for academic work in biology and geography and emphasis is placed on ecology and ecological issues in both subjects. Students studying them are able to work at the site throughout the four years of their degree course, and many small scale research projects have been undertaken.

However, it is also seen as important for all students, not only those who are specialising in biology and geography, to have some experience of teaching about, and in, the environment. In order to achieve this, wherever possible, tutors arrange for school children to visit the site, students plan small pieces of fieldwork and then work with small groups of children, gaining first hand experience 'beyond the classroom'. Analysis and evaluation of the planned activities are then undertaken in curriculum courses. All students training in the early years programme pursue cross-curricular environmental topics. Geography and science curriculum courses are integrated for this work. The whole group, approximately seventy-five students and tutors, work together, ensuring that some activities are pursued in each of the habitats. The organisation and management of such work at Key Stage 1 is discussed, appropriate fieldwork activities experienced and the results are then collectively displayed. This year an extra dimension was added to the usual fieldwork activities when a post graduate certificate group used their visit to focus on language development and the potential for art and craft work. The most pleasing outcome of all of these experiences amongst the trainee teachers is the number of students now introducing new schools to the wetlands area, bringing their classes during periods of teaching practice.

So far, the large majority of students on initial teacher education courses and of experienced teachers working with their own classes on the wetlands have been primary specialists enhancing science and geography related themes at Key Stages 1 and 2. However, within the National Curriculum, there is a progressive widening and deepening of the environmental concepts to be addressed, both explicitly and implicitly and this has implications for the training of science teachers who, in many cases, enter the profession from relatively narrow academic backgrounds, but who are required to teach broadly based science in school. For example, when considering within "Life Processes and Living Things" at KS 4 that *pupils should be taught how the distribution and relative abundance of organisms in a habitat can be explained in terms of adaption, competition and predation,* the student teacher might naturally see a justification for fieldwork activities. However, within the physical sciences attainment targets, chemical themes such as *how nitrogenous fertilisers are manufactured, and their effects on plant growth and the environment* also suggest how experiences outside the laboratory can enhance teaching and learning. With imagination, physics topics on energy resources and energy transfer can also be developed through environmental contexts. When engaged in Experimental and Investigative Science, a key component of the science curriculum, the work of pupils can be enhanced by wetlands based investigative work. From the more general skills and attitudes being inculcated, to the highest levels within the national curriculum such as recognising contexts where variables are less easily controlled and where judgements have to be made on real evidence available, we are beginning to see PGCE students become increasingly willing to extend their teaching beyond traditional boundaries.

At GCE A-level many chemistry syllabuses include environmental chemistry and so the potential for these students, who have not traditionally ventured outside the laboratory, can be exploited. The large group of students on our secondary PGCE Science programme are making an increasing use of the facilities. Chemists and physicists, who have traditionally shied away from such experiences are being encouraged through co-operative tasks with support from biology graduates who are naturally more at ease with fieldwork techniques. It has been a concern to us that when PGCE students are working in school on teaching practice, a very few of the chemists and virtually none of the physicists have until now engaged with their pupils in activities outside the immediate school confines. Fieldwork frightens them. It is at the initial training stage that we can best change attitudes and allow such students the opportunities to develop confidence in a structured way.

Use of the site is not however confined to student teachers and school children. Two PhD studies are also focusing on the area. An interesting outcome of the development has been the attraction to the water area of species of bats and one study is monitoring bat species throughout the wetlands site and woodland area - with special attention given to Daubenton species. A second study is monitoring the colonisation of the wild flower meadows by butterflies. Thus a full spectrum of field studies has now evolved.

## Concern for the environment

While such courses have emphasised the importance of developing subject knowledge for both teachers and children, alongside confidence in fieldwork techniques, the need to deepen concern for the environment is also crucial. The use of broad environmental themes such as 'change', 'growth', 'habitats' and 'physical processes' has provided opportunity for planning appropriate structured learning experiences which focus not only on animal and plant adaptation, the similarities and differences between localities and the study of weather patterns, but also on environmental damage and pollution and the effects of human influence on the environment. Such work, involving information collection and data handling and storage, now provides the foundation for studying environmental change, a requirement at Key Stage 2, and will help to raise environmental issues for discussion at Key Stage 3. This kind of study not only increases awareness of the special nature of certain environments, but also their vulnerability.

Through environmental monitoring, from chemical and physical as well as from biological perspectives, a range of fundamental skills and science concepts can be developed through contexts which, for pupils, are more relevant and related to their own concerns than more traditional approaches. Sampling methods, analytical techniques, instrument familiarisation using the sorts of equipment available at the university but rarely in school, data collection, its analysis, preparation and dissemination can be undertaken in the context of real applications and situations related to the social concerns of young people.

During the past twenty years the expansion of provision of courses at undergraduate and postgraduate level in universities has accelerated. In addition to the proliferation of environmental science degree programmes it is now common for higher education institutions to offer a diverse range of degree programmes, for example, environmental chemistry, environmental systems or monitoring combined with physics, business studies, sports science, or tourism. The combinations seem endless. The potential, therefore, for using the wetlands with a whole new clientele is vast. Our objectives now include opening up the resource for the development of undergraduate coursework in such degrees. At the higher degree level, we have introduced modules into the MSc programmes in Science Education and in Geographical Education for both primary and secondary school teachers which will further expand the use of the area for our own teaching and for school based research projects.

Today, it is important that students and pupils look beyond the immediate environment of the wetlands. Based on their experiences, activities and investigations here, we are beginning to plan more extensive work for our students, as a starting point in the European dimension of their education. As we, and the nations around us, become increasingly more integrated, it is essential that young people develop closer links with their peers in other countries, in other environments. As more schools are able to communicate across Europe via the electronic links freely available, through schemes such as Europe in the School, The School in Europe (Bell and Dransfield, 1990) and the European

Development Awareness Project (1993) they increasingly use environmental contexts for co-operative study. We are anxious that our trainee teachers become involved in such initiatives. We have established links between our PGCE students following Science, Economics or Modern Foreign Languages courses and their counterparts in France, Germany and Belgium so that together they can develop curriculum materials for use with pupils across the continent. Other countries are sometimes more environmentally aware than our own and already have well established curriculum development projects in place. Proposals for a new curriculum in Sweden, for example, include environmental studies as one of the three principal areas for teaching in subject studies and in interdisciplinary work and a German initiative "Europe - Materials for Teaching" includes a substantial environmental package (Kastner, 1993). The wetlands resource will provide our students with some of the data for multinational exchange - one contribution to a developing programme.

## Public awareness of the site

Members of the public are encouraged to use many of the University facilities; a sculpture trail and several campus walks are popular features in the grounds. The medieval woodland, although part of the campus, is owned and managed by Warwickshire Wildlife Trust and organised walks and study days are regularly programmed. The ornamental lake with its luxuriant vegetation and varied bird population also attracts many visitors. The wetlands site opened up whole new habitats and their developments have been watched with interest and enthusiasm. In order to maintain this interest, further funding was made available by the National Rivers Authority in 1994, for information boards to be erected near to Tocil Pool. Additionally, guided walk and identification leaflets were produced. These are available for resident students, conference visitors and members of the public. Open studies programmes exploring the various habitats are popular and shortly a major national conference on the bat population is to be held there. These features enable many visitors to the University to appreciate this facility.

## Summary

The need to conserve and enhance the quality of the countryside has been very well stated by The Countryside Commission in its own policy statement 'Sustainability and the English Countryside' (1993) published in response to the UK Government's consultation paper on the 'UK strategy for sustainable development'. The Commission argues that it is not just 'the best and most important' parts of the countryside that need to be considered within policies for sustainability, but that different properties of the countryside, such as natural resources, landscape features, wildlife habitats and human artefacts have their own distinct importance, forming together 'a complete and dynamic whole'. These cultural and natural features, it is argued, enrich our lives and are essential components of sustainability. It is suggested that where development takes place in the countryside any loss or damage should be fully compensated by environmental enhancement. The following quotation from the RSNC report highlights the particular need to focus on the development of wetland habitats:

> Since 1945 we have lost 97% of our moist key meadows and 60% of lowland mires, mostly to land drainage.                         (RSNC, 1992)

The University wetlands area was initially created in response to this situation, however it has proved to be a source of ongoing inspiration in the planning of teaching programmes. From an area of no special ecological significance, a stimulating environment has been created, promoting conservation and enhancement of the water area through teaching programmes. It is only through creative and imaginative teaching approaches that young people can be engaged effectively in environmental study. It is our aim to continue to encourage teachers to use this area to promote in their children a lasting concern for the environment.

## Bibliography

Barker, S. and Platten, L. (1994) *The Wetland Experience*. Solihull National Rivers Authority.

Bell, G.H. and Dransfield, R. (1990 *Europe in the School, The School in Europe*. London: Shell Education Service.

Countryside Commission (1993) *Sustainability and the English Countryside*. Cheltenham: Countryside Commission.

DES (1991a) *Science in the National Curriculum*. London HMSO

DES (1991b) *Geography in the National Curriculum*. London: HMSO

DES (1995a) *Science in the National Curriculum*. London: HMSO

DES (1995b) *Geography in the National Curriculum*. London: HMSO

European Development Awareness Project (1993) *The European Dimension*. London: Central Bureau for Educational Visits and Exchanges.

Green, P. and Platten, L. (1994) Returning to the National Curriculum through Field Studies. *Journal of Teacher Development* **3** (2).

Green, P and Platten, L. (1995) The Wetlands at the University of Warwick: a Partnership which changed the Environment.

*Environmental Education* **48**. Walsall: National Association for Environmental Education.

Kastner, H. (1993) European Teaching Materials in Germany. *EDIT* **3** London: Central Bureau for Visits and Exchanges.

NCC (1990) *Curriculum Guidance No. 7 Environmental Education.* York: National Curriculum Council.

RSNC (1992) Wildlife Trust Partnership Report. *Natural World* **35** London: Royal Society for Nature Conservation.

# 9 The role of agricultural colleges in environmental education: the Seale-Hayne perspective

*Hayley Randle and Ian Kemp*

## Abstract

This paper examines how the teaching of environmental issues in higher education institutions has evolved over the last fifty years, using the Seale-Hayne Faculty of Agriculture, Food Studies and Land Use in the University of Plymouth as an illustration. The development of environmental education at Seale-Hayne, originally an independent college of agriculture, is followed and linked to national issues and policies relating to the countryside. Key influences shaping the provision of environmental education are identified and related to the prevailing agricultural climate. Influences identified include production maximisation, the Scott report evaluating agricultural use of the countryside, the unseen side effects/implications of profit making and exploitation of land in the 1960s, the Silsoe Conference in the 1970s which made the first serious attempt to reconcile the accumulated conflict between farmers and conservationists and finally, in the 1980s intensification and implications of the Common Agricultural Policy dictated by membership of the European Economic Community. The development of non-agricultural HND and degree programmes in response to changes outside of the educational sphere is also examined.

# Introduction

Many UK colleges and university departments, which until recently specialised in agriculture and horticulture, are now offering a much wider range of courses (Bond, 1995). A large number of these are either based on the study of environmental issues or integrate these with more traditional agricultural teaching. The introduction of environmental courses has been in response to the changing agricultural climate, increasing interest in landscape and nature conservation and growing participation in countryside recreation. This chapter will follow the development of environmental education at Seale-Hayne Faculty of Agriculture, Food and Land Use, University of Plymouth.

Seale-Hayne College was endowed under the will of the Rt. Hon. Charles Seale-Hayne (1833-1903) who left a large legacy along with a request to build a 'Technical and Agricultural College in the County of Devon' (E.J. Sobey, personal communication, December 1981). It was further specified that the college was to be

> in the neighbourhood of Newton Abbot, for the technical education of artisans and others, without distinction of creed, and for the special encouragement of the industries, manufacturers and products of the county of Devon.
>
> (Sells, 1978)

On gaining the consent of the Court of Chancery to found Seale-Hayne as an independent college of agriculture, two hundred and twenty five acres situated on a hill overlooking the river Teign in South Devon were purchased for the trust. Seale-Hayne is unique in the UK in that its buildings were designed specifically to be an agricultural college (Cattermull, 1951).

The foundation stone of Seale-Hayne was laid in 1912 by the Rt. Hon. W. Runciman, MP who at the time was the president of the Board of Agriculture and Fisheries. By 1914 the construction was completed and the college ready for occupation, but it was immediately commissioned by the Home Office to be used as a Royal Naval Hospital. During the first world war, although there were no formal courses in agriculture, Seale-Hayne ran a course in 'farm work for girls'. An article in the Countryman documents the memories of one participant, Gwen Stenning, who left being proficient in early morning milking and working heavy horses amongst other things (Hall, 1994).

# The inter-war period

In 1919 Seale-Hayne was handed back to the college governors by the War Office and on 5th January 1920 opened to students for the first time. There were thirty seven students and ten staff. The courses on offer reflected the post-war national need to maximise production. Many of the students were ex-service men preparing to make a career in farming (Cattermull, 1951). Rosemary Sells (1978) describes the time spent by her father, Frank Horne , at Seale-Hayne between 1920 and 1923. She refers to the lack of clear syllabuses and the need to cram three term's worth of work into two so that the academic year could begin in time. Sells concludes that Horne gained a greater knowledge and love of the countryside, the ability to work 'hard and well', confidence and a thirst for learning from his three years in the pioneering community at Seale-Hayne.

Between 1920 and 1930 student numbers at Seale-Hayne increased steadily to between seventy and eighty (Edwardes-Ker, 1931). The seven courses on offer were still centred on agriculture. There was a three or four year degree in Agriculture, a three year college diploma course in General Agriculture, a two year college certificate course in General Science of Agriculture, a one year certificate in General Poultry Husbandry, a twenty week short course in the Science of Agriculture, a twelve week summer course in Dairying and finally a farm pupil course in Practical Farming.

By the early 1930s there was a fall in the number of students, to around forty five, partly because of limited accommodation available to young students at Seale-Hayne and a depression in agriculture in general (Cattermull, 1951). Nevertheless, between 1930 and 1940 there was a general increase in academic standards, and in 1935 the college opened to women.

# The second world war

In 1940 growth was curtailed as students disbanded at the outbreak of the second world war. Some of the staff were assigned to War Agricultural Committees, and many of those who weren't resigned. Teaching still went on at Seale-Hayne, mainly the training of land girls undertaking a four week course which included skills such as milking and tractor driving.

# After the second world war

Courses began again at Seale-Hayne before the end of the second world war. In 1942 there were sixty students studying agriculture or agriculture-related areas. By 1946 student numbers had grown to one hundred and forty three. The student profile following the end of the second world war was similar to that following the first world war, with a large number of ex-service personnel. As to be expected, owing to the continuing national need to maximise food production after the war, the type of courses running at this time were similar to those in operation after the first world war. In short, like many other agricultural colleges, the ethos at Seale-Hayne was 'Production Maximisation', which severely restricted the development of non-agricultural courses.

Even in the early 1940s, there were concerns about the validity of the 'Production Maximisation' approach and its associated policies. In 1941 Lord Justice Scott was appointed by the Minister of Works and Building in consultation with the Minister of Agriculture to lead a committee on 'Land Utilisation in Rural Areas'. The aim of this committee was to obtain a view of the future land requirements of British agriculture. The first part of Scott's brief was to provide factual information on the nature of the land, the countryside and changes that had been brought about in land use patterns and population distribution. The second part of his brief was to consider the growing impact of urban growth and of townspeople on the countryside. The precise terms of reference he and his committee were to work to were as follows:

> to consider the conditions which govern building and other constructional development in country areas consistent with the maintenance of agriculture, and in particular the factors affecting the location of industry having regard to economic operation, part-time and seasonal employment, the well-being of rural communities and the preservation of rural amenities.
>
> (Rogers, Blunden and Currey, 1985)

Scott concluded first, that 'farming is good for the countryside', second, that there should be an injection of capital into farming in order to establish stability in the agricultural industry and third, that the 'better' land should be retained in farming unless it could be proved that it was in the national interest for any change to take place. As to be expected there were a number of objections to this view, including those made by Professor Dennison. In his 'minority' report, Dennison concluded that matters were not as simple as Scott had indicated; improvements in agricultural productivity were capable of overcoming problems posed by the loss of land to development, and thus agriculture need not be granted a prior right to rural land (Rogers, Blunden and Currey, 1985). Although the debate generated by the Scott and Dennison reports continued, the primary role of agricultural colleges remained the training of students to contribute to the national goal of maximising food production.

# The 1950s and 1960s

The 1950s saw the introduction of the first non-agricultural courses at Seale-Hayne. This inevitably was accompanied by a rapid expansion of student numbers. By 1952 there were two hundred and three students, one hundred and forty eight men and fifty five women, one hundred and three of whom were resident. This sudden growth inevitably resulted in rapid expansion at Seale-Hayne, in terms of construction, provision of facilities and of course the farm. In the period following the second world war courses included agriculture, dairying, horticulture, forestry and rural studies.

A course entitled 'Rural Studies for Teachers' was developed in 1952. This was a one year course leading to a diploma in rural Studies (Moore, 1964). It was intended that teachers participating in the Rural Studies course would, when trained, be able to

> instill in their pupils a deep love of the countryside and an appreciation of the problems faced by farmers.
>
> (Moore, 1964)

It was intended that these student teachers could help to create a closer bond between town and countryman, and as a consequence help to achieve fuller cooperation. It is important to note that Rural Studies students could also competently manage pigs, poultry and bees, through their training in basic agriculture during the course.

In the early 1960s the words 'business' and 'profit' became inextricably linked with agriculture. By the mid 1960s, however, concern about the implications of this type of farming were being voiced. Rachel Carson published her book 'Silent Spring' dealing with the effects (both short and long term) of pesticides on wildlife (Carson, 1962). Five years later E.J. Mishan published his book 'The Costs of Economic Growth' in which other environmental concerns such as pollution were raised (Mishan, 1967). Towards the end of the decade even stronger calls were being made to consider the implications of intensive 'agri-business'. At the same time membership of some voluntary conservation groups began to grow rapidly reflecting the increased public concern over changes in the British countryside. Between 1965 and 1970 for example, membership of the County Naturalist's Trusts increased by one hundred and seventy two percent rising from 20,965 to 57,000 (Green, 1981).

The continuing intensification of UK agriculture throughout the 1960s and the concomitant rise in the environmental movement led to a situation where conflicts were frequent. On the one hand conservationists condemned farmers and farming practice and on the other hand farmers tended to see conservation as

> an abstract subject, put over by emotional people who spent much time wringing their hands over the destruction of hedgerows
>
> (Barber, 1970a)

# The 1970s

The need for closer communication and understanding between farmers and conservationists prompted the organisation of the 'Silsoe conference' in 1969. It played an important part in helping to reconcile conflicting interests in the countryside; ideas first aired at the conference were to shape the development of new courses at Seale-Hayne and at other higher education institutions.

In his keynote speech to the conference J. Winnifrith, an ex-Minister of Agriculture and then director of the National Trust stressed the compatibility of farming and conservation saying that

> for a properly balanced countryside we need not only prosperous agriculture, but a countryside which keeps its natural beauty and interest
>
> (Winnifrith, 1970)

Whilst the reconciliation of farming and conservation conflicts was the central theme of the conference, Winnifrith also drew attention to a relatively new, but already major, pressure being exerted on the countryside: the impact of leisure activities. He recognised the great explosion of the motor car owning population and the potential for damage to the countryside as it increasingly fulfilled the role of 'town persons playground'.

There was considerable interest in the outcome of the 'Silsoe Conference'. 1970 was European Conservation year; the relationships between farming and conservation explored by the conference were widely reported in the media and were a focus of interest for the rapidly expanding environmental movement. Carter (1988) suggests that the subsequent development of the Farming and Wildlife Advisory Group (FWAG) was a direct result of discussions which took place at the conference.

Although the relationship between farming and conservation concerns, and to a lesser extent the impact of leisure in the countryside, were brought clearly into focus by the conference, in 1970 agriculture and conservation were still entirely separate disciplines within higher education. Few courses dealt with the growing field of countryside recreation, although courses were emerging which examined environmental issues, one of the earliest being the conservation course offered by University College London. There was however little attempt at integration, to look at the impact of countryside recreation or landscape issues within a single programme. Many of the institutions offering established agriculture courses were in an ideal position to change this situation.

At Seale-Hayne the change came in 1973 with the introduction of a new Higher National Diploma in 'Natural Resources and the Rural Economy', subtitled 'Land Use and Environmental Studies'. The introduction of the new course was justified on the grounds that it provided a response to the pressing need for technologists educated in the various aspect of natural resource use and rural economy which had been created by increasing competition for land use (Seale-Hayne, 1972).

The need to produce students who had a good understanding of ecological principles was clearly identified in the proposal document, but at this stage environmental subjects did not form a core area of interest. Only eleven percent of the total teaching hours was devoted to environmental studies, with the same amount for recreational studies, but forty five percent was devoted to agricultural science and technology. In fact, the introduction of the new diploma had been as much a reaction to the perceived need for farmers to diversify and enlarge their businesses as it was to the increasing environmental concerns. There was particular emphasis on the establishment of farm tourism and recreation enterprises.

Students completing the new diploma found employment in a variety of fields. Some returned to traditional agricultural holdings, but developed new recreational enterprises on them, whilst others helped with the development of new enterprises in an employed capacity. A substantial number became involved in the expanding voluntary conservation sector or took posts in the public sector working as countryside rangers or project officers. Employment opportunities for the course finalists were good and demand for places on the HND was buoyant with student numbers steadily rising.

In 1979 the first BSc in Agriculture was introduced at Seale-Hayne, within which the increasing importance of environmental issues was acknowledged. G.J. Dowrick, Seale-Hayne principal from 1971 to 1988, in an evaluation of the educational needs of the agricultural industry, stressed the importance of the study of crops and animals in relation to their environment (Dowrick, 1979). In 1983 Presswell observed that Seale-Hayne college now contributed to a much wider field than just agricultural education, with courses in Rural Resources and their Management. Recognition of the importance of the environment and the inclusion of environmental issues within the new courses may have helped to maintain the demand for places at Seale-Hayne at a time when other institutions were closing down their agricultural departments.

## The 1980s and 1990s

The rural land use debate which had helped to generate the new courses at Seale-Hayne intensified during the 1980s. Wibberley (1980) questioned the desirability of ever increasing areas of land devoted to agricultural production. He suggested that agriculture had been allowed to become too dominant in the British countryside at the expense of other non-agricultural land uses. Barber (1981) drew attention to public concern at the changing face of the countryside resulting from agricultural activities such as straw burning and hedge removal. He outlined the apparent failure of farmers to integrate wildlife conservation and landscape protection with the farming process. McInerney (1986) pointed out that by the mid 1980s the European Economic Community (EEC) had got to the stage where it was over-supplied in all temperate agriculture commodities. The implications of this were far reaching. The public perception of dependence on farmers to supply enough food for the nation was lost, and public attention was turning to the costs of the Common Agriculture Policy (CAP), which at this time stood at over two billion pounds. McInerney argued that one of the major failings of the CAP was its concentration on agricultural products and its disregard of non-agricultural land use. He concluded that the non-agricultural uses such as conservation, amenity and maintaining the quality of the rural environment, whilst not provided for by the CAP, should nevertheless be complementary to the supply of agricultural goods. Slee (1988) discussed the importance of providing training for the management of these non-agricultural land uses in higher education. He argued that the countryside is more than just a food factory but that educationalists had generally failed to come to terms with the structural changes in agriculture associated with the CAP.

The changing pattern of rural land use throughout the 1980s, with shifts in demand between agriculture, conservation, recreation, forestry and urban development underlined the importance of providing courses which would produce students with a wide range of knowledge and experience. The market for people with a thorough grounding in these fields was growing, particularly in the public and voluntary sectors. Local authorities and organisations such as the National Trust were seeking to employ more people in the field of 'Countryside Management'. This has been defined as

> getting things done to conserve and enhance the landscape both visually and as a wildlife habitat and to increase informal recreation and public awareness of access to the countryside whilst protecting the legitimate interests of land users and other rural people.
>
> (Burnham, 1985)

At Seale-Hayne the need to provide training for these countryside managers had already been recognised and provided for in part through the introduction of the HND in Natural Resources and Rural Economy. By the 1980s this course had become the HND in Rural Resource Management and the balance of teaching had shifted away from agriculture towards the environment and countryside recreation. This shift in emphasis reflected the increasing importance of an understanding of these subjects in the management of the British countryside and the changing needs of employers in the field. There was by the mid 1980s a growing demand for degree level graduates from the Rural Resource Management discipline. In 1988 the first students were recruited for the four year BSc in Rural Resource Management. The course aimed to equip students to understand and resolve conflicting interests in the rural environment and to effectively manage rural resources. Students studied the physical, biological and planning basis of the countryside, in addition to landscape and habitat management and the changing demands of the countryside.

An important part of the new degree, as with the established HND, is the requirement to complete a sandwich period. On the degree route the placement comes at the end of the second year. Students are required to complete a minimum of forty eight weeks full-time employment in work relevant to the programme before their final year at Seale-Hayne. The placement is an integral part of the degree or HND programme, providing students with an opportunity to apply knowledge acquired during the first part of their programme and to acquire additional practical skills which are often required by employers. Over the years a broad range of work has been undertaken by placement students. Initially many worked within the traditional rural industries of agriculture and forestry, but they have increasingly found work in countryside management, conservation, recreation and rural planning. This change reflects the growing importance of environmental and recreation knowledge and experience in securing employment within these areas over the last twenty years.

Demand for both of the Rural Resource Management courses (HND and BSc) was high from the outset and the courses have continued to thrive. This is demonstrated by the number of applicants for places on these course for the 1995/1996 intake. There were 104 applicants for 55 places on the HND and 118 applicants for 38 places on the BSc.

Between the late 1980s and early 1990s, Seale-Hayne underwent substantial organisational changes. In April 1989 the college merged with Polytechnic South West, now the University of Plymouth. This merger presented opportunities for students to engage in the Credit Accumulation and Transfer Scheme (CATS) in which they could obtain credits from different degree programmes which contribute to an overall qualification. Just four years later, in the September of 1993, Seale-Hayne Faculty underwent another major change with the arrival of semesterisation and modularisation. Each degree programme was re-organised to consist of a number of modules; this also resulted in greater flexibility and presented an opportunity for the relatively straightforward development of new degree programmes. At the same time the Seale-Hayne Faculty was restructured into two departments, Agriculture and Food Studies and Land Use and Rural Management.

The continuing growth of environmental education is nationwide. In the 1995/1996 edition of the 'Directory of Courses in Land-based Industries', there are forty nine courses falling under the 'Landbased/ Countryside Studies' category in eighty three UK educational institutions and thirty nine in the 'Land Management' category.

Environmental education continues to evolve at Seale-Hayne. Courses are constantly being updated to take into account the current and future needs of employers. The close contact with employers, which is a requirement for successful industrial placements, also plays an important part in identifying these needs. In 1994, an employers' survey for the Rural Resource Management HND revealed that the six most common careers of Rural Resource Management HND students were recreation management, environmentally sensitive agriculture, countryside management projects, providing countryside interpretation and information, environmental education and environmental consultancy. Inspection and subsequent comparison of the modules constituting the Rural Resource Management programme in 1988 and 1994 showed a distinct transition towards 'rural' and 'environmental' themes. This is illustrated by the following module changes: the Foundation Unit was replaced by the 'Rural Environment Issues in Perspective' module, the

'Environmental Pollution: Policies and Problems' module became 'Environmental Monitoring' and 'Public Sector Management' was replaced by the 'Environmental Impact Assessment'.

A student who enters the BSc Rural Resource Management degree in 1995/1996 will be exposed to a wide range of modules, including 'Rural Economics', 'Components of Change in the Countryside', 'Aspects of Landscaping', and the 'Management of Factors Impinging on the Countryside and Environment', such as tourism and recreation.

Rural Resource Management is not the only programme run at Seale-Hayne featuring environmental components. Other degree programmes containing environmental modules include Agriculture and Countryside Management and Rural Estate Management. The Agriculture and Countryside Management degree currently introduces its students to 'Evaluating Change in the Rural Environment', 'Habitat and Management' and 'Landscape Design and Maintenance'. The Rural Estate Management student on the other hand is introduced to other environmental aspects such as 'Rural Planning and Development', 'Diversification and Integrated Land Use' and 'Pollution of the Rural Environment'. One of the newest programmes at Seale-Hayne, Tourism Management, includes a module which examines the impact of tourism on the environment.

Two new degree programmes will start in September 1996. The first, BSc Agriculture and the Environment contains relatively little business and management training, focusing instead jointly on agriculture and the environment. The second, BSc 'Agriculture with Rural Estate Management' is based on the general agriculture degree with many of the specialised agriculture modules being replaced with modules from the Rural Estate Management programme, some of which have an environmental content. In addition to the undergraduate programmes available at Seale-Hayne, an MSc in Rural Development will start in September 1996.

## Conclusion

In common with other agricultural colleges in Britain the evolution of environmental courses at Seale-Hayne was initially a slow process and has accelerated rapidly only recently. The need to maximise food production in the years immediately following the first and second world wars gave a clear purpose to the agricultural industry. The primary role of agricultural colleges was therefore to provide well trained agriculturalists to service the industry and remained so well into the 1960s.

New demands on the countryside brought about by increased leisure time and the growing environmental movement in the 1960s and 1970s were recognised at Seale-Hayne with the introduction of its HND in Natural Resources and the Rural Economy. This departure from courses with a purely agricultural base proved successful and represented the start of an important trend for Seale-Hayne. Changing priorities for rural land throughout the 1980s and 1990s have reinforced this trend. Seale-Hayne has, through the introduction of its HND and degree in Rural Resource Management and the inclusion of environmental subjects within other degree programmes, provided students to meet the growing demand for people able to balance the conflicting requirements of agriculture, development pressures, recreation, tourism and the environment.

Today, as a faculty of the University of Plymouth and with a growing range of programmes, Seale-Hayne is in a strong position to build upon its experience in providing environmental education and to supply students able to tackle the emerging environmental issues in the British Countryside in the late 1990s.

## Acknowledgements

We would like to thank Paul Brassley for his help unravelling the history of Seale-Hayne. We would also like to thank Linda Tiley for digging out archive material on demand.

## Bibliography

Anon (1962) 1912-1962 Seale-Hayne *In Caelo Salus*. Agriculture **69** (9), pp. 410-411.

Barber, D.C. (1970a) What it's all about. In Barber, D., *Farming and wildlife: a study in compromise*. Proceedings of the Silsoe Conference, Silsoe, Bedfordshire.

Barber, D.C. (1970b) What farmers can do. In Barber, D., *Farming and wildlife: a study in compromise*. Proceedings of the Silsoe Conference, Silsoe, Bedfordshire.

Barber, D.C. (1981) The countryside - where now? *Agricultural Progress* **56** pp. 74-79.

Bond, N. (1995) Colleges widen their horizons. *Farmers Weekly*, 30th June.

Burnham, P. (1985) What is countryside management? *Ecos* **6** pp. 24-27.

Carson, R.L. (1962) *Silent Spring*. London: Hamish Hamilton.

Carter, E.S. (1988) Farming and wildlife advisory groups - conservation advice through partnership. *Agricultural Progress* **63** pp. 52-57.

Cattermull, C.C. (1951) In the beginning: 18. Seale-Hayne Agricultural College. *Agricultural Progress* **XXVI** (1) pp. 61-67.

Dowrick, G.J. (1979) Meeting the education needs of the agricultural industry. *Agricultural Progress* **54** pp. 66-73.

Edwards-Ker, D.R. (1931) Seale-Hayne Agricultural College. *Journal of the Bath and West and Southern Counties Society* **V** pp. 59-64.

Green, B (1981) *Countryside conservation: the protection and management of amenity ecosystems.* London: George Allen and Unwin.

Hall, C. (1994) One countryman to another. *The Countryman* **99** pp. 127-131.

McInerey, J. (1986) Agricultural policy at the crossroads. *Agricultural Progress* **62** pp. 11-25.

Mishen (1967) *The costs of economic growth.* London: Pelican Press.

Moore, H.I. (1964) Seale-Hayne Agricultural College. (Unpublished document)

Presswell, P.J. (1983) The Seale-Hayne saga. (Unpublished document)

Richards, S. (1994) *Wye College and its world - a centenary history.* Kent: Wye College Press.

Rogers, A., Blunden, J. and Currey, N. (1985) *The Countryside Handbook.* The Open University in association with the Countryside Commission. London: Croom Helm.

Seale-Hayne College (1972) Proposal to offer a Higher National Diploma in Natural Resources and Rural Economy (Land Use and Environmental Studies). Newton Abbot: Seale-Hayne College (Internal document).

Sells, R. (1978) *From seedtime to harvest: the life of Frank Horne.* Cambridge: Hobsons Press.

Slee, R.W. (1988) The development of higher level courses in rural resource management. *Agricultural Progress* **63** pp. 39-43.

Wibberley, G.P. (1980) Is agriculture being given too dominant a place in British land use? *Agricultural Progress* **55** pp. 98-102.

Wibberley, G.P. (1985) Agricultural careers and course evaluation. *Agricultural progress* **60** pp. 70-73.

Winnifrith, J. (1970) The clash between conservationists and farmers. In Barber, D., *Farming and wildlife: a study in compromise.* Proceedings of the Silsoe Conference, Silsoe, Bedfordshire.

# 10 Environmental policy in further and higher education

*Jonathan Horner*

## Abstract

There has been considerable interest shown by employers in improving environmental performance and developing environmental policy. Whilst early progress in this field tended to come from larger businesses and industry, smaller employers and educational establishments are now beginning to develop policies. This paper briefly reviews the development of UK corporate environment policy, considering both environmental management systems and environmental reporting. Educational environmental policy development is then examined, including reference to relevant aspects of the Toyne report on environmental responsibility in further and higher education (DFE, 1993). Roehampton Institute London is used as a case study, being considered a fairly typical higher education establishment as regards environmental policy development. Environmental policy-related undergraduate work at the Institute is used to illustrate one way in which some progress on Toyne's recommendations has been made. It demonstrates that students can play a significant role in the development of environmental policy not only within educational establishments, but also to some extent in local business and industry, by providing advice on environmental improvements.

# Introduction

Early progress in developing environmental policy by UK employers came mainly from large industries which have major impacts on the environment. The focus was particularly on reducing pollution of the local environment and minimising health and safety risks for employees. Whilst the stimulus for improvement often came from legislative authorities, industry has increasingly recognised the marketing and public relations benefits of improving environmental performance. More recently, a wider range of non-industrial organisations have begun to examine their environmental performance. This has been considered from a wider view point, to include issues such as the conservation and sustainable use of resources and the maintenance of biodiversity.

The increased interest shown by organisations in environmental policy has led to a demand for systematic advice and standardised procedures for assessment. Such environmental management systems are now in existence, although the methodology for their implementation and verification/certification is still evolving. British Standard 7750 Specification for Environmental Management Systems came into effect in March 1992 (BSI, 1992). This was followed in 1993 by the European Community Ecomanagement and Audit Scheme (EC, 1993). The latter requires site-specific environmental statements which must be validated by an external accredited verifier. An International Standard, ISO 14001, which is the international equivalent of BS 7750 and bears considerable resemblance to it, is currently being prepared. Verification of such systems and consequent environmental reports by an independent third party would clearly help to improve the credibility of environmental performance with shareholders, customers and the general public. Further details concerning the verification of environmental reports is provided by Evans and Warris (1995). Organisations now have recognised, structured procedures for demonstrating environmental commitment and for judging their environmental performance.

Increasingly, companies are reporting annually on their environmental performance. Frequently, this is in the form of an environment section in the Company Annual Report, although some companies produce a separate environment report. In 1994, sixty-six of the one hundred Financial Times top companies reported on the environment in their annual report, thirty four producing separate reports (KPMG, 1995). Reports are becoming more objective, including details of emissions and in some cases, the inclusion of quantitative targets for improving environmental performance. More companies are providing assessment of individual sites and adopting environmental management systems such as those already mentioned. In 1994, six of the Financial

Times top companies sought independent verification of the content of their environment reports (KPMG, 1995).

A number of environmental award schemes have been initiated to reward companies for good environmental reporting and performance. For example, the British Business Commitment to the Environment Awards were established as long ago as 1975. At that time, there were few environmental policies and relatively few entrants for the awards. There has been a steady increase in the number and quality of entrants. The judges look for long term environmental commitment extending beyond legal requirements and commercial necessity. In 1992, British Telecom plc launched their Environmental Supplier awards. It rewards supply companies for innovation in minimising the environmental impact of their processes and activities. All such awards provide an added incentive for companies to improve their environmental performance.

# Environmental policy development in further and higher education

There has been increasing awareness in educational establishments of the need for greater environmental responsibility and many are now investigating ways of improving their environmental performance. One major initiative came from the Committee of Directors of Polytechnics (CDP). It declared an intention to promote greater awareness of environmental issues through curricular developments and by reducing the environmental impact of institutional practice. They appointed a National Co-ordinator for the Greening of Polytechnics and several publications including *Greening Polytechnics* (CDP, 1990) and *Greening the Curriculum* (CDP, 1991) ensued. The former report described the greening of institutional practice whilst the latter considered the introduction of environmental criteria into the curriculum. Both provide a range of examples of existing environmental initiatives in the then Polytechnics (now 'new' universities). A guide to environmental action in Further Education Colleges soon followed, produced by the Further Education Unit in collaboration with the Council for Environmental Education (FEU, 1992). Three important criteria for developing environmental policy in further education colleges were stressed:

> the need to develop a sustainable future, the need for a whole-institution response and environmental education for all
>
> (FEU, 1992)

159

In 1991, the Greening of Higher Education Council (GHECO) was established to promote a greater awareness of environmental issues in universities and colleges. Its first newsletter was published in October 1993. They have recently undertaken a survey of environmental management in UK universities, results of which are likely to be published towards the end of 1995.

The importance and significance of greening further and higher education was stressed by a Department for Education report (DFE, 1992) on Environmental Responsibility - a report of a Committee on Environmental Education in Further and Higher Education chaired by Peter Toyne. Amongst its recommendations of relevance to this paper were that:

1　Every FHE institution, after consultation with its staff and students, should formally adopt and publicise, by the beginning of the academic year 1994/95, a comprehensive environmental policy statement together with an action plan for its implementation.
2　Institutions should seek to improve their dialogue with employers (who should be willing to reciprocate).
3　Each institution should adopt a policy for the development of environmental education.
4　The Department for Education, the Welsh Office and the Department of the Environment should investigate the feasibility of establishing a national awards scheme to recognise outstanding progress by individual institutions in the development of environmental education, and in the improvement of their overall environmental performance as institutions.

(DFE, 1992)

The report recommends that the strategies adopted in further and higher education should be:

akin to the corporate environmental strategies which a rapidly increasing number of companies are adopting

(DFE, 1992)

At the time of writing, response to the Toyne report amongst colleges and universities would appear to have been somewhat patchy. Many establishments have agreed some form of environmental policy, but whether there has been much co-ordinated action as regards implementation and actual introduction of environmental initiatives is debatable. Willis (1994) suggests that where progress is being made, it is often in the form of *ad hoc* measures which are unofficial and have only a short term future. Only a few establishments have officially appointed environmental co-ordinators/managers. A recent survey of eighty-five universities indicated that just twelve of them have an officially appointed member of staff to advance environmental issues, of which four are only part-time appointments (Willis, 1994). The majority of the posts in question appear to be of fixed duration. Successful environmental policy is a continuous and evolving process which is not suddenly going to be completed after a fixed period of time!

A few universities have made notable progress in developing environmental policy. For example, the University of Central Lancashire published an Environmental Audit Project in 1993 (University of Central Lancashire, 1993). The University of Manchester has an 'Environmental Project Assistant' and the University of Cambridge appointed a full-time Environmental Officer in 1995, albeit only for a three year period. The University of Greenwich has appointed an 'Environmental Development Officer' and De Montfort University has an 'Environmental Audit Officer'. Perhaps the most ambitious and praiseworthy attempts at greening universities have occurred at the Universities of Strathclyde and Edinburgh. The former has introduced an Environmental Management System to meet the requirements of BS 7750, the most important part of which is an environmental management manual which encompasses general management, management system and environmental procedures (McDonach et al, 1994). The latter opened an 'Environmental Teaching and Research Office' in 1994 with two full-time staff members (De la Coeur, personal communication). As de la Coeur (1995) points out, new building programmes provide an obvious opportunity for adopting best environmental practice. He refers to new buildings at the University of East Anglia and Linacre College, Oxford, as examples. Cheltenham and Gloucester College of Higher Education and Farnborough College of Technology are referred to in the same article as not only having environmentally sound buildings, but also as being good examples of what can be achieved in terms of overall institutional 'greening'. For example, he notes that Cheltenham and Gloucester College has been implementing a comprehensive environmental strategy including energy efficiency and transport policies and that Farnborough College also has comprehensive environmental management. The latter is considered especially praiseworthy for composting most of its food waste in wormeries and in running a comprehensive independent recycling programme. Peter de la Coeur is Director of GHECO, which was referred to earlier, and its newsletter 'Greening Universities' provides regular updates on environmental policy development in higher education.

In FE Colleges, the DFE (1992) refers to a number of establishments which have made some progress in developing environmental policy. For example, environmental policy statements are cited for Accrington and Rossendale College and Barnet College, and the former was undertaking an environmental audit/review. Colleges with 'green working groups' are also listed. Irvine and Ponton (1991) describe some of the factors which might be considered in promoting green policies in colleges. A further report on developing the environmental education curriculum in further education colleges, being prepared by the Further Education Development Agency (FEDA), should be published by the end of 1995. In response to the Toyne report, the Further Education Funding Council (FEFC, 1993) noted that PICKUP funds in 1993-94 have included allocations for a number of professional development projects in the environmental area and that environmental criteria would be taken into account in its assessment of applications for capital projects (FEFC, 1993).

The introduction of an environmental award scheme, as recommended by Toyne, could provide an incentive for environmental policy development by management. In the short term, colleges might be able to introduce their own form of awards scheme based on competition between classes or departments. However, as Toyne also suggests, an even greater stimulus could be provided by Funding Councils if colleges and universities were to be assessed on environmental performance, and were awarded funding based on their environmental ratings.

## Roehampton Institute London's developing environmental policy

Having briefly reviewed the development of corporate and educational environmental policy, consideration will now be given to environmental policy development in the Roehampton Institute London, an Institute of the University of Surrey, where the author is employed. The Institute, sited in South West London and having over 6000 full- and part-time students, consists of four colleges each set in attractive landscaped gardens with listed buildings. It is fortunate in having sites of considerable ecological interest with species of note including badgers, newts and herons. The environment is recognised as being important both from an educational point of view (there are long established biology, environmental studies, geography and social biology undergraduate programmes) and for enhancing recruitment and developing community relationships.

Roehampton Institute London is perhaps typical of many educational establishments with regard to its environmental policy development. It has made some progress on specific environmental initiatives and has a draft environmental policy statement awaiting approval and adoption by Council. As long ago as 1990, a presentation on environmental strategy was made to the Institute management by the author and a representative from a company of environmental management consultants. In the same year, a brief section on environmental issues appeared in the Annual Report of the Institute. However, this was very much a one-off occurrence and no progress had been made with regard to either regular annual reporting or adoption of an environmental management system which, as referred to earlier, is becoming increasingly common in business and industry.

The Institute established a Strategic Advisory Group on the Environment (SAGE) in 1993, to develop an environmental policy and to initiate environmental improvements. The group consists of academics from a range of subject disciplines (including the author) and management staff. Included are biologists, who have been recognised as having an essential role to play in developing environmental policy (Horner, 1994). A draft environmental policy statement as shown in Figure 10.1 has been prepared after considerable discussion and is currently awaiting approval by the Institute governing body (Council). The intention is that by drawing on available expertise within the Institute, SAGE will place before the Health and Safety Committee appropriate development programmes for consideration. The Committees will determine the most appropriate means of consultation with all appropriate parties within the Institute before recommending such programmes, suitably amended where necessary, for adoption by Council. In meeting its statutory obligations, Council has vested in the Rector, as Chief Executive, responsibility for the management of environmental issues and he will formally report to Council on an annual basis, and more frequently as may be necessary, on the Institute's environmental performance. Council should now have a strategic plan for the environment identifying the manner in which environmental issues are to be developed over the next three years, together with a method of monitoring progress against the standards set in individual documents which will be produced as the need arises.

As with many educational establishments, whilst a policy is being agreed, greater management commitment is ideally required to encourage the initiation of environmental improvements and to develop a full environmental strategy (Horner, 1993). A number of environmental initiatives have already been introduced regardless of environmental policy both by management and by environmentally concerned individuals. Collaboration with, and sponsorship by, business and industry has played an important role for some of the initiatives (Horner,

This Environmental Policy has been produced to reflect the commitment of Council to the need for progressive development of environmental care by the conservation and sustainable use of natural resources and minimisation of pollution. This will require the development of environmental awareness amongst staff and students with everyone being given the opportunity of suggesting ways of improving our Institute's environment. Individual roles and responsibilities for achieving these objectives will be reflected in the production of a range of environmental guidance documents identifying the personal and departmental performance standards to be achieved.

Central to the above will be the Council's commitment to achieving the following:

1 Optimising energy use
2 Reducing waste
3 Developing an environmentally appropriate buildings policy
4 Maintaining and improving the quality of college grounds
5 Encouraging the use of less environmentally damaging modes of travel
6 Ensuring an environmental input into purchasing
7 Promoting the status of environmental issues within the academic life of the Institute

Council's duties will be conducted in accordance with the requirements of the relevant statutory provisions and best practice. In accepting its responsibilities it wishes to draw the attention of all staff and students to the need for cooperation in achieving the objectives contained in this policy.

In establishing this positive and progressive approach to the management of the environment, Council recognises the need for staff and students to be consulted and involved. Essential tools in this process are Campus Health and Safety Committees which facilitate management, staff and students working together to achieve the common objectives of an environmentally friendly place in which to work and study. This will require personnel receiving an appropriate level of training and clear identification of responsibilities.

**Figure 10.1  Roehampton Institute London -**
             **Draft environmental policy statement**

1993). For example, considerable success has been achieved with recycling initiatives thanks to efforts made by the author - who considers himself, and is considered by many, as the Institute's (unofficial) Environmental Advisor! Thanks to a grant from the Shell Better Britain Campaign and funding from one of the College Student Unions, bottle banks have been established at two of the colleges. A local London borough collects the glass and the money generated is sent to local and national charities. An added bonus is the considerable saving made on waste disposal costs. Similar schemes are operating successfully for the recycling of paper, drink cans and laser toner cartridges. Students and staff clearly have an important role to play in contributing to the success of these schemes. Roehampton Institute students formed a 'Roehampton Environment and Conservation Team' (REACT) several years ago which has organised meetings and environmental activities which have helped to contribute to increasing environmental awareness and environmental improvements. For example, one project involved the restoration of a pond and fountain in a grade II listed garden in one of the colleges. As students become more environmentally aware, colleges which have a 'green' profile will be seen as more attractive places in which to study.

## Environmental policy and student projects

To demonstrate the application of the curriculum to environmental policy development, some possibilities for student work in this field will now be described. The author has developed a new module for the undergraduate Environmental Studies Programme which provides students with a practical introduction to environmental policy. The overall objective of the module is for students to produce an environmental case study report of a specific business or industry. The case study selected must be a discrete site, not a whole company in general (for example, the Abbey National Building Society Putney branch as opposed to The Abbey National plc). The emphasis of the case study is on the practical investigation of environmental considerations of the chosen business or industry. Students produce a structured, appropriately referenced report under the sections listed in Figure 10.2. There is scope for obtaining information from a wide variety of sources as suggested in Figure 10.3, but the major emphasis is on collaboration with the selected business or industry and observation of resource use and environmental impact. In many cases, students select an organisation where they are employed part-time or have been employed in the past. This is commonly either an employer local to the Institute or local to the student's accommodation.

Abstract

Introduction - including aims, product details, process descriptions, environmental impacts of similar establishments

Method - including location map and sources of information

Environmental Impacts - including pollution, conservation and legal aspects

Recommended Improvements

References

Appendices - including correspondence record and any data generated

**Figure 10.2   Case study section headings**

Textbooks/Journals

Newspapers/Magazines

Local Library/Local Maps

Local Councils - especially Planning and Environmental Health Departments

Local Population - for example a brief questionnaire survey might be conducted

National Rivers Authority (NRA)

Her Majesty's Inspectorate of Pollution (HMIP)

Site Visit/Conducted Tour

Employee Interviews/Questionnaire

Similar Business/Factory

**Figure 10.3   Possible information sources**

However, since the module encompasses a vacation period, employers in student's home towns are often selected. Employment provides a useful head start with existing knowledge of products and processes as well as contacts within the company. However, parental or relative employment, or frequent visits (for example to a shop or leisure centre) can also be helpful in this respect. Contact with employers can actually provide future employment possibilities for students.

Complementing the case study investigation, students attend a structured series of lectures dealing with topics such as environmental impact assessment, case studies of business and industrial greening, environmental policy and environmental management systems. An important component of this is the invitation of guest speakers from business and industry to talk about environmental policy development in their own organisations. For example in 1995, speakers included representatives from ICI plc and the London Borough of Richmond Upon Thames. As a result of the latter, collaborative links have developed between the Institute and the Borough with regard to Local Agenda 21 and a final year student research project involving an investigation of suspected contaminated land is being established. Figure 10.4 lists examples of more than 100 projects which have been completed for this module since its inception in 1993. It has certainly helped to increase dialogue with employers as recommended by the Toyne report.

Several students have selected one of the Institute's own colleges as a case study for this module, resulting in some useful recommendations for environmental improvement. However, perhaps more useful in terms of educational environmental policy are student projects dealing with more specific aspects of the environment, and involving much more in-depth coverage of topics, including appropriate monitoring. A number of possible study areas of relevance to environmental policy development are listed in Figure 10.5. The precise nature of the work carried out could be geared to projects in either further or higher education. For example, an undergraduate project might involve monitoring certain environmental parameters within the establishment requiring careful attention to experimental design and statistics. Some form of population survey might be involved, which would require the construction of appropriate questionnaires to allow subsequent statistical analyses. A number of such projects have been conducted at Roehampton Institute as final year research dissertations. For example, one recent study investigated current recycling facilities to assess their effectiveness and to discover the attitudes of staff and students to recycling. An attempt was made to compare the college's performance on a number of recycling parameters based on a five star system. The dissertation concluded with recommendations for improving the future management of recycling facilities.

---

Champion Timber, New Malden

Cheltenham General Hospital

Chester Zoo

Fujitsu Factor, Durham

Hand-In-Hand Public House, Wimbledon

Kitfair Textiles, East London

Leisure Centre, Barnstaple

Lloyds Bank, Sandown, Isle of Wight

Oxfam Shop, Putney

Tesco, Colchester

---

**Figure 10.4   Some examples of case studies 1994/1995**

---

Catering and the Environment

Environmental Attitudes and Awareness

Heating Survey

Lighting Survey

Litter Survey

Mail Survey (eg. to what extent are reusable envelopes used?)

Open Windows Survey

Recycling Survey

Transport to Work Survey

Wildlife Audit

---

**Figure 10.5   Some ideas for project themes in developing educational environmental policy**

This type of project work is increasingly being undertaken in a number of colleges and universities. For example, Merritt (1994) refers to a number of student projects conducted at the University of Greenwich, which included a waste audit of the Deptford Campus, a study of environmental impacts of university buildings and a study of energy and environmental performance of new homes built by a local company. In further education, students at Langley College produced plans for landscaping a quadrangle and at Farnham College, students conducted a project to establish a small company within their college to recycle aluminium cans (FEU, 1992).

## Conclusions

It seems very likely that by the turn of the century all further and higher education colleges will be expected to have environmental policies in place, and that there may be financial rewards for those exemplifying good practice. Some colleges and universities have already established policies and practices. However, in many cases environmental initiatives have been *ad hoc* measures, or have been introduced by staff who are only part-time or on fixed term contracts. While environmental management systems are becoming increasingly common in business and industry, there is as yet only one example of a nationally recognised system operating in an educational establishment. In developing environmental policy, colleges and universities need to involve all staff and students in the greening process. Considerable assistance and progress can be achieved by students conducting environmental policy related projects, some ideas for which have been presented in this paper.

## Acknowledgements

I would like to thank Richard Fisk, Health and Safety Adviser, and Professor Vince Gardiner, Head of Environmental and Geographical Studies, Roehampton Institute London for commenting on the draft of this article. Thanks are also due to Peter de la Coeur (The Greening of Higher Education Council (GHECO)) and Chris Parkin, FEDA, for providing useful information.

GHECO is at 120A Marlborough Road, Oxford, OX1 4LS.

# Bibliography

British Standards Institute (1992) *Specification for Environmental Management Systems*. BS 7750. Milton Keynes: BSI.

Committee of Directors of Polytechnics (1990) *Greening Polytechnics*. London: CDP

Committee of Directors of Polytechnics (1991) *Greening the Curriculum*. London: CDP

de la Coeur, P. (1995) The Green Teams are Coming to Your Town. *Times Higher Education Supplement* 1169 vii.

Department for Education (1993) *Environmental Responsibility - an Agenda for Further and Higher Education*. London: HMSO

European Community (1993) Eco-Management and Audit Scheme. *Official Journal of the European Communities* 36 L168.

Evans, D.E. and Warris, A. (1995) Verification of Corporate Environmental Reports. *Environmental Assessment* 3 (1) pp. 12-14.

Further Education Funding Council (1993) Further Education Funding Council Report Number 8. London: FEFC.

Further Education Unit (1992) *Colleges Going Green - a Guide to Environmental Action in Further Education Colleges*. London: FEU.

Horner, J.M. (1993) Business Collaboration and Sponsorship of Environmental Initiatives at the Roehampton Institute of Higher Education. *Greener Management International* 3 pp. 35-40.

Horner, J.M. (1994) Environmental Policy - The Biologists' Contribution. *Biologist* 41 (5) pp. 188-190.

Irvine, S. and Ponton, A. (1991) Towards a Greening of FHE. *National Association of Teachers of Further and Higher Education Journal* 16 (1) pp. 14-17.

KPMG (1995) *UK Environmental Reporting Survey 1994*. London: KPMG.

McDonach, K., Yaneske, P.P. and Emslie, S.V. (1994) *FHE and BS7750: Environmental Management Systems*. In Summary of Talks from Greening the Campus: Environmental Management in Higher Education, Conference, Regent's College, London. Oxford: Greening of Higher Education Council.

Merritt, Q. (1994) Greener Which. *Greening Universities*. 1 (2) p. 13.

University of Central Lancashire (1993) *Environmental Audit Project*. Preston: University of Central Lancashire.

Willis, K. (1994) Environmental Initiatives in British Universities. *Greening Universities* 1 (2) pp. 1-2.

# 11 Environmental education and the general public

*Robert Stephenson*

## Abstract

The growing importance of the concept of environmental sustainability has given renewed emphasis to the need to inform the general public and involve them in the environmental debate. As yet there is no nationally agreed mechanism for this process. The public encounter information from a variety of sources; those examined here are the media, suppliers of goods, employers, environmental organisations and local government especially through their actions on Local Agenda 21. Examples are examined in order to consider their ability and enthusiasm to provide information to a wide cross-section of the public. Particular emphasis is placed on the limitations on information transmission imposed by social and economic factors, and their effect on limiting personal action for the environment.

## Introduction

This chapter is concerned with the ways in which the public receive information on environmental issues. It specifically excludes direct involvement in vocational and academic education courses.

It is now twelve years since the United Nations asked Gro Harlem Brundtland to establish and chair the World Commission on Environment and Development (WCED). This event marked the point at which the intimate connection between environmental issues and development issues was firmly acknowledged at an international level. The final report of the WCED brought environment and development together, in what is still one of the best known definitions of sustainable development, as

> development that meets the needs of the present without compromising the ability of future generations to meet their own needs.
> (WCED, 1987)

Since then the 1992 United Nations Conference on Environment and Development at Rio brought together 179 countries as signatories to an agreement for a programme of wide consultation designed to draw up international, national and local agendas of action which will be necessary to move us towards sustainability. This 'Agenda 21' process is due to be completed in 1996. Given the importance of this process it would be a retrograde step to consider the general public's encounters with environmental education without reference to the role of sustainability.

## The three strands of effective environmental education

In 1990 the UK government published 'This Common Inheritance' (HMSO) as a statement of Britain's environmental strategy

> It is essential, if environmental policies are to achieve their objective, that there is a wide public awareness of the issues at stake and their importance to the future of the planet and future generations. Education has an essential part to play.
> (HMSO, 1990)

This statement appears to require no more than raised awareness amongst the population, in order that they be willing to go along with the established environmental policies. This kind of language, which appears to separate the population from the decision-making process, and which assumes a hierarchical structure controlled from the top, is a long way from the active involvement assumed in the elements of environmental education as stated by the National Curriculum Council (NCC). In 'Curriculum Guidance 7' (1990) the NCC state that environmental education comprises three linked components:

- education **about** the environment - to provide awareness, knowledge and understanding
- education **in** or **through** the environment - to develop curiosity about, and a personal response to, the environment
- education **for** the environment - to promote active participation and finding solutions.
  (NCC, 1990)

These three strands build upon each other, the combination of knowledge and emotional involvement leading to the need to take action. The best environmental education will embrace all three strands.

## Factors influencing the effectiveness of environmental inputs

Many of the routes through which people receive environmental information are not intended as educational in the manner described above. This will have an influence on the effectiveness of the information received. In addition, different groups within the population will encounter different environmental inputs and their initial circumstances will affect the way they respond to the experiences. These key factors will be addressed as each of the sources of environmental inputs are examined but the initial conditions of the individuals is also worthy of separate consideration.

Are there any preconditions which must be met before individuals feel able to participate in any or all of the three stages of effective informal environmental education? The work of Maslow (1954) suggests that most people need to have resolved their basic physiological needs (food, warmth and shelter) safety needs (security, stability, freedom from fear and anxiety) before they recognise the need to belong. Belonging to a small group, such as a family or close-knit community, can help to meet the more basic needs, but belonging to more distant or abstract groups is unlikely to occur until the basic physiological and safety needs are met. It is exactly these abstract and distant forms of belonging which are necessary in order for anything but the most local and immediate forms of environmental concern to grow. If this is accepted, it should come as no surprise that, in recent structured interviews, young men on Youth Training Schemes and unemployed men showed little enthusiasm for the 'quality of life' issues underlying sustainability. They felt they needed more 'quantity of life' first. As one said:

> What it boils down to is if you've got nothing you've not got a quality of life, have you?
>
> (MacNaglen et al, 1995)

The meeting of basic needs forms several chapters in Agenda 21, as is emphasised in the Local Government Management Board's summary (LGMB, 1993), but this broader view of environmental issues is not yet the mainstream interpretation, possibly because it challenges views accepted by many in the current political climate.

173

# Informal educational channels: the media

The media are a major source of environmental information, embracing local issues in regional and sub-regional papers and going up to national and international issues in the national press and television. Television news coverage tends to be shallow, rarely exploring the background to an item in any depth. Greater detail is provided in documentary programmes, but these tend to have small audiences, usually of people who have an existing interest in the issue.

The national newspapers do not all give equal weight to the environment. This has clear implications for access to information in different readership groups and was well illustrated in coverage of the meeting of the United Nations Framework Convention on Climate Change, held in Berlin from the 28th March to the 7th April 1995. According to a report in the Guardian (Russel-Jones, 1995) there was no mention of the conference, or the information coming from it, in the Daily Express, Daily Mail, Daily Mirror and Today. The Sun similarly failed to find space for it. The Daily Telegraph made only a brief mention of the conference though the Sunday Telegraph carried an article on rising insurance costs and climate change. The Times and Independent carried no reports but both had articles which seemed designed to reduce the importance of the issue (The Independent did allow a reply from the Chair of Friends of the Earth). Only the Guardian and the Financial Times produced several articles on the range of news coming from the conference.

The poor dissemination of information is highlighted when the daily circulation of these papers is considered (Table 11.1).

**Table 11.1    Daily circulation of newspapers with coverage of the United Nations framework convention on climate change**

| Good coverage | | No coverage | |
|---|---|---|---|
| Guardian | 397,139 | Sun | 4,085,828 |
| Financial Times | 290,954 | Daily Mirror | 2,488,807 |
| | | Daily Mail | 1,813,645 |
| | | Daily Express | 1,287,400 |
| | | Today | 563,565 |
| TOTALS | 688,093 | | 10,239,245 |

Source: Audit Bureau of Circulation, data for April 1995

The fact that well known environmental journalists such as Geoffrey Lean, David Nicholson-Lord and John Vidal work for the broadsheet newspapers and that Greenpeace advertise on the cover of broadsheet papers suggests that it is the better educated, professional and better paid classes which have more time for environmental concerns. The membership profile of many environmental pressure groups is also significantly weighted towards better educated, professional people.

## Environmental action and social class

Some evidence supporting the idea that the higher social classes have more time and money for environmental concerns can be found in the Department of the Environment's Survey of Public Attitudes to the Environment (HMSO, 1994). Table 11.2 is a list of personal actions taken for environmental reasons and shows (amongst other breakdowns) the percentage of each social group taking each action "on a regular basis". Many of the actions can be grouped under one of three headings,

- actions having a financial cost
- actions having storage and time costs
- actions having a financial benefit.

Organically grown food and bottled water impose direct costs which will have smaller impacts on the professional and managerial classes. Those same classes may also have more space at home to store materials for recycling. Raised environmental concern (possibly linked to high consumption) may also motivate them. The steeper fall in composting activity through the classes may relate to availability of time for gardening; it does not relate to absence of gardens because only households with gardens were included in the analysis. Household fuel use shows little class-related variation, perhaps because it offers direct financial savings which can be achieved with very little expenditure. The last two actions show an interesting reverse in trend with the unskilled class showing greatest action in situations where environmental benefits go hand in hand with financial benefits. One broad brush summary of this information would be as in the following paragraphs:

Personal action for the environment is reported across all social classes. The more popular actions are those without financial costs, though other factors (available time, domestic space, guilt) lead to higher participation amongst the higher social classes. Actions which offer financial savings without significant inconvenience are popular with between 25% and 35% of all social classes whilst actions with direct financial costs are more common in the higher classes.

**Table 11.2  Personal actions taken for environmental reasons:**
**the percentage of each social class taking action on a regular basis**

| | *Percentage taking regular action* | | | |
|---|---|---|---|---|
| | Social Class I/II | Social Class III | Social Class IV | Social Class V |
| FINANCIAL COST | | | | |
| Bought organically produced food | 18 | 9 | 10 | 12 |
| Used bottled or filtered water | 35 | 26 | 25 | 19 |
| EXTRA STORAGE AND TIME COSTS | | | | |
| Saving paper for recycling | 56 | 49 | 38 | 40 |
| Use a bottle bank | 58 | 45 | 34 | 30 |
| Made compost | 30 | 24 | 17 | 17 |
| FINANCIAL BENEFIT | | | | |
| Kept down use of electricity/gas | 35 | 32 | 31 | 34 |
| Cut down car use for short domestic journeys | 25 | 27 | 25 | 32 |
| Used low energy bulbs in the home | 15 | 16 | 17 | 19 |

Source:  HMSO (1994)

Finally it is worth noting that the one regular action (not shown in the above table) with most potential for environmental good ('deliberately used public transport instead of a car') was carried out by either seven or eight per cent of each social class. The combination of extra financial cost and inconvenience was too much for over ninety per cent of the sample groups. The importance of these negative factors is revealed elsewhere in the survey, where there was overwhelming support (92%) for more, and more reliable, public transport, but only one third of respondents wanted drivers to be charged for using certain roads and less than one in five (19%) felt there should be an energy tax on fuels.

# Reaching the people: environmental education initiatives

There is clearly a widespread interest in behaving in an environmentally sound manner provided financial cost and inconvenience can be minimised. This has certainly been the aim of many businesses supplying our consumer goods.

## 1   Retailer and manufacturer initiatives

Annual surveys of green activism conducted by MORI and reported by Worcester (1994) reveal why manufacturers and retailers now promote products for their environmental qualities. Each year a sample of 2000 people were asked if they had 'selected one product over another because of its environmentally friendly packaging, formulating or advertising'. The following percentages responded positively:

**Table 11.3  Percentage of individuals selecting products on perceived environmental qualities**

| YEAR | 1988 | 1989 | 1990 | 1991 | 1992 | 1993 |
|------|------|------|------|------|------|------|
| %    | 19   | 47   | 50   | 49   | 40   | 44   |

Source:  Worcester (1994)

A more recent survey, by Mintel and reported by Nicholson-Lord (1994), found that the proportion of consumers who look for green products and are willing to pay more for them rose from 53% in 1990 to 60% in 1994. On average they would pay 13% more for green products. Over the same period the proportion claiming to be unaware of, or unconcerned about green issues fell from 18% to 10%. In addition there has been a significant rise in the number of green consumers in the manual worker category.

Examples of the type of education provided by retailers include the entrance exhibitions in B&Q stores explaining their policies on offering peat substitutes in composts, avoiding peat extracted from sites of special scientific interest and moving to sourcing tropical timbers from sustainably managed forests. In addition many stores have an in-store broadcast system to promote particular lines. These are also used to explain why the store now stocks a range of low organic solvent paints. The store also requires its suppliers to minimise unnecessary packaging and is working towards full 'cradle to grave' audits on all its products.

Such a policy raises awareness about environmental issues in a very large audience and helps to increase interest in going green, but it should also be remembered that the company is profit driven. When the company commenced its move towards more environmental information in 1991, it was reported that they would not ban products with known environmental impacts, but would seek products with as small an impact as possible and provide customers with information to make up their own minds (ENDS, 1991).

The Co-operative Wholesale Society (CWS) recently commissioned a Gallup survey of 30,000 people, which has confirmed that green consumerism is still a real issue for many people (Buckley, 1995). The results of the survey were clear enough to encourage the CWS to embark on a new policy of openness. Battery farm eggs will cease to be 'farm fresh' and will become 'intensively produced'; if a customer wants to know who produces the CWS brand goods, then that information will be given. Buckley quotes Bill Shannon, general manager of Co-op Brands, as saying,

> Consumers are not asking us to nanny them. They want us to give them the information that allows them to take decisions for themselves.

## 2 Organisations as educators of employees

Environmental management of business started in the USA in the early 1970s, where developments are often designed to demonstrate compliance with regulations and to avoid litigation. The early stages of US environmental quality management are well covered in Sewell (1975). A significant development in European environmental management, and a change from using the process as an in-house management tool to an open, public document, occurred when Norsk Hydro published its first environmental audit report in 1990. Their report not only published an audit of environmental impacts but also set targets for improvement and published their progress in reaching those targets. Charles Duff, Development Manager of Norsk Hydro UK, said of their UK report:

> ... we want our environmental report to show everyone from the shop floor upwards that they work for a caring and responsible company.

The process of awareness raising involved all the employees and they were also involved in the regular process of data gathering, which is necessary to monitor progress towards targets (ENDS, 1990).

e 1990 both the European Community and the British Standards
ie have developed formal procedures for implementing
mental management systems (the Environmental Management and
Scheme (EMAS) and BS7750) and, though neither have the
ement for full and open reporting, both schemes include setting
ets and allocating responsibilities; EMAS has a compulsory wide-
ging initial environment review stage which involves examination of
environmental impacts of all the activities of the organisation. Whilst
would be possible to comply with the requirements of either scheme
without fully involving all employees, development work carried out with
the staff of Brighton Health Promotion Unit shows that the system
becomes more properly integrated into an organisation if all the staff
participate (Stephenson, 1993). Following individual interviews with all
the staff, a short series of meetings not only shared existing knowledge
about environmental impacts but also provided an opportunity to broaden
and deepen understanding. Staff were then able to assess the impact of
their own activities (using a specially prepared initial environmental
review checklist) and, at a subsequent meeting, identify potential targets
for improvement. Only at this stage was it necessary to involve the
specialist staff from the Health Authority such as energy, waste and
water managers as well as maintenance and grounds staff. This method
of working allowed the staff of the Health Promotion Unit to feel a sense
of ownership of the process. Informal discussions suggest that this
'bottom-up' approach had the advantage of encouraging staff to adopt
some of the ideas into their home lives.

This 'bottom-up' approach to environmental management has been
adapted and developed for use in schools. Considerable emphasis is put
on involving the wider community through high profile activities which
draw in local businesses and Council departments and attract local media
coverage for the school and its environmental management system
(Stephenson and Mares, 1994). The project, known as Eco-Schools, has
recently been adopted by 'Going for Green', the Government's initiative
for taking the sustainability message to individuals and community
groups.

Whether a school or a business, the adoption of an environmental
management system is not lightly undertaken. The Institute of
Environmental Assessment (France, 1991) reported that (excluding the
chemical industry) only 8% of companies they surveyed had introduced
comprehensive environmental audits. Even the less demanding process of
adopting environmental policies is proving to be slower in the UK than
elsewhere in Europe. A survey by Touche Ross found that 30% of UK
companies had formal environmental policies, compared with 100% in
Germany and 70% in Eire (Touche Ross Associates, 1990). Although

progress may be slow, there is evidence that it has been happening, and more companies are defining environmental policies, though the growth rate has fallen. In 1993, when the Royal Society of Arts introduced their Environmental Management Awards, there were 103 entries; in 1994 there were 71; and in 1995 just 65, although 1995 saw a record number of small firms entering (Clover, 1995). As Clover observed

> The question now is how far other companies lag behind the trend-setters.

## 3    Environmental organisations and public education programmes

Worcester (1994) showed that environmental protection organisations are in an excellent position to inform the public; he reported in the Eurobarometer survey of 1992 that such organisations are trusted by the public eleven times more than public authorities and five times more than the media. Three recent projects involving environmental organisations will be described.

a)   The Global Action Plan (GAP) started in 1990 and was operating in nine countries by the time it was introduced into the UK in 1993. The first GAP UK newsletter (Church, 1990) described it as 'a decentralised action programme' with three main aims:

- To translate global environmental goals into measurable household, workplace and community actions.
- To provide skills and support to enable people to achieve those actions at the personal and local level.
- To collect the results of those actions and feed them back to everyone involved in the programme and to the media.

(Church, 1990)

The original scheme planned to establish teams of households which would use the purchased handbook to examine their production of refuse, use of domestic fuels, water and transport, and shopping habits. The programme would then help them set targets to reduce their impacts and quantify the change. In addition to the mutual support of the team they would have access to a Community Co-ordinator who would be able to help resolve problems and supply local information.

By the time the scheme came to Brighton (in February 1994) there had been several changes. The expensive handbook had become a series of loose-leaf packs, including charts and record cards to simplify data collection. This appeared to be in response to a reluctance amongst UK households to form teams which could share the cost of the handbook. It also aimed to encourage households to record more information. The other main change aimed to offer more support for individual households, with the training of 15 Guides who would make contact with households joining the programme and support and encourage them as each month they gathered and sent in their data and embarked on the next pack. This function was possible because GAP had linked up with the local authority, which had agreed to publicise the scheme in the regular, existing Council mailings to householders. Even with Council publicity the scheme had attracted fewer than 100 households by November 1995 and only four teams consisted of more than one household.

At the end of the first year, GAP Guides in Brighton suggested that many households had not felt able to complete the whole programme and a significant proportion of those who did complete elements of it did so in a partial manner, often failing to complete and return the record cards. This was a particular disappointment because the feedback was designed to encourage continued participation. In contrast, greater success seems to have occurred where GAP was established within companies which could offer support and an ideal situation for people who already knew each other to work together.

What kind of people join GAP? There is no information on the Brighton GAP participants but 77 members of Cumbria GAP returned a questionnaire (GAP, 1994) which revealed that:

- Nearly two thirds (61%) of the lead individuals were female.
- 80% were living with a partner.
- 55% were between 36 and 55 years old with a further 32% over 55 years.
- Nearly two thirds (62%) had a pre-tax annual family income over £15,000.
- 24% had a gross income over £30,000 p.a.

Their newspaper readership tends to confirm that they are mainly better educated, middle classes. Forty per cent read the Guardian, Independent, Telegraph or Times, 10% read the Daily Mail and only 9% read Today, the Express, Mirror or the Sun. A relatively large 22% read no daily paper, which may be related to the 26% who are retired.

It would seem that GAP is probably reaching those with existing environmental concerns, though it may well be increasing their knowledge of environmental matters.

b)  The Small Changes Project, although still in its pilot stage, has gone further than GAP in trying to reach existing groups of people who come together for reasons other than environmental interests. Small Changes was established in June 1994 by the Newcastle-upon-Tyne based New Consumer Ltd, with partial funding from the European Community, with the aim of researching and developing effective methods of providing environmental and lifestyles information to existing women's groups. It is currently (in 1995) working with four national women's organisations on a pilot project which started with a lifestyle survey (3021 sent out, 1571 returned and currently being analysed) to establish baseline data about respondents, their shopping habits, leisure activities, energy and waste related home activities and opinions relating to a range of environmental and ethical issues. A second questionnaire will be administered after groups of women have had an opportunity to work through and discuss the information and ideas in two workpacks. The first workpack, 'The Kitchen', has already been distributed. A second pack, 'The Garden', is now going out. One problem identified by Monica Frisch, the Small Changes project consultant, is preparing material to suit a wide spectrum of initial knowledge (Frisch, 1995). The main innovation of the Small Changes approach seems to be the careful targeting and study of an identifiable group to allow specifically tailored awareness-raising and behavioural change resources to be created. It is therefore unfortunate that the tight timetable has not allowed full analysis of one stage before the next stage has been commenced. It is in the nature of a pilot project that problems of this sort are identified; hopefully there will an be opportunity to make changes for the next phase of Small Changes.

The second questionnaire will provide a measure of the project's success in changing behaviour. In the longer term it is likely that the participants will need to know that their changes have made a difference, a need that was identified early by the Global Action Plan, though their method proved rather too complex for many participants. Perhaps the existing teams of Small Changes can be used to gather locally relevant information and disseminate it to other parts of the women's organisation, to build interest and spread action.

c)  Eco-feedback is a method of involving households in a locality in a high profile scheme to reduce their use of household fuels. It differs from GAP and Small Changes in being a single issue campaign and in offering weekly targets for energy use. The weekly targets are published in local papers, with individual households identifying their target figure by looking for the target against an annual fuel use closest to their own. The tables are based on fuel used in the previous year, adjusted to take account of different weather conditions and incorporating a fuel-saving reduction. Households take weekly meter readings and complete a simple record card. Comparing their figures with the published targets gives a rapid feedback on success. The weekly tables also offer information on energy conservation methods and sources of advice to help participants get closer to the targets.

In the UK Eco-feedback was piloted in Leicester between February and July 1993, under the title 'Save Energy at Home'. The programme involved over 6000 households, initially contacted through a letter and publicity leaflets included in the local free newspaper. The partnership of Leicester Environment City Trust, the New Economics Foundation, British Gas and East Midlands Electricity helped to ensure the scheme received much local media attention as well as coverage by Radio 4 and the Independent (Dawe and Wood, 1993).

A second Eco-feedback project was run in Middlesbrough in the winter of 1993/94. Fifty-six thousand households were invited to participate, 2600 registered and 360 completed the project. The low response is particularly disappointing as the potential barrier to participation (of having to find old records to calculate the previous year's fuel use) was removed in this project because the energy supply companies provided the figures for all registered households. The returned record cards indicated that the 360 households averaged a 5% gas and 2.5% electricity saving with no significant investment costs (Wood, 1995).

Both of the above schemes targeted a large population, but elsewhere in the UK Eco-feedback has been run on a smaller, local community scale. A report on all these schemes found that smaller ones tended to have a better registration rate and higher completion rate. Walker (1995) felt that local support within smaller schemes was a significant factor in accounting for this difference. The face-to-face doorstep contact used in a small Nottinghamshire scheme was correlated with higher participation. Walker also reported that Dutch Eco-feedback schemes attract people from all social classes. This was supported, in Cardiff, by the fact that there was a fifty-fifty split between participants from owner-occupied and rented accommodation. The prime motive given by the Cardiff owner-occupiers was 'saving the environment', whereas the rented sector gave 'saving money' as their prime motive.

# Local government, local agenda 21 and environmental education

Local government, both within the UK and internationally, has taken a leading role in the movement towards sustainability, as defined by the Agenda 21 process. In the UK the Local Government Management Board is disseminating information and promoting action on sustainability on behalf of the Local Authority Associations and the Local Government International Bureau. The scope of Agenda 21 can be summarised by paraphrasing the chapter headings of section one of the Agenda 21 document (summarised by the Local Government Management Board (1993)). It involves the integration of the following environment and development issues (international co-operation, combating poverty, changing consumption patterns, demographics, health and sustainable human settlements) into decision-making at all levels in order to protect and improve natural and built environments. Given the enormity of the task it is not surprising that progress is slow, but the emphasis on involving the whole community (Bishop, 1994) has provided a range of broadly educational projects.

Although every community has its own particular detailed approach for adopting the Local Agenda 21 process, many use a model based on the Environment City approach (Wood, 1994). This model establishes Specialist Working Groups (SWGs) for issues such as built environment, waste and transport. Each Group has a balance of members representing the public, private and voluntary sectors plus ordinary citizens. Representatives of each Group sit on a Forum with senior members of each community sector. The Forum deals with strategic policy matters and ensures co-ordination between the SWGs. An administrative and service function should be provided by the Council, though it is important that the whole is not seen as owned by the Council.

This structure can support a wide variety of activity, from academic debate to grassroots action, but the latter is usually the more powerful way to reach the community, especially where the SWGs recognise that their role includes informing and involving the wider community. Even the best attempts to involve the public cannot reach everyone. Wood (1994) reports that a summer 1994 public attitude survey in the four Environment Cities (Leeds, Leicester, Middlesborough and Peterborough) showed that 47% of the total population knew that their city was an Environment City but only 7% had changed their behaviour, to benefit the environment, as a result of Environment City.

The emphasis on wide community participation arises from the role of capacity building in the UN Agenda 21 document. Capacity building is a central concept of the Agenda 21 process; it is the process of resourcing and developing the abilities of institutions so that they are able to make the necessary changes to move towards sustainability. Capacity building:

> ... is as much concerned with enabling people and organisations to make the necessary changes as with the changes themselves.
>
> (LGMB, 1993)

It has been taken up in a range of advisory publications aimed at local government (Hams et al, 1994, Wood, 1994 and Bishop, 1994) and many parts of the voluntary sector are aware of the need and are demanding greater involvement. Full involvement of the wide local community is still fraught with difficulties; unless it is very carefully presented, there is still a tendency for only a narrow slice of the community to become involved in any issue, for example the consultation process of a planning inquiry. Thomson (1990) quotes US research by Estel (1979) on the make-up of people attending public planning meetings:

- 13% not educated beyond secondary school level
- 38% had done college work
- 48% had college degrees
- 45% had attended over 5 public meetings in the previous 5 years
- 37% held elective or governmental positions.

An interesting model for encouraging wide neighbourhood involvement has been developed by Reading Borough Council with the World Wide Fund for Nature and the Community Education Development Centre (Welsh, 1994). Neighbourhoods are defined by areas with local and common interests: they are typically smaller than wards, having populations of between 2000 and 2500. Defining a neighbourhood tends to identify the local issues and key local individuals. Existing contacts between the Council and key local people are used to introduce the idea of Neighbourhood Agenda 21 and the mechanism to introduce it. Local people are identified to act as facilitators, and are given the necessary training in background environmental matters and group-work skills. The facilitators and key officers work with local groups to explore linkages between existing interests and the Agenda 21 process. These linkages are then developed with local groups through 'capacity building' exercises.

This process should help members of different groups recognise that they have common concerns which can be tackled in partnership with others in their community and representatives from other local bodies. It is intended that this process should lead to a Neighbourhood Agenda 21, written by local people and identifying their priorities for an improved and sustainable quality of life. This will lead to target setting, the identification of easily understood indicators of progress and a monitoring system to chart, and if necessary adjust, progress towards the targets. Once the model has been trialled it will be taken to other local authorities, initially in Wirral, Coventry and Bradford.

## Conclusion

The success of any environmental education programme, in bringing about action for improvement (the third and most important stage of effective environmental education), depends on the balance of concerns of the audience. Those on low incomes will generally be less interested in lower consumption. Holman (1995) suggests that their interests may be in neighbourhood projects such as credit unions, food co-ops, youth clubs, furniture stores, community businesses and play schemes. These projects can be run by the community and meet immediate needs, and are generally compatible with the concept of sustainability. However, if government is still struggling to find ways of getting wide public participation, it is even further from facilitating the empowerment of communities at a neighbourhood level. As Holman concludes:

> The issue is not whether a national neighbourhood fund could be afforded but whether politicians regard local groups as of such value that they should be properly funded.
>
> (Holman, 1995)

The other large sector of society, the middle and higher income groups, generally have a different agenda, one that has been defined, by Galbraith (1992) as the Culture of Contentment. Galbraith defines three requirements for the maintenance of this culture.

- a presumption against government intervention
- a social justification for the untrammelled, uninhibited pursuit and possession of wealth
- a reduced sense of public responsibility for the poor.

(Galbraith, 1992)

These requirements are in conflict with the basic philosophy of sustainability - that all people should work together (consensus building) to ensure everyone has a decent environment (from adequate housing to climatic stability) whilst ensuring the viability of resources for future generations (meeting need but not greed). The selfish nature of the Galbraith model is not in conflict with the actions which the middle classes are willing to take, the question being one of whether they are willing to go beyond simple 'feel-good' actions to ones which challenge the 'culture of contentment'.

In the last few years many public sector, voluntary sector and commercial initiatives have appeared which aim to increase the general public's level of environmental awareness. Very few, however, attempt to explain all the facets of the issues they address. Whilst many encourage modest, light green environmental action, it is the exception which explores the full ramifications of sustainability. Perhaps the ultimate effective tool for promoting effective environmental action is what Porritt (1992) has called 'a necessary supply of disasters'.

## Bibliography

Bishop, J. (ed.) (1994) *Local Agenda 21 Roundtable guidance No 1: Community participation in Local Agenda 21.* Luton: LGMB.

Buckley, N. (1995) Rise of the ethical consumer. *The Financial Times.* London: 27 April.

Church, C. (ed.) (1990) GAP Newsletter No. 1. London: GAP UK.

Clover, C. (1995) Greenery goes from gimmick to a philosophy. *The Times* London: 25 May.

Dawe, G. and Wood, C. (1993) *Stepping stones, the BT environment city review of sustainability.* Lincoln: RSNC The Wildlife Trusts Partnership.

ENDS (1990) Norsk Hydro: a corporate initiative in environmental reporting. *ENDS Report* **185** pp. 13-15, June.

ENDS (1991) B&Q: passing green consumer pressure down the supply chain. *ENDS Report* **203** pp. 12-15, December.

Ertel, M.O. (1979) A survey of research evaluation of citizen participation strategies. *Water Resources Research* **15** pp. 757-763.

France, D. (ed.) (1991) *Auditing: a practical perspective.* Horncastle: Institute of Environmental Assessment.

Frisch, M. (1995) Personal communication, consultation with new consumer. Newcastle-upon-Tyne, 23 June.

Galbraith, J.K. (1992) *The Culture of Contentment.* Harmondsworth: Penguin.

GAP (1994) *Analysis of Global Action Plan questionnaires sent out in August 1994.* London: GAP.

Hams, T., Jacobs, M., Levett, R., Lusser, H., Morphet, J. and Taylor, D. (1994) *Greening your local authority.* London: Longman.

HMSO (1990) *This common inheritance: Britain's environmental strategy.* CM1200, London: HMSO.

HMSO (1994) *1993 Survey of Public Attitudes to the Environment.* London: Government Statistical Service.

Holman, B. (1995) Locals can do it for themselves. *The Guardian.* London: 14 June.

LGMB (1993) *Earth Summit: Rio 92, Supplement No. 2: Agenda 21.* Luton: Local Government Management Board.

MacNaglen, P., Grove-White, R., Jacobs, M. and Wynne, B. (1995) *Public perceptions and sustainability in Lancashire.* Lancaster, Centre for the Study of Environmental Change, for Lancashire County Council.

Maslow, A.H. (1954) *Motivation and personality.* New York: Harper and Row.

NCC (1990) *Curriculum Guidance 7: Environmental Education.* York: National Curriculum Council.

Nicholson-Lord, D. (1994) Green wave washes over mainstream shopping. *The Independent.* London: 14 December.

Porritt, J. (1992) from BBC Radio 4's programme 'Analysis', 15 April.

Russel-Jones, R. (1995) Too hot to handle. *The Guardian.* London: 5 April.

Sewell, G.H. (1975) *Environmental Quality Management.* New Jersey: Prentice-Hall.

Stephenson, R.A.J. (1993) *Developing an assessment method for identifying and measuring the environmental impacts of a community building,* unpublished dissertation, MSc Environmental Impact Assessment, University of Brighton.

Stephenson, R.A.J. and Mares, C. (1994) *Eco-Schools: towards a sustainable lifestyle.* Wigan: Tidy Britain Group.

Thomson, M.A. (1990) Determining impact significance in EIA: a review of 24 methodologies. *Journal of Environmental Management* **30** pp. 235-250.

Touche Ross Consultants (1990) *European management attitudes to environmental issues.* London.

Walker, P. (1995) Personal communication, author of the report on eco-feedback for the Building Research Establishment.

WCED (1987) *Our Common Future.* Oxford: OUP.

Welsh, R. (1994) Neighbourhood Agenda 21: going local in Reading. *Streetwise* **5** (3).

Wood, C. (1994) *Painting by numbers.* Lincoln: RSNC.

Wood, C. (1995) *Stepping Stones II.* Lincoln: RSNC.

Worcester, R. (1994) The sustainable society: what we know about what people think and do. *Values for a sustainable future*, a symposium organised by UNED-UK, RSA and WWF. London: 2 June.

# 12 Education for the environment: from rhetoric to realisation

*Roger Firth and Malcolm Plant*

## Abstract

In response to the socio-ecological crisis and the national and international calls for social transformation towards more sustainable societies, how do we know as environmental educators that we are being effective? As environmental education moves towards greater institutionalisation and a concern for sustainability, are there 'indicators' that environmental educators can use in their efforts to improve effectiveness? Cade (1992) suggested that there is a need for research to identify appropriate 'performance indicators' as a way of taking stock of our investments in young people. The authors argue, however, that performance indicators are both inappropriate and unrealisable. Instead, through their work as teacher educators, they identify the possibility of 'process indicators'. More significantly than indicators, it is argued, if environmental education at all levels is to fulfil the high expectations now being pinned on it, research and pedagogy needs to recover the potential of environmental education from an over-simple equation being made between education, society and 'sustainable development' as defined by the UNCED process and the dominant discourse of development.

We are at a watershed in environmental education. As we move from marginal status towards institutionalisation with much more universal practice we are searching to improve its quality and effectiveness. However, there is no standardised gauge of these improvements - no widely used set of performance indicators or evaluation tools, no agreed standards of quality or

national audit ... Unless research is urgently carried out to find these
indicators, the future health of environmental education is at risk.

(Cade, 1992)

# The proposition

In response to the socio-ecological crisis and within the context of the
international and national calls for social transformation towards more
sustainable lifestyles and societies, how do we know as environmental
educators that we are being effective? Can 'indicators' be identified
which demonstrate improved effectiveness? Cade (1992) argues that the
search for 'performance indicators' is a way of taking stock of our
investments in young people. He also suggests that it is politically
expedient, because it is widely accepted that education and research
which focuses on the tools and methods of evaluation gain greater
political support. He asks whether easily measured, standardised
indicators of the state of environmental education could be identified.
This, he argues, would enable government departments, organisations
and institutions to regularly use these indicators as a means of evaluating
their own performance in environmental education as well as the state of
environmental education at local and national level. The indicators would
provide:

- a common national framework
- a tool for self-evaluation
- accountability and access to information
- a political debating tool
- evidence for publicised claims
- a component of 'state of the environment' reports.

Cade (1992) also points out that this is a timely search for
'performance indicators' with the commercialisation of the OFSTED
inspection of educational institutions, with the continuing government
call for accountability and the growing emphasis on environmental
education and training as a result of the 1992 Earth Summit and
*Agenda 21*.

# The context

Numerous reports indicate that public concern for the environment is at
unprecedented levels in many parts of the world (Dunlap, Gallup and

Gallup, 1992). There is a growing public awareness that human economic activity is increasingly undermining its own future and that of other life-forms, through unsustainable patterns of living. This growing awareness had predictably led to calls for changes to improve the situation, and so profound are the desired changes that they have been termed social transformation, although the notion of transition may be more appropriate. The environment has become a major issue in the political arena both nationally and internationally.

Calls for social transformation need to be placed within wider discussions of social change, which have pointed to changes in a range of elements of contemporary society. Huyssen (1986) refers to a noticeable shift in sensibility, practices and discourse formations which distinguish a postmodern set of assumptions, experiences and propositions from that of a preceding period. By its very nature, talk of social change on such a grand scale is imprecise, even speculative. However, whether these changes mark the end of the modern era and the advent of postmodernity, or at least the beginning of the end, or a more radical phase of modernity (what Giddens (1990) has called high modernity and Beck (1992) calls reflexive modernity), there is sufficient evidence to suggest that the changes which underlie the concept of postmodernity are real and that while it is difficult to gauge their extent and their future, they are more likely to continue than not.

A number of international governmental conferences and reports of the last decade (such as WCED, 1987; IUCN/UNEP/WWF, 1992; UNCED, 1992) have recognised the interdependence of environmental and development issues. The central concern of these reports is the search for sustainable patterns of development and living that can redress present day environmental degradation without jeopardising ecosystems or the resource base for future generations. These international calls for action demonstrate that sustainable development has been legitimated by key decision makers. They reflect the growing awareness of the manifestation of development and other social issues in the bio-physical environment and the complex ways in which patterns of social relationships, cultural forms, political practices and economic institutions are all implicated in the production of a global socio-ecological crisis.

In parallel, the education sector has witnessed the development of environmental education and environmental education research and an exposition of their aims and purposes. However, as Greenall Gough (1993) points out, a Western, Eurocentric and developed worldview articulated by white, middle class English speaking males has dominated the discourse of environmental education for much, if not all, of the past twenty five years. Environmental educators must be aware of this critique of the assumptions upon which environmental education has both developed and is still articulated.

During this time environmental education has progressed from relative obscurity to being widely regarded as a key instrument in response to the socio-ecological crisis and in the development of more sustainable societies. Yet, as Popkewitz (1984 and 1991) points out, this is despite sobering historical analyses to the contrary.

## The context within schools

In Britain, the political and educational rhetoric has been similar:

> Environmental education will need to permeate all levels and aspects of education, beginning with the National Curriculum in schools, continuing in colleges and universities and extending into professional and vocational training. For education the challenge will never be bigger.
> (Chris Patten, former Secretary of State for the Environment, 1990/91)

The Government has endorsed the importance of sustainable development (DoE, 1993) and has paid lip-service to education for sustainability (HMSO, 1990; HMI/DES/BP, 1991; DFE, 1993). The status of environmental education in schools has risen in recent years with this increasing official recognition and more attention has been paid to all aspects of its theory and practice (Sterling, 1992). But the reality for many schools in England and Wales is the very limited entitlement of environmental education within the National Curriculum. The government's commitment to environmental education or education for sustainability can be seriously questioned as a result of the recent pruning of the National Curriculum (the Dearing Report: DFE, 1994) and the publication of *Sustainable Development: The UK Strategy* (DoE, 1993). Neither document makes reference to environmental education within the school curriculum.

The recent NFER (1994) briefing paper *Environmental Education: Teaching Approaches and Students' Attitudes*, funded under phase III of the ESRC Global Environmental Change Programme, which is investigating the effectiveness of environmental education in schools, reported that:

> ... environmental education is delivered in a wide range of ways across secondary schools in England and Wales partly because it is not a statutory element within the National Curriculum. Although recognised as a vital part of compulsory education, it is currently constrained by the pressure to cover large amounts of statutory 'content'.                      (NFER, 1994)

Gayford (1993) further suggests that as a result of the revised subject Orders following the Dearing review, geography becomes almost the exclusive means of formally including environmental education in the curriculum. As the NFER (1994) report argues, this can hardly be regarded as a positive step for environmental education if only because, under the latest proposals for the last two years of compulsory schooling, geography is optional; there is the prospect of those pupils opting out of geography receiving very little if any environmental education in these two years. As Osborn-Jones (1994) has pointed out, there is a very real danger that environmental and development education will become specialist areas, studied for a limited period by a minority of students.

## Contrasting paradigms

Issues of environment, social justice and sustainability pose important questions for the future of human society. They are also important for those who wish to teach for a just and more sustainable future and those who are involved in the education of such teachers (Fien, 1995).

There have been many attempts over the years to outline and classify the sets of coherent values and beliefs (ideologies) which shape environmental education and educational research activity generally. Recent activity (Fien, 1993; Huckle, 1995; Kemmis, Cole and Suggett, 1983; Kemmis, 1991; McTaggart, 1991; Sterling and Cooper, 1992) has been helpful in the identification of different forms of environmental education and environmental education research, and of their potential to contribute to processes of social change. Each of these is related to a philosophical stance that questions what knowledge is, how it is acquired and how it is used. For convenience of argument the classification used here is based on Habermas's (1972 and 1974) theory of knowledge constitutive interests:

- empirical/analytic-technical control and prediction
- interpretive-mutual understanding and communication
- socially critical-empowerment and emancipation.

This classification is widely recognised across the social sciences and is grossly oversimplified in the following summary.

The empirical/analytic approach presumes that knowledge is objective and is produced by causal explanation from outside, and is able to be generalised into theories/theorems that may be used to predict or control future events. Such knowledge is based on evidence gleaned by meticulous and controlled observation. The observer is believed to be dispassionate and detached from the observed.

The interpretive approach presupposes that knowledge is subjective and is constructed by mutual negotiation. Such knowledge is specific to particular situations and localities. The purpose of such knowledge is greater understanding rather than prediction and control.

While sharing some of the assumptions of the interpretive approach, socially critical education declares that knowledge is problematic and reflects structures of power and social inequalities. Such knowledge cannot be value-free. It always embodies the interests of some social group. The preferable outcome of this form of education is social action to improve human life. Knowledge is seen not as adornment but as interventionary ability. Knowledge for its own sake is unconvincing. Knowledge to make the world a better place becomes the only acceptable purpose. But, it should be pointed out that all knowledge has the potential to oppress or emancipate (Foucault, 1977).

These orientations are often not construed as discrete categories by environmental educators, but rather as 'shifting territories' - which are closer or further apart from each other, and to a greater or lesser extent contested - highlighting the inconsistencies and ambiguities within any individual's standpoint (Janse van Rensburg, 1994).

Much recent activity, as a result of the endorsement of sustainable development, has been an attempt to encourage environmental educators to engage in the socially critical or reconstructionist traditions of environmental education, to promote approaches to curriculum planning and pedagogy that can help integrate social justice and ecological sustainability into the educational process of personal and social change, rather than giving their uncritical support to existing educational realities.

## Environmental education

The recent inter-governmental reports have all recognised the importance of education in helping to bring about the extensive social changes needed for sustainable development (WCED, 1987). The 1992 Earth Summit expresses extensively the role of education in relation to sustainable development and concluded:

> Education is critical for promoting sustainable development and improving the capacity of the people to address environment and development issues ... It is critical for achieving environmental and ethical awareness, values and

attitudes, skills and behaviour consistent with sustainable development and for effective public participation in decision making.

(UNCED, 1992)

It appears that one of the challenges for the 1990s is to translate the rhetoric of the reports into reality; to turn the principles of sustainable development into practice.

This appealing rhetoric expresses a common and now conventional view of environmental education and what it needs to accomplish. Yet, the reports seem to be formulating an instrumental or deficit view of environmental education, one in which the aim is to feed more information and awareness-raising experiences into a rather linear process of fairly passive learning. Underpinned by the belief that raising awareness will lead to appropriate changes in attitudes and values and eventually behaviour, the implicit assumption is that there are 'sustainable development' experts who know best; the elements of technicism, reductionism, individualism and behaviourism are conspicuous (Janse van Rensburg, 1994). The belief in an instrumental rationality[1] and the solubility of environmental problems by the application of appropriate techniques (sustainable development) is the context, and the product is an uncritical formulation of environmental education.

## Education for sustainability

The social, economic, political and ecological imperatives of the concept and processes of sustainable development have established a renewed agenda for environmental education which links it very closely with development education. The International Union for the Conservation of Nature (IUCN) has described this new direction for environmental education as 'education for sustainable living' while others prefer to use the term 'education for sustainability' (Fien, 1995).

Education for sustainability requires a reconceptualisation of environmental education and some of the assumptions upon which it has often been based. Much of the dominant discourse in environmental education has been based upon a technocentric or instrumental rationality and approach to environmentalism, which aims to enhance environmental management and control by seeking scientific and technological solutions to urgent environmental problems. In serving this paradigm, young people are initiated into the concepts and technical skills for such solutions to environmental problems without addressing their root social, political and economic causes (Huckle, 1983 and 1995; Fien, 1993 and

1995). In this way, environmental education uncritically supports the way society is currently organised.

We agree that it is vital for educators, researchers and policy-makers to seek ways to ameliorate critical socio-ecological conditions through a critical exploration of sustainability, but we question whether the promotion of a 'sustainable development' perspective in schools will actually contribute in some way to social transformation, or will in the longer term command the professional and social consensus which is necessary to establish environmental education as a major and stable dimension of the school curriculum.

## Sustainable development

The concept of sustainable development has become a significant part of the debate on global environmental-development issues. However, the meaning of sustainable development and the means whereby it is to be realised remain contested (Firth and Plant, 1994). The concept has been shaped through the UNCED process and the dominant discourse of development, which has uncritically connected the two terms 'development' and 'sustainability'. In consequence, this continues to advance an instrumental rationality. The United Nations and national governments have adopted sustainable development without questioning the assumption that growth and further development were necessary, let alone the assumption that they were possible (Chatterjee and Finger, 1994). The concept is being used to politically engineer a social consensus about the core values which ought to govern human interaction with the environment across all sectors of society: business and commercial, institutional, community and individual. We argue that we must collectively un-learn much of the dominant development paradigm of which modern society is both the product and the victim - much of which has been absorbed within environmental education. This also seems a more appropriate focus for research concerned to improve the effectiveness of environmental education.

## Environmental education as social processes of change

Thus, rather than jumping on the sustainable development bandwagon, it is important for environmental educators to assess which ways and forms of education and research are most likely to stimulate, inform and contribute in some way to social transition.

Equally significant, any reconceptualisation of environmental education will have to be extended to an analysis of the relationship between education and the reproduction of the environmental values and practices of capitalist societies. Trainer (1990 and 1994) has argued that both the overt and implicit (hidden) curricula of schools play a major role in reproducing the ecologically unsustainable values of industrial, affluent consumer society. We need to recognise that the education system is part of the instrumental rationality of late modernity (Firth, 1995).

## Starting points

In recognising the significance of the concept of sustainability, we do not support the current formulation of national and international policies around the idea of sustainable development. Nor do we consider that an 'education for sustainability' that promotes a pre-specified and prescribed set of goals and content is an appropriate, or the most likely, form of education to contribute in some way to social transition.

The concern through our own teaching and research (within higher education, although what is said here has direct relevance to schools) is to argue that how human beings live in relation to the environment is so important that the questions and issues it poses can only be properly addressed through a reflexive educational process, which allows such questions and issues to be critically and contextually reviewed and become generative of curricula and social action. In this way social processes of change become a focus of education and research for teachers and young people, with the emphasis on developing the capacity for change, rather than having it imposed upon them (from outside - from experts - whether teachers, curriculum agents or whoever). Environmental education is a process of developing capacities for intelligent social action rather than one of transmitting discrete elements of knowledge.

The reflexive orientation is inevitably socially critical, as it is concerned with a critical understanding of society and an informed commitment to the improvement of society (Greenall Gough and Robottom, 1993). It is an orientation which draws attention to the dominant political and social practices and consumer-led economic systems and is aimed at understanding both the nature of our contemporary environmental predicament and the means by which we can collectively transform our roles within it. However, the possibilities of social change are realised through the interaction of teachers and young people within the educational process rather than by external intervention.

Such a process model of curriculum design is open-ended and necessitates the continual development of a curriculum through attempts to realise, in the practice of teachers, its educational values. What such a curriculum design specifies are the educational processes, not the learning outcomes or the contents of study. It offers criteria that might best provide occasion for learners to construct their own understanding and action. The most appropriate contexts for developing the learners' understanding and action are the ones in which they will need to be employed in adult life. The knowledge that characterises an environmentally aware and active citizen cannot be prescribed but only determined by the learner in the process of engaging with the issues and questions concerning society-environment relations.

This process design does not preclude offering up those concepts, structures and goals thought to be relevant to environmental education, such as sustainable development, but they should be offered in different terms from those which imply they are learning objectives (Elliott and Rice, 1990). Such concepts, structures and goals need to be seen as part of the available pre-specified resources for an educational process. Other concepts and structures may be discerned as the need becomes apparent to teachers and/or students in the course of developing the curriculum through the educational process. They can all be seen as explicit or implicit theories, attitudes, values and abilities held by teachers and students which make up the wide body of resources of environmental education. What follows from abandoning a coherent structure of goals and concepts for environmental education is the need to re-establish the problematic and socially constructed nature of knowledge. From this perspective the process of environmental education is, by its critical and reflexive nature, oriented towards processes of social change.

At the root are notions of interconnectedness and subjectivity. It is an attempt to connect the everyday lives of teachers, how their sense of themselves and their relations with others is given meaning within the discourses of everyday life. How people see themselves in terms of their community and environment is at the core of the issue of identity and of our educational programmes. Making sense of the world and our place in it is not achieved through abstract, rational thought and ideas, but by reflecting on the realm of everyday experiences and how it constructs our sense of ourselves. In this regard, environmental education is seen in marked contrast to the static modernist theory of knowledge which has traditionally underpinned the construction of educational (school) knowledge and the curriculum (transmissive, subject-based, objective and rational) and which is enshrined in our liberal tradition of education.

Instead, knowledge is seen as dynamic and generative, emphasising the human authorship of social reality, and education becomes a reflexive process, action oriented and situated in the experiences of everyday living. Postmodernist, poststructuralist and feminist thought is seen as having an epistemological effect of profound importance for the way in which knowledge is implicated in society and the socio-ecological crisis.

If schools and environmental educators wish to find the answer to the motivations of young people towards participation in the issues of society then they need to understand how the experiences of the young, their sense of themselves and their social location are represented to them by the cultures in which they live and those which they construct themselves. The cultural emphasis is seen as particularly important, both in terms of the forms in which young people experience the social world and the forms in which they are likely to feel most empowered.

There are often wide discrepancies between a 'formal representation' of their experiences and themselves, through the abstract rational thought of their formal educational learning, and a 'semiotic representation' which increasingly reflects the fragmented, decentred and diffused nature of society, within which the capacity of the individual to locate her/himself is somehow being lost and replaced by the mass media and its images, virtual and real. The experiences of young people and their own self-constructions increasingly seem to reflect a 'semiotic representation', in the apparently inescapable features of information and consumer societies, that is the production of demand through the manipulation and consumption of images. There may be much greater scope for effective participation by young people in the issues of society, through the kinds of local knowledge and experience that is both part of the everyday experience of young people, and yet which is also in need of development, if they are to be able to re-make that experience in ways that are more satisfying to them. Education for sustainability must address the problems of participation in ways that acknowledge the characteristics of contemporary culture. By focusing primarily on abstract rational thought and ideas of sustainable societies or sustainable communities, this approach may seldom touch the real contexts and issues of young people's experience within an increasingly diverse and changing society. In consequence, education becomes hypothetical and distanced from everyday life, and is therefore likely to be largely ineffective.

# Principles before indicators

Clearly there is no general understanding or agreement about what constitutes indicators for effective environmental education. The formulation of specific indicators or criteria by which we may evaluate the improved effectiveness of environmental education seems a very daunting task. Indeed, in terms of the way that environmental education has been formulated above, it is questionable whether indicators are appropriate or formally realisable. Cade (1992) himself offers several cautions in the use of performance indicators, including over-quantification and the significant fact that the most important indicators may be too complex or 'qualitative' to identify.

It is beyond the scope of this paper to attempt to demonstrate the range of 'performance indicators' that environmental educators might want to use in an attempt to assess the effectiveness of their professional practice. We would suggest that the first step in considering indicators/criteria for judging the effectiveness of environmental education is to look critically at the paradigmatic principles we would wish to embrace. Once these principles have been made explicit, indicators or criteria appropriate to the paradigm could be formulated. It must be stressed however, that there are no all-encompassing and detached indicators or criteria which allow the existence of universal dialogue within, or yet between, paradigms.

There do appear to be certain 'threads of commonality' within our own work with teachers which could be used as possible indicators of improved effectiveness, which are now the focus for further discussion and research. In simple terms, our aim is to develop the potentialities of the teachers, both as individuals and as members of the community (the term is not being used in any abstract functionalist sense, but rather is embedded in the experiences of everyday living), to live in reasonable harmony with their surroundings, to think for themselves and to cope with problems as they can now foresee them.

The 'process indicators' identified reflect components of the developing thought and action of teachers. They inevitably take time to evolve within the thought and action of individual teachers and feature a requirement for continuous refinement, even reconceptualisation. These components are being used to evaluate the improved effectiveness of our own professional practice. They offer a possible structure for us to integrate curricula and the development of teacher professional practice with social action. As components of the thought and action of the individual teacher, and in drawing out the relations between the environment and the learner, they are likely to be of relevance to environmental education within schools. They are summarised in terms of the learner's experiences through the educational process:

1   Interconnectedness and subjectivity: how does the educational process give meaning to the learner's sense of her/himself and their every day relations with others and the environment?

2   Complexity: how does the educational process allow the learner to experience the environment in all its complexity?

3   Change, uncertainty, controversy and risk: how does the educational process also accommodate the notions of change, uncertainty, controversy and risk?

4   Relational: how does the educational process relate the learner's experiences of their local environment to the local community and to the wider global context?

5   Transformative learning: how does the educational process develop capacities for the intelligent, individual and collective reflexive action to transform current situations and experiences?

6   Advocacy: how does the educational process generate advocacy through a life-style that demonstrates commitment to others and a real concern for the environment?

## The need for more research

Many environmental educators will regularly use some form of 'indicators' as a means of evaluating the effectiveness of their own professional practice. As yet, there are few documented or 'official' recommendations, although Ali Khan's (1993) proposals offer one way to evaluate further and higher education programmes that serve vocational needs.

Cade (1992) has argued that research is needed to identify easily measured, standardised indicators of effective environmental education. This would, he argues, enable groups, government departments and other organisations as well as educational institutions to regularly evaluate their own performance in environmental education, as well as the state of environmental education at local and national level. If indicators are to be used, there will need to be a range of such indicators, applicable to different people, in different contexts and for different purposes; but does this qualification become self-defeating of the need for standardised performance indicators?

Qualitative or process indicators may be more appropriate. However, within our own experiences of working with environmental educators, we are aware of the danger of such indicators becoming self-defeating. In emphasising the reflexive nature and the social-situatedness of learning, it is very likely that the emerging indicators are at best transitionary and will be reconceptualised.

If environmental education is to fulfil the high expectations now being pinned on it, then research, along with a reorientation of educational thinking and structures, is a priority. We doubt, however, whether a major investment in research to identify standardised performance indicators as a means to evaluate the effectiveness of environmental education is a way forward. What is needed, as Sterling (1992) argues, is research that might recover the potential of education from its present direction, with the danger of an over-simple equation being drawn between education, society and sustainability.

The promotion of a 'sustainable development' perspective in schools is also unlikely to improve the effectiveness of environmental education. Huckle (1991) emphasises that much of environmental education as presently constructed is part of the problem rather than the solution. It is based on inadequate theory and practice, yet is receiving increasing support from powerful elites who seem to be hijacking it in order to manage the global socio-ecological crisis in their own interests. What is required is a critically reflexive orientation within environmental education and environmental education research: one that would expose the instrumental rationality of sustainable development and offer reconceptualisations of ways of engaging with the socio-ecological crisis. In this way, possible social processes of change, that is social transition, becomes a focus of both education and research.

We have outlined one reconceptualisation of environmental education, which is neither abstract or formalised as a grand narrative, and does not represent the key relations between people and the environment as anonymous and rational (people) and universal (the environment). Grand narratives lack the specificity of culture, class, ethnicity, gender and place. If environmental education is to develop an environmental citizenship as a status endowed with social and ecological entitlements which people can legitimately claim, then to be a citizen is to regard these entitlements as one's own, part of one's identity and personhood. If environmental citizenship is something to which people are to be committed, its involvement in the discourses of people's everyday lives needs to be shown. No approach to environmental education concerned with social transition is likely to succeed if it does not connect with the way in which people see themselves and their positions in the discourses of everyday life, that is with the subjectivity in which they recognise their identity as persons and as members of a variety of shifting group memberships.

1.  Instrumental rationality is considered in more detail in Firth, 1995. Briefly, it is a modernist or Enlightenment rationality which advances the unquestioned desirability of economic growth, the importance of individual self-advancement over community and environmental well-being, and the [im]-moral imperative of the profit motive and the market to determine social, environmental and economic priorities.

# Bibliography

Ali Khan, S. (1993) *Environmental Issues in Further and Higher Education*. Coombe Lodge Report, The Staff College.

Cade, A. (1992) Measuring the State of Environmental Education. *Environmental Research Seminar Report*. ESRC Global Environmental Change Research Programme: Policy Studies Institute, London, 3 December 1991.

Chatterjee, P. and Finger, M. (1994) *The Earth Brokers*. London: Routledge.

DFE (1992) *Environmental responsibility: an agenda for further and higher education*. HMSO, 'The Toyne Report'. London: HMSO.

DoE (1993) *Consultation Paper on the UK Strategy for Sustainable Development*. London: HMSO.

Dunlap, R., Gallup, G. and Gallup, A. (1992) *The Health of the Planet Survey*. Princeton, NJ: The George H.Gallup International Institute.

Elliott, J. and Rice, J. (1990) The relationship between disciplinary knowledge and situational understanding in the development of environmental awareness. In Maarten Pieters (ed.) *Teaching for sustainable development*. Enschede: Institute for Curriculum Development, Workshop Report, Veldhoven, Netherlands, 23-25 April.

Fien, J. (1993) *Environmental Education: a pathway to sustainability?* Geelong: Deakin University Press.

Fien, J. (1995) Teaching for a sustainable world: the Environmental and Development Education Project for Teacher Education. *Environmental Education Research* 1 (1) pp. 21-33.

Firth, R. (1995) Postmodernity, rationality and teaching environmental education. *International Research in Geography and Environmental Education* 4 (2).

Firth, R. and Plant, M. (1994) *Environmental Education Through Action Enquiry*. MA programme, module study guide 7-8. Nottingham Trent University.

Foucault, M. (1977) *Discipline and Punishment: the birth of the prison*. London: Allen Lane.

Gayford, C. (1993) Environmental Education. In G.K. Verma and P.D. Pumfrey (eds.) *Cultural Diversity and the Curriculum, Vol 2: Cross-curricular Contexts, Themes and Dimensions in secondary schools*. London: Falmer Press.

Greenall Gough, A. (1993) *Founders of Environmental Education*. Geelong: Deakin University Press.

Greenall Gough, A. and Robottom, I. (1993) Towards a socially critical environmental education: water quality studies in a coastal school. *Journal of Curriculum Studies* 23 (4) pp. 301-16.

Habermas, J. (1972) *Knowledge and Human Interests*. London: Heinemann.

Habermas, J. (trans: J. Viertel) (1974) *Theory and Practice*. London: Heinemann.

HM Government (1990) *This Common Inheritance: Britain's Environmental Strategy*. London: HMSO.

HMI/DES/BP (1991) *Conference Report*: International Conference on Environmental Education. Manchester 18-22 March.

Huckle, J. (1983) Environmental Education. In J. Huckle (ed.) *Geographical Education: reflection and action*. Oxford: Oxford University Press.

Huckle, J. (1991) Education for Sustainability: Assessing Pathways to the Future. *Australian Journal of Environmental Education* 7 pp. 43-62.

Huckle, J. (1993) Environmental Education and Sustainability: A view from critical theory. In J. Fien (ed.) (1993) *Environmental Education: A Pathway to Sustainability*. Geelong: Deakin University Press.

Huckle, J. (1995) *Reaching Out: Education for Sustainability*. Part One. Goldalming: WWF UK.

Huyssen (1986) *Again the Great Divide: modernism, mass culture, postmodernism*. Bloomington, IA: Indiana University Press.

IUCN/UNEP/WWF (1991) *Caring for the Earth*. Gland: International Union for the Conservation of Nature.

IUCN Commission on Education and Communication (1993) *Education for Sustainability: a practical guide to preparing national strategies*. Gland: International Union for the Conservation of Nature.

Janse van Rensburg, E. (1994) Social Transformation in Response to the Environmental Crisis: The Role of Education and Research. *Australian Journal of Environmental Education* 10 pp. 1-20.

Kemmis, S. (1991) Emancipatory Action Research and Postmodernisms. *Curriculum Perspectives* **11** (4) pp. 59-65.

Kemmis, S., Cole, P. and Suggett, D. (1983) *Orientations to Curriculum and Transition: Towards the Socially Critical School*. Melbourne: Victorian Institute of Secondary Education.

McTaggart, R. (1991) Action research is a Broad Movement. *Curriculum Perspectives* **11** (4) pp. 44-47.

NCC (1990) *Curriculum Guidance 7: Environmental Education*. York: National Curriculum Council.

O'Donoghue, R. (1993) Clarifying Environmental Education: A Search for Clear Action in Southern Africa. *Southern African Journal of Environmental Education* **13** pp. 28-38.

Osborn-Jones, T. (1994) Stand up for local heroes. *Times Educational Supplement* (Extra) **4067**, 10 June.

NFER (1994) *Environmental Education: Teaching Approaches and Students' Attitudes*. Briefing paper, September. Slough: NFER.

Popkewitz, T.S. (1984) *Paradigm and Ideology in Educational Research: The Social functions of the Intellectual*. London: Falmer Press.

Popkewitz, T.S. (1991) *A Political Sociology of Educational reform*. London: Teachers College.

Sterling, S. (1992) A Critical Review of Environmental Education Research. *Environmental Education Research Seminar Report*, ESRC Global Environmental Change Research Programme: Policy Studies Institute, London, 3 December 1991.

Sterling, S. and Cooper, G. (1992) *In Touch: Environmental Education for Europe*. Goldalming: WWF UK.

Trainer, T. (1990) Towards an ecological philosophy of education. *Discourse* **10** pp. 92-117.

Trainer, T. (1994) If You Really Want to Save the Environment. *Australian Journal of Environmental Education* **10** pp. 59-70.

UNCED (1992) Promoting Education and Public Awareness and Training. *Agenda 21, Conference on Environment and Development*. Conches, Chapt. 36.

UNESCO-UNEP (1990) Environmentally Educated Teachers: the priority of priorities? *Connect* **XV** (1) p. 1-3.

WCED (1987) *Our Common Future* (The Brundtland Report). Oxford: Oxford University Press.

# COMPETENCE & ACCOUNTABILITY IN EDUCATION

### Edited by
### Peter McKenzie, Philip Mitchell and Paul Oliver

## MONITORING CHANGE IN EDUCATION

In a world of apparently diminishing resources, there have been consistent calls for more effectiveness and efficiency in education, and there can be no question that those involved in education will face calls for increased accountability.

Meanwhile the competence 'movement' has stressed the idea that education and training should be primarily concerned with achieving measurable outcomes, particularly those which have credence in the workplace. Opponents suggest that this is often to the detriment of the knowledge and understanding normally regarded as crucial to competent performance, yet it is likely that this kind of measurement will increasingly become an index of accountability.

The papers presented in this volume examine these concepts in a variety of contexts, ranging from school-based teacher training to the assessment of NVQs, and from recent government legislation to the Smithers Report. A variety of views are expressed, which should be of interest to all those concerned with current trends in education.

**1995    168 pages    1 85742 279 1    £25.00**

*Price subject to change without notification*

# The Dictionary of

# Educational Terms

## David Blake & Vincent Hanley

Contact ratio, Key Stages, hidden curriculum, opting out – but what does it all mean? If you have ever felt bewildered by the constantly changing language in the school world this is the book for you!

This convenient and easy-to-use book of reference to education in England and Wales brings together information on the National Curriculum, the world of schools, the legal framework of education, key educational ideas and much more. The extensive cross-referencing and comprehensive list of abbreviations and acronyms make it an ideal tool for teachers, governors and parents alike. **The Dictionary of Educational Terms** is an invaluable guide to a complicated field – can you afford to be without it?

*David Blake* and *Vincent Hanley* are Principal Lecturers in Education at the West Sussex Institute of Higher Education.

**1995    203 pages**
**Hbk**    1 85742 256 2    **£30.00**
**Pbk**    1 85742 257 0    **£14.95**
*Prices subject to change without notification*

*arena*

# GOLDMINE

## Finding free and low-cost resources for teaching

## 1995–1996

## Compiled by David Brown

*"It can be highly recommended because the choice of subjects, the organisation of the entries, and an index make a mass of information very easily accessible. Having used this directory to acquire resources for a couple of ad hoc topic areas, I can confidently state that it works - with ease and practicability. In the saving of teachers' time, let alone in access to materials, it really is a goldmine. I would advise any school to acquire this book. The title of the book is wholly accurate and the outlay is modest compared with the returns."* **School Librarian**

David Brown has been teaching in primary, middle and secondary schools for 23 years. It was through David's need to find resources within a limited school budget that he began to uncover a wealth of low-cost, good quality material which was just what he was looking for.

**Goldmine** places these resources into topic areas, describes them and tells you where you can get them from. Since the first edition in 1985, **Goldmine** has developed into the country's leading directory of free and sponsored teaching resources, providing the wherewithal to obtain over 6000 resources from some 235 suppliers.

Budget-conscious schools will find it saves its purchase price many times over, and parents and teachers are safe in the knowledge that all the items described in here ar personally recommended by a teacher, the compiler himself.

1995     **329 pages**     1 85742 137 X     £15.00

*Price subject to change without notification*

*arena*